ROLE OF WOMEN IN NATION BUILDING

ROLE OF WOMEN IN NATION BUILDING

By

Rajiv Sagar

2008

CYBER TECH PUBLICATIONS
4264/3, Ansari Road, Daryaganj, New Delhi-110002 (India)
Ph.: 011-23244078. Fax: 011-23280028
E-Mail: cyberpublicationsdelhi@yahoo.com

ROLE OF WOMEN IN NATION BUILDING

Rajiv Sagar

First Edition 2008

Published by :

G.S. Rawat for **Cyber Tech Publications**
4264/3, Ansari Road, Daryaganj, New Delhi-110002 (India)
Ph.: 011-23244078. Fax: 011-23280028
E-Mail: cyberpublicationsdelhi@yahoo.com

Printed at : **Amit Enterprises**, Maujpur, Delhi, (9810878184)

Preface

The soul of Indian nation is the symbol of integrity. Our centre-point is family and not an individual. Our concept of family is based on the principle of mutuality and not individuality. It is also necessary that men should change their mind-set, understand the importance of women's role in family as well as nation building and make all the avenues open to them for fulfilling the divine mission as the architect, of the nation.

Women in India have come along way by carving a niche for themselves in various fields in our male-dominated society. Over the years, they have won more rights and freedom to choose the way they wanted to live their lives without being discriminated against. However, the ground realities still seem to be hostile to women.

Unless we impart education about a value based work ethics we cannot ensure a safe atmosphere for women. It is only when we rise above the identities based on body consciousness such as gender, status, caste etc. and identify each individual as a spiritual entity having unique qualities, that we can truly give respect to each other. Real empowerment of women can come about only when they become the embodiments of shakti.

Woman is the architect of the whole society and the architect of humanity's destiny. She builds the home; she establishes the institution of family life; she brings up the children and makes them good citizens with her devotion compassion, meditative nature, concentration and dhyana. Women are the emblem of living temples of shakti, the natural energy. The most ancient scriptures say that without shakti, without the female power, it is not possible for humankind to survive. The female power has been the force behind all the great leaders of the world.

"The success of the World, particularly West, United States, China, Japan, Korea and other Asian Tigers is attributable to the participation of their women resource in the national development. India has once again realize the role and importance of women resource in the development, & nation building. Hope that this book will be informative enough to the readers.

—*Author*

Contents

1

Nation Building

Nation-building is a normative concept that means different things to different people. The latest conceptualization is essentially that nation-building programs are those in which dysfunctional or unstable or "failed states" or economies are given assistance in the development of governmental infrastructure, civil society, dispute resolution mechanisms, as well as economic assistance, in order to increase stability. Nation-building generally assumes that someone or something is doing the building intentionally.

But it is important to look at the evolution of theories of nation-building and at the other concepts which it has both supplanted and included. Many people believe that nation-building is evolutionary rather than revolutionary, that is takes a long time and is a social process that cannot be jump-started from outside. The evolution of the Italian city-states into a nation, the German city-states into the Zollverein customs union and later a nation, the multiple languages and cultural groups in France into the nation of France, the development of China from the warring kingdoms, took a very long time, and were the result, not only of political leadership, but of changes in technology and economic processes (the agricultural and then industrial revolutions), as well as communication, culture and civil society, and many other factors.

In what Seymour Martin Lipset has called The First New Nation, the United States, at first 13 colonies with diverse origins, came together to form a new nation and state. That state, like so many in contemporary times, faced the prospect of secession and disintegration in 1865, and it took another 100 years for the integration of black and white, North and South,

East and West. This was a new type of nation-state, because its people were not all of the same ethnicity, culture, and language, as had been thought to be the case in the early defining of the concept of nation-state.

But nation-building by one nation may destroy others. In the building of the US nation and others, aboriginal nations were erased or marginalized. The Six-Nations Confederacy of the Iriquois had existed before the US nation (and was thought by some to be a model for it). Today many "First Nations" are in the process of nation re-building, re-building the social, cultural, economic and political foundations for what is left of self-governance. First nations seek to re-build cultural identities as nations in order to challenge their disintegration by others in the creation of their own states.

Association of First Nations National Chief Matthew Coon cited the Harvard Project on American Indian Economic Development (released in 2001 by the Kennedy School of Government at Harvard) proposal of a Nation Building Model of Economic Development. The project defined Nation-building as: "Equipping First Nations with the institutional foundation necessary to increase their capacity to effectively assert self-governing powers on behalf of their own economic, social and cultural objectives." The study identified four core elements of a nation building model: (1) genuine self rule (First Nations making decisions about resource allocations, project funding and development strategy), (2) creating effective governing institutions (non-politicized dispute resolution mechanisms and getting rid of corruption), (3) cultural match (giving first nations institutions legitimacy in the eyes of their citizens), and the need for a strategic orientation (long-term planning).

One of the reasons for the difficulties of what many consider "failed states" is that some peoples who had been integrated were taken apart by European colonialism, while others who were separate peoples were integrated together in new states not based in common identities. Particularly in Africa and the Middle East, new political borders paid little attention to national identities in the creation of new states. Thus the notion of nation-state, a nation which developed the governmental apparatus of a state, was often nonsense. While in Europe nation-building historically preceded state-building, in post-colonial states, state-building preceded nation-building. The aftermath of colonialism led to the need for nation-building.

WHAT IS NATION-BUILDING?

A 2003 study by James Dobbins and others for the RAND Corporation defines nation-building as "the use of armed force in the aftermath of a conflict to underpin an enduring transition to democracy." Comparing seven historical cases: Germany, Japan, Somalia, Haiti, Bosnia, Kosovo, and Afghanistan, "in which American military power has been used in the aftermath of a conflict to underpin democratization elsewhere around the world since World War II," they review the lessons learned. This definition of nation-building is substantially different than those which see nation-building as the province of people within a nation. The definition centers around the building of democratic processes, but many argue that the use of the military to bring about democracy may be inherently contradictory. Whether nation-building can be imposed from outside is one of the central questions in this field, and whether that can be done by the military is a further part of the question.

WHAT IS A NATION?

To understand the concept of nation-building, one needs to have some definition of what a nation is. Early conceptions of nation defined it as a group or race of people who shared history, traditions, and culture, sometimes religion, and usually language. Thus the United Kingdom comprises four nations, the English, Irish, Scottish, and Welsh. The people of a nation generally share a common national identity, and part of nation-building is the building of that common identity. Some distinguish between an ethnic nation, based in (the social construction of) race or ethnicity, and a civic nation, based in common identity and loyalty to a set of political ideas and institutions, and the linkage of citizenship to nationality.

Today the word nation is often used synonymously with state, as in the United Nations. But a state is more properly the governmental apparatus by which a nation rules itself. Max Weber provided the classic definition of the state:

> *Today, however, we have to say that a state is a human community that (successfully) claims the monopoly of the legitimate use of physical force within a given territory. Note that "territory" is one of the characteristics of the state. Specifically, at the present time, the right to use physical force is ascribed to other institutions or to individuals only to the extent to which the state permits it.*

In approaching the question of nation-building, and in particular its relationship to state-building, it is important to keep in mind that this definition specifies the legitimate use of force.

EVOLUTION OF NATION-BUILDING THEORY

The term nation-building is often used simultaneously with state-building, democratization, modernization, political development, post-conflict reconstruction, and peace-building. But each concept is different, though their evolution is intertwined. The concept of nation-building came to be used especially among American political scientists a decade or so after World War II, to describe the greater integration of state and society, as citizenship brought loyalty to the modern nation-state with it. Reinhard Bendix focused on the expansion of citizenship and of rights to political participation. Karl Deutsch focused on the role of social communication and national integration in nation-building in Western societies. Others began to apply it to non-Western societies as well.

Almond and Coleman argued for the functional approach to understand and compare the political systems of developing countries. They argued for the interdependence and multi-functionality of political structures, and argued especially that the input functions of political systems could help to distinguish stages of political development.

They defined input functions as: (1) political socialization and recruitment, (2) interest articulation, (3) interest aggregation, and (4) political communication. Output functions were: (5) rule-making, (6) rule application, and (7) rule adjudication. Most nation-building after the end of the Cold War seems to focus more on the output functions.

Lucian Pye linked modernization with Westernization and "the diffusion of a world culture," what we might today call globalization. He identified political development with:

> *A world culture based on advanced technology and the spirit of science, on a rational view of life, a secular approach to social relations, a feeling for justice in public affairs, and, above all else, on the acceptance in the political realm that the prime unit of the polity should be the nation-state.*

Pye identified multiple meanings of political development, among them:

- as prerequisite to economic development,
- as politics typical of industrial societies,
- as political modernization,
- as administrative and legal development,
- as mass mobilization and participation,
- as the building of democracy, and
- as stability and orderly change.

He identifies equality as one of the basic themes running through all of these. While nation-building after 9/11 still incorporates many of these meanings of political development, equality does not seem to play a major role in practice.

Dudley Seers, in his presidential address to the Society for International Development in 1969, presaged what has become the concept of human development. He said:

> *The questions to ask about a country's development are therefore: what has been happening to poverty? What has been happening to unemployment? What has been happening to inequality? If all these have declined from high levels, then beyond doubt this has been a period of development....*

In the 1990s the UN Development Program brought out the Human Development Report and the Human Development Index to focus on those aspects of development other than economic, including in the index both health and education. Many UN programs, as well as NGO efforts, focus on these aspects, and the World Bank has begun to focus on poverty, but to date there seems no effort by the US in either Afghanistan or Iraq to include poverty, unemployment, or inequality in nation-building efforts.

Almond and Verba in 1963 introduced the concept of The Civic Culture to the development literature. The civic culture, which combines tradition and modernity, is one of the processes that sustain democracy. Almond and Verba defined as part of this civic culture the obligation to participate and the sense of civic competence and cooperation. They also noted the importance of the role of education in the development of a civic culture. Alexis de Toqueville had noted the importance of associations in sustaining Democracy in America at its earliest stages. Robert Putnam, in exploring the civil traditions in modern Italy that make democracy work, includes in his notion of the civic community: civic engagement, political equality, and solidarity, trust, and tolerance, in addition to associations. He finds the presence of choral societies in Italy, bowling leagues in the US, and other associations, to be important, but in Bowling Alone, finds such associations to be reducing in the US today.

The importance of civil society also became clear as a factor in the movement from authoritarianism toward democracy in the former Soviet Union and Eastern Europe at the end of the Cold War. The role of civil society received much support in early nation-building/democratization efforts in the former Soviet Union and Eastern Europe, but has drastically declined since then. This notion of the importance of civil society as an underpinning to democratic nation-building seems to be given lip-service in current efforts, but in reality it is not seen as significant by nation-builders if one measures this by any spending measure. If nation-building in the 20th century is to be successful, it may want to return to look at some of its early theorists. The importance of democratic values, of the civic culture and civil society that develop and sustain them, the importance of increasing social, political, and economic equality, and of human development, rather than just economic development or state-building, are key in any successful strategy for long-term democratic nation-building. Nation-building is more than just state-building. To be a sustainable force for peace-building, it must incorporate more than just the Western appendages of democracy. Voting systems and free market development and increasing the GNP per capita are not likely to bring stable peace.

WHY DOES NATION-BUILDING MATTER?

Nation-building matters to intractable conflict because of the theory that a strong state is necessary in order to provide security, that the building of an integrated national community is important in the building of a state, and that there may be social and economic prerequisites or co-requisites to the building of an integrated national community.

Further, when nation-building implies democratization, there is the further hypothesis known as the democratic peace hypothesis. Originally explicated by Immanuel Kant in the 17th century, the democratic peace hypothesis says that perpetual peace can be achieved by developing a federation or league of free republican nations. Representative democracies, organized in an international organization, would bring peace. Political scientists who have explored this hypothesis have focused on one of two versions: democracies don't make war against each other, or democracies don't initiate war at all. There is certainly evidence of the former, and some evidence of the latter.

The other side of the coin is that nation-building may sometimes be simply another name for external intervention and the extension of empires. If it can be said that failed states are the cause of national, regional, or world security problems, or that human rights abuses are so extensive that the need to overcome them in turn overcomes the traditional sovereignty rights of states under international law, then intervention in the name of nation-building can be seen to be justified. Sometimes nation-building may simply be used as a justification for the expansion of imperial control. So nation-building matters, but what is meant by nation-building matters even more.

WHAT CAN BE DONE?

The first major question that needs to be asked is whether nation-building should be done at all. In the context of intractable conflict, is nation-building an appropriate method of providing stable peace and a secure community, which can meet the needs of the people within it? There are mixed conclusions here. The democratic peace hypothesis argues that democratic states do not initiate wars, or alternatively, in its more limited version, do not initiate wars against each other. Immanuel Kant's original statement of the hypothesis in his essay on Perpetual Peace in the 17th century argued both for the necessity of republican (or representative democracy) governments, and for their participation in a league of peace, or federation of free nations. This would mean that the simple creation of democratic nations would not be enough; peace would require also the creation of some sort of international governance and international law.

There is disagreement among current theorists of nation-building as to the relationships between the development of a free market economy and the development of democratic participation, as well as over the necessity of building a civil society as a prerequisite for the development of state institutions for democratic participation. Different theories of nation-building emphasize different parts of the arguments. Different versions of nation-building benefit different groups. Some appear to benefit more the outside countries, and/or the international governmental and nongovernmental organizations which are involved. Some benefit elites in the nation being built or rebuilt. Some spread benefits widely in the society; some do not.

Nation-building that will be likely to contribute to stable international peace will need to emphasize the democratic participation of people within the nation to demand rights. It will need to build the society, economy, and polity which will meet the basic needs of the people, so that they are not driven by poverty, inequality, unemployment, on the one hand, or by a desire to compete for resources and power either internally or in the international system. This does means not only producing the formal institutions of democracy, but the underlying culture which recognizes respect for the identities and needs of others both within and outside. It means development of human rights--political, civil, economic and social, and the rule of law. But it also means development of sewer systems, and roads, and jobs. Perhaps most important, it means the development of education. Nation-building must allow the participation of civil society, and develop democratic state institutions that promote welfare. Democratic state-building is an important part of that. This is a multi-faceted process that will proceed differently in each local context.

MILITARY OR CIVILIAN?

The second major question in what can be done about nation-building is the question (if it should be done) of who should do it, and who CAN effectively do it. The literature is divided over these issues. Clearly the US leadership of the years 2001-4 believes that nation-building in Iraq is primarily the province of the US military. It has shut out even much of the US State Department in this effort, let alone other countries, let alone Iraqis themselves. But the US military itself remains divided on the issue of whether the military should be involved in peacekeeping, peace-building, and nation-building. Some argue that this is not the function of the military; it is to exert force, or as retired Colonel Fred Peck announced in an NPR interview October 22, 2001: "Our job is to kill people and smash things." Some argue that this would weaken the military and make them less capable of doing their primary task of defending US national interests. Some argue that the institution that projects force cannot at the same time build peace or build a nation.

The U.S. Army Training and Doctrine Command's "Mission Statement and Commander's Intent" says that it develops competent and adaptive leaders..., imbu[ing] the qualities and skills necessary to dominate across the spectrum of conflict." Is it possible to dominate across the spectrum of conflict at the same time as helping to build a nation?

There are others in and out of the US military who argue for a kinder, gentler military, and argue that military training needs to be changed to reflect these new tasks. In a 2003 article in The Atlantic Monthly, Robert Kaplan laid out 10 rules for "Managing the World." The first rule: "Produce More Joppolos," refers to Major Victor Joppolo, from John Hersey's novel, A Bell for Adano. Kaplan argues that Joppolo, a US civil affairs officer who became the post-WW-II military mayor of Adano, and worked to settle internal disputes, return fishermen to the sea, and find a replacement for the bell Mussolini had melted down for arms, can be a model for soldiers in military occupations and peacemaking operations.

US Army Lt. Colonel Patrick Donohoe argues that the Army must prepare leaders for nation building, by providing training in "culture; basic law and civics; city planning and public administration; economics; and ethics," as well as language, and "how a free, democratic government is supposed to work." He argues that ethics training must include knowledge of the Geneva Conventions and the Law of Armed Conflict. While all of these may be important, one is still left with the question of whether the military is the best institution for nation-building.

THE US OR THE UN?

Another question is whether an outside country can build a nation in another country. Is nation-building more effectively done by a single country, by the UN or UN-related organizations, by regional organizations, or by some combination of these? Michael Ignatieff, in a cogent article critiquing "nation-building lite" in Afghanistan, prior to the start of the second Iraq war, argues for "imperial nation-building," for the importance of sufficient US application of force and sufficient and much larger application of dollars in development aid to make a difference in a critical period. He acknowledges this as imperialism, arguing that "nation-building is the kind of imperialism you get in a human rights era, a time when great powers believe simultaneously in the right of small nations to govern themselves and in their own right to rule the world." He argues that Afghans "understand the difficult truth that their best hope of freedom lies in a temporary experience of imperial rule."

The 2003 RAND study by James Dobbins and others reviews the lessons learned in US nation-building efforts. Comparing seven historical cases: Germany, Japan, Somalia, Haiti, Bosnia, Kosovo, and Afghanistan, "in which American military power has been used in the aftermath of a conflict to underpin democratization elsewhere around the world since World War II," Dobbins and colleagues come to the following conclusions:

Lessons Learned in U.S. Nation-Building Efforts

- Many factors--such as prior democratic experience, level of economic development, and social homogeneity--can influence the ease or difficulty of nation-building, but the single most important controllable determinant seems to be the level of effort, as measured in troops, money, and time.
- Multilateral nation-building is more complex and time-consuming than a unilateral approach. But the multilateral approach is considerably less expensive for individual participants.
- Multilateral nation-building can produce more thorough transformations and greater regional reconciliation than can unilateral efforts.
- Unity of command is as essential in peace operations as it is in war. This unity of command can be achieved even in operations with broad multilateral participation when the major participants share a common vision and tailor the response of international institutions accordingly.
- There appears to be an inverse correlation between the size of the military stabilization force and the level of casualties. The higher the proportion of troops relative to the resident population, the lower the number of casualties suffered and inflicted. Indeed, most of the post-conflict operations that were generously manned suffered no casualties at all.
- Neighboring states can exert significant influence, for good or bad. It is nearly impossible to put together a fragmented nation if its neighbors try to tear it apart. Every effort should be made to secure their support.
- Accountability for past injustices can be a powerful component of democratization. Such accountability can be among the most difficult and controversial aspects of any nation-building endeavor, however, and therefore should be attempted only if there is a deep and long-term commitment to the overall operation.

- There is no quick fix for nation-building. None of our cases was successfully completed in less than seven years.

Dobbins and colleagues recognize the advantages of a multilateral approach, arguing that while it is more complex and time-consuming, it is less expensive for any one participant and, more important, is better at producing both transformation and regional reconciliation. They also recognize the important role of neighboring countries. They make no mention of the US attempt to win hearts and minds in Vietnam.

The United Nations has participated in nation-building efforts both through the Security Council's authorization of peacekeeping missions involving primarily military, but also civilian and police participants as well. Among these have been Cambodia, Angola, and Bosnia in the early 1990s, and Kosovo and East Timor. Some have been more, some less, successful. It has also participated in development and human rights efforts completely aside from peacekeeping. Efforts range from those of UNICEF in fostering children's rights, to the UN Development Program in providing human development aid, to the Ad Hoc Criminal Tribunals on Rwanda and the former Yugoslavia, to the World Food Program, to UNESCO's Education for All program.

These are also an important component of nation-building. Economic, social, and political development, and institutions which protect human rights and provide for the rule of law, are important not only to post-conflict peace-building, but to nation-building at any stage of development or any stage of conflict. And it may well be that the international legitimacy that can be provided by a global institution may be better for nation-building than efforts by any single country, or a regional organization, or a "coalition of the willing." Accusations of "imperial nation-building" are reduced when there is greater international consensus.

But Donini, Niland and Wermester question whether Western approaches, military and technological, can foster just outcomes, whether through individual countries efforts or through UN agencies. They raise questions of how UN agencies and international NGOs interact with national and local communities in the process of providing aid for political reconstruction and human rights development. Can nation-building really come from outside at all? It may be necessary to go back to the debates over the definition and purposes of nation-building to answer that question.

IGOS, STATES OR NGOS?

NGOs and state development agencies have also played important roles in nation-building projects. Mary Anderson has argued that foreign development aid has often fostered the propensity for greater conflict rather than reducing it. She urges that state development agencies first be certain to "do no harm." As states began both to realize the costs of development aid, both financial and otherwise, NGOs became increasingly involved. Supposedly NGOs, with smaller budgets and staffs, could have a greater likelihood of actually reaching the needs of people. But both IGOs and NGOs have now become big business, and many now have the same disadvantages of states.

The issue is not so much which agency, but how the agency functions. Does it simply throw money at the problem? Does it exacerbate tensions by providing money or projects unevenly across ethnic groups or regions in such a way as to generate competition or, worse, security fears? Is its presence so big that it overwhelms the local or national governing structures it is trying to nurture? Is it culturally knowledgeable and sensitive? If one of the components of nation-building is to nurture the further development of civil society, how does an outside organization interact with civil society? This brings us to our final question: can nation-building be done by external actors, or is it only effective when done by those whose nation is being built?

INDIGENOUS OR EXOGENOUS ACTORS?

Nation-building is an evolutionary process. It takes a long time. One of the problems with outside actors is that they come and they go. While it may be considered useful for an outside military occupation or peacekeeping force to provide the temporary stability and security necessary in order to allow the process of nation-building to proceed, the question of whether this is the best method remains. If a military stays too short a time, expectations of a dependable peace for the foreseeable future may not develop, and thus people will be unlikely to invest in the future. If, on the other hand, a military stays too long, people will rely on the security provided by outsiders and fail to develop their own institutions for providing it.

The same questions may be asked about outside civilian actors, whether a single state, a regional organization, a global organization, or an NGO. While a significant influx of resources may be necessary, especially in the period immediately following a violent conflict, the right amount, the right methods, and the right length of time are critical. In general, it appears that nation-building is best left in the hands of those whose nation it is or will be, and that outside organizations support, rather than direct, nation-building.

The nation-builders to bet on are those refugee families piled onto the brightly painted Pakistani trucks moving up the dusty roads, the children perched on the mattresses, like Mowgli astride the head of an elephant, gazing toward home. The nation-builders to invest in are the teachers, especially the women who taught girls in secret during the Taliban years. I met one in an open-air school right in the middle of Kabul's most destroyed neighborhood. She wrote her name in a firm, bold hand in my notebook, and she knew exactly what she needed: chalk, blackboards, desks, a roof and, God willing, a generation of peace. At her feet, on squares of U.N.H.C.R. sheeting, sat her class, 20 upturned faces, all female, having the first reading lesson of their lives.--Michael Ignatieff. "Nation-Building Lite," New York Times Magazine, 28 July 2002.

Arguing for the importance of indigenous nation-building does not mean that outside actors should ignore the process. If an outside military is to be involved, it must be funded and supplied sufficiently so that it can bring order and security following conflict. Or it must stay out. Similarly, if there is to be outside civilian involvement, whether state-based, IGO or NGO, it must also have sufficient funding and technical skills in order to provide what is needed and to stay the course. Arguing for the indignity of the process should not be an excuse for exiting the process where there is need for outside help.

WHAT IS A MENTOR?

The notion of mentoring is ancient. The original Mentor was described by Homer as the "wise and trusted counselor" whom Odysseus left in charge of his household during his travels. Athena, in the guise of Mentor, became the guardian and teacher of Odysseus' son Telemachus.

In modern times, the concept of mentoring has found application in virtually every forum of learning. In academics, mentor is often used synonymously with faculty adviser. A fundamental difference between mentoring and advising is more than advising; mentoring is a personal, as well as, professional relationship. An adviser might or might not be a mentor, depending on the quality of the relationship. A mentoring relationship develops over an extended period, during which a student's needs and the nature of the relationship tend to change. A mentor will try to be aware of these changes and vary the degree and type of attention, help, advice, information, and encouragement that he or she provides.

In the broad sense intended here, a mentor is someone who takes a special interest in helping another person develop into a successful professional. Some students, particularly those working in large laboratories and institutions, find it difficult to develop a close relationship with their faculty adviser or laboratory director. They might have to find their mentor elsewhere-perhaps a fellow student, another faculty member, a wise friend, or another person with experience who offers continuing guidance and support.

In the realm of science and engineering, we might say that a good mentor seeks to help a student optimize an educational experience, to assist the student's socialization into a disciplinary culture, and to help the student find suitable employment. These obligations can extend well beyond formal schooling and continue into or through the student's career.

The Council of Graduate Schools (1995) cites Morris Zelditch's useful summary of a mentor's multiple roles: "Mentors are advisors, people with career experience willing to share their knowledge; supporters, people who give emotional and moral encouragement; tutors, people who give specific feedback on one's performance; masters, in the sense of employers to whom one is apprenticed; sponsors, sources of information about and aid in obtaining opportunities; models, of identity, of the kind of person one should be to be an academic." In general, an effective mentoring relationship is characterized by mutual respect, trust, understanding, and empathy. Good mentors are able to share life experiences and wisdom, as well as technical expertise. They are good listeners, good observers, and good problem-solvers. They make an effort to know, accept, and respect the goals and interests of a student. In the end, they establish an environment in which the student's accomplishment is limited only by the extent of his or her talent.

THE MENTORING RELATIONSHIP

The nature of a mentoring relationship varies with the level and activities of both student and mentor. In general, however, each relationship must be based on a common goal: to advance the educational and personal growth of the student. You as mentor can also benefit enormously.

There is no single formula for good mentoring; mentoring styles and activities are as varied as human relationships. Different students will require different amounts and kinds of attention, advice, information, and encouragement. Some students will feel comfortable approaching their mentors; others will be shy, intimidated, or reluctant to seek help. A good mentor is approachable and available. Often students will not know what questions to ask, what information they need, or what their options are (especially when applying to graduate programs). A good mentor can lessen such confusion by getting to know students and being familiar with the kinds of suggestions and information that can be useful.

In long-term relationships, friendships form naturally; students can gradually become colleagues. At the same time, strive as a mentor to be aware of the distinction between friendship and favouritism. You might need to remind a student-and yourself-that you need a degree of objectivity in giving fair grades and evaluations. If you are unsure whether a relationship is "too personal," you are probably not alone. Consult with the department chair, your own mentor, or others you trust. You might have to increase the mentor-student distance. Students, for their part, need to understand the professional pressures and time constraints faced by their mentors and not view them as merely a means-or impediment-to their goal. For many faculty, mentoring is not their primary responsibility; in fact, time spent with students can be time taken from their own research. Students are obliged to recognize the multiple demands on a mentor's time.

At the same time, effective mentoring need not always require large amounts of time. An experienced, perceptive mentor can provide great help in just a few minutes by making the right suggestion or asking the right question. This section seeks to describe the mentoring relationship by listing several aspects of good mentoring practice.

Careful Listening: A good mentor is a good listener. Hear exactly what the student is trying to tell you-without first interpreting or judging. Pay attention to the "subtext" and undertones of the student's words, including tone, attitude, and body language. When you think you have understood a point, it might be helpful to repeat it to the student and ask whether you have understood correctly. Through careful listening, you convey your empathy for the student and your understanding of a student's challenges. When a student feels this empathy, the way is open for clear communication and more-effective mentoring.

Keeping in Touch: The amount of attention that a mentor gives will vary widely. A student who is doing well might require only "check-ins" or brief meetings. Another student might have continuing difficulties and require several formal meetings a week; one or two students might occupy most of an adviser's mentoring time. Try through regular contact-daily, if possible-to keep all your students on the "radar screen" to anticipate problems before they become serious. Don't assume that the only students who need help are those who ask for it. Even a student who is doing well could need an occasional, serious conversation. One way to increase your awareness of important student issues and develop rapport is to work with student organizations and initiatives. This will also increase your accessibility to students.

Multiple Mentors: No mentor can know everything a given student might need to learn in order to succeed. Everyone benefits from multiple mentors of diverse talents, ages, and personalities. No one benefits when a mentor is too "possessive" of a student.

Sometimes a Mentoring Team Works Best: For example, if you are a faculty member advising a physics student who would like to work in the private sector, you might encourage him or her to find mentors in industry as well. A non-Hispanic faculty member advising a Hispanic student might form an advising team that includes a Hispanic faculty member in a related discipline. Other appropriate mentors could include other students, more-advanced postdoctoral associates, and other faculty in the same or other fields. A good place to find additional mentors is in the disciplinary societies, where students can meet scientists, engineers, and students from their own or other institutions at different stages of development.

Coordinate Activities with other Mentors: For example, a group of mentors might be able to hire an outside speaker or consultant whom you could not afford on your own.

Building Networks: You can be a powerful ally for students by helping them build their network of contacts and potential mentors. Advise them to begin with you, other faculty acquaintances, and off-campus people met through jobs, internships, or chapter meetings of professional societies. Building a professional network is a lifelong process that can be crucial in finding a satisfying position and career.

PROFESSIONAL ETHICS

Be alert for ways to illustrate ethical issues and choices. The earlier that students are exposed to the notion of scientific integrity, the better prepared they will be to deal with ethical questions that arise in their own work.

Discuss your policies on grades, conflicts of interest, authorship credits, and who goes to meetings. Use real-life questions to help the student understand what is meant by scientific misconduct: What would you do if I asked you to cut corners in your work? What would you do if you had a boss who was unethical?

Most of all, show by your own example what you mean by ethical conduct. You might find useful the COSEPUP publication On Being a Scientist: Responsible Conduct in Research (1995), also available on line.

POPULATION-DIVERSITY ISSUES

In years to come, female students and students of minority groups might make up the majority of the population from which scientists and engineers will emerge. Every mentor is challenged to adapt to the growing sex, ethnic, and cultural diversity of both student and faculty populations.

Minority Issues: Blacks, Hispanics, and American Indians as a group make up about 23% of the US population, but only about 6% of the science and engineering labour force. Many minority-group students are deterred from careers in science and engineering by inadequate preparation, a scarcity of role models, low expectations on the part of others, and unfamiliarity with the culture and idioms of science. Mentors can often be effective through a style that not only welcomes, nurtures, and encourages questions, but also challenges students to develop critical thinking, self-discipline, and good study habits. Expectations for minority-group students in science have traditionally been too low, and this can have an adverse effect on achievement. A clear statement that you expect the same high performance from all students might prove helpful. Be aware of minority support groups on your campus and of appropriate role models. Link minority-group students with such national support organizations as the National Action Council for Minorities in Engineering.

Cultural Issues: You could find yourself advising students of different cultural backgrounds (including those with disabilities) who have different communication and learning styles. Such students might hail from discrete rural or urban cultures in the United States or from abroad; in many programs, foreign-born students are in the majority. If you are not familiar with a particular culture, it is of great importance to demonstrate your willingness to communicate with and to understand each student as a unique individual. Are you baffled by a student's behavior? Remember that a cultural difference could be the reason. Don't hesitate to ask colleagues and the students themselves for help. Finding role models is especially important for students from a culture other than yours. Examine yourself for cultural biases or stereotypical thinking.

Female Representation: In some fields-notably psychology, the social sciences, and the life sciences-females are well represented as students but underrepresented in the professoriate and are not always appointed to assistant professor positions at a rate that one would expect on the basis of PhD and postdoctoral student representation. In other fields-such as mathematics, physics, computer science, and engineering-females are underrepresented at all levels. In all fields, the confidence of female students might be low, especially where they are isolated and have few female role models. If you advise female students in one of these fields, be aware that they could need extra support. Wait for cues from students, however, to avoid singling out anyone for special treatment. Be familiar with campus support groups and of female role models on and off campus.

Family Issues: Both women and men can face challenging family issues; mentors should be alert to students who need extra support when having a child, raising a child alone, returning to school after child-rearing, caring for a parent, suffering marital problems, or juggling the challenges of a two-career family. You might want to send a student to a colleague or counselor with special competence in family issues.

Sexual Harassment: If you mentor a student of the opposite sex, extra sensitivity is required to avoid the appearance of sexual harassment. Inappropriate closeness between mentors and students will produce personal, ethical, and legal consequences not only for the persons involved but also for the programs or institutions of which they are part.

Be Guided by Common Sense and a Knowledge of Your Own Circumstances: Is it appropriate to invite the student to discussions at your home? During meetings, should you keep the office door closed (for privacy) or open (to avoid the appearance of intimacy)? Make an effort to forestall misunderstandings by practicing clear communication. If you do have a close friendship with a student, special restrictions or self-imposed behavior changes might be called for. But do not restrict students' opportunities to interact with you because of sex differences. In a respectful relationship, mutual affection can be an appropriate response to shared inquiry and can enhance the learning process; this kind of affection, however, is neither exclusive nor romantic. For additional guidance, talk with your department chair, your own mentor, or other faculty.

Disability Issues: Students with physical, mental, emotional, or learning disabilities constitute about 9% of first-year students with planned majors in science and engineering. Be careful not to underestimate the potential of a student who has a disability. Persons with disabilities who enter the science and engineering workforce perform the same kinds of jobs, in the same fields, as others in the workforce. You should also keep in mind that persons with disabilities might have their own cultural background based on their particular disability, which cuts across ethnic lines.

As a mentor, you might be unsure how to help a student with a disability. Persons with disabilities can function at the same level as other students, but they might need assistance to do so. You can play a pivotal role in finding that assistance, assuring students that they are entitled to the assistance, and confirming they are able to secure assistance. Another very important role of the mentor is in making colleagues comfortable with students who have disabilities.

Many campuses offer programs and aids such as special counseling, special equipment (adaptive computer hardware, talking calculators, and communication devices), adapted physical education, learning disability programs, and academic support.

Further, your institution's specialist in Americans with Disabilities Act (ADA) issues might provide help (for example, in securing funding from the National Institutes of Health [NIH], the National Science Foundation [NSF], and other sources). However, keep in mind that this person might know less than you do about the needs of a student in your field--for example, in the use of particular equipment.

2

Militarisation, Nation and Gender

INTRODUCTION

Recent feminist theories of nationalism have pointed out that the Qaum (nation) is essentially feminine in construction. The nation is narrated on the body of women who become an emotionally-laden symbol of the nation, self, the inner, spiritual world and home. One's motherland or maadar-e-watan, as it comes to be called, becomes invested with the kind of erotic attraction felt towards women, especially in the figure of the mother.

The country comes to be appropriated, represented and contained within words which have strong romantic, erotic as well as maternal connotations. The desire for this land/woman/dharti is constructed as masculine desire; the desire to possess it, see it, admire it, love it, protect it and die fighting for it against rivals.

Since the desire for women gets transferred on to the nation and women's bodies come to signify the nation, communal, regional, national and international conflicts come to be played out on women's bodies. These bodies thus become arenas of violent struggle. Women are humiliated, tortured, brutally raped, and murdered as part of the process by which the sense of being a nation is created and reinforced.

The first part of this chapter will examine the ways in which gender ideology lies at the heart of the production of nationalist and militarist thought in Pakistan. The second part will look at how women's bodies were used during Partition as part of a national battle to create Pakistan and India.

MILITARISATION AND THE EROTICS OF NATIONALISM

Pakistan complicates and enriches a more general understanding of the gendered construction of the nation. Pakistan as an idea was imagined in opposition to Hindu/India within the parameters of the two-nation theory. There are constant attempts at the level of popular and official discourse to assert Pakistan's and Islam's difference from India and Hindus; in fact these two are often represented as the exact opposite of each other.

When self-definition depends so desperately on real or imagined difference, this difference has to be asserted aggressively, consistently and violently. Most States maintain large standing armies for the purpose of protecting and maintaining the boundaries of the Self against encroachment, conquest, invasion and intrusion by the 'enemy'. These armies are provided with the latest weapons of mass destruction to enable them to enforce internal cohesion and integration, while sealing off the borders against the threatening and polluting outsiders. Militarisation thus becomes the foremost imperative of the nation-state, frequently its number one priority even at the expense of the welfare and happiness of its citizenry which it claims to protect.

The concept of militarisation is being used here not merely to denote a large, standing army equipped with the latest nuclear and conventional weapons. Militarisation, in a wider and more comprehensive sense, entails the effects of militaristic thinking on an entire society.

This happens when the whole society becomes so permeated by violent imagery, thought, emotion, cognition and imagining, that it becomes inconceivable to solve any conflict without resorting to the force of arms. All institutions of society become saturated with violence and ideas of combat, battle, fighting, blood, martyrdom, victory, defeat, heroes and traitors become a part of everyday life even in civilian matters. In such cases, even the language of the military is borrowed and internalised by the civilian institutions, for example, words such as 'strategy', 'plan of action', 'targets' have become part of common usage in the departments of population, education and social welfare. Violence becomes so much a part of everyday consciousness that its brutal effects, its painful consequences and its tragic outcomes are obliterated.

The nation-state, as a form of legitimised violence, inscribes itself on the mind at both the conscious and unconscious levels. This is done through imagery which has immense evocative power through its associations with other objects which are invested with desire. The desire for objects of love is displaced on to the nation-state which becomes a highly erotic entity. It becomes the object of desire, the subject of poetry and song and it comes to be eulogised in the mass media, textbooks and public monuments.

A complex and intricate relationship develops between the predominance of military values, love and desire for the nation-state and gender ideology. This relation is articulated through the construction of the nation state as mother. As Saba Khattak writes "The nation state is portrayed as the mother which needs protection against the outside enemy. This appeals... to a male macho psyche that is called for defence and survival." As an example of the 'protector' and 'protected', she quotes Sardar Assef Ali, the former foreign minister, as having said that "to us the nuclear programme is similar to the honour of our mothers and sisters, and we are committed to defending it at all cost."

This kind of imagery is clearly evident in our nationalistic songs, poetry, taranas, milli naghmas, television plays and popular films. A song from the old movie Aag Ka Darya, (River of Fire), which became very popular, goes: Ay Watan hum hain teri shama key parwanon mein (Oh, Country you are the candle around which we, your lovers, hover). Shama (candle) and parwana (the lover) are commonplace images used generously in Urdu poetry to denote the beloved and the lover who yearns for her and burns in the pain of her love. In the song, the country becomes the beloved, therefore feminine, and the lover represents male desire. It reflects the displacement of private passion on to the public sphere of the nation.

There is ample evidence of the appropriating and desirous male gaze in other nationalist songs. One of the oldest comes from the national poet, Allama Iqbal, who wrote:

Saaray Jehan say Acha, Hindustan Hamara
Hum bulbulain hain is ki, yeh gulsitan hamara
Hindustan is better than the entire world
We are its nightingales and the land is our garden

Similar feelings are echoed later in a famous song: Chaand meri zamin, phool mera watan (My land is the moon, My country is a flower). These songs are extremely well-known and popular. They are often sung in schools and are printed in school textbooks next to pictures of war heroes, guns, tanks, fighter jets and submarines. In all three examples above, the country/land is compared to something considered beautiful in local folklore and national imagery. In the first case, the land/beloved is a candle/light around whom the burning lover hovers; in the second case the land is a garden and the lovers are bulbuls who sing love songs for the beloved; and in the third case the land is compared with the moon (usually considered beautiful) and the country with a flower, another symbol of beauty and romance.

The use of such romantic metaphors for the country is widespread in nationalistic poetry. Massive amounts of passion is displaced on to the land which is invested with images normally used for women and hardly ever used to describe men. The subject of desire is male and the gaze is also that of a male looking upon a beloved. The active/passive relation is easily discernible in the above poems as the candle is passive and it is the masculine parwana who hovers around her, the garden is passive and the active bulbul sings to it.

The connection of woman with inanimate objects, whether the moon, land, or candle is also common in our society as is obvious in the common saying that most troubles are caused by zan, zar and zamin, that is, woman, money and land. Here two inanimate objects are placed side by side with woman, a living being whose connection with land is once again asserted. The important thing to remember is that all three are commodities which males desire and exchange among themselves in the form of transactions and alliances.

The imagery of nation-as-mother and motherland evokes even more passionate responses. Nalini Natarajan argues that the image of the mother is used because it "suggests common mythic origins. Like the land (which gives shelter and 'bears'), she is eternal, patient, essential." There seems to be a primordial sense of connection between land (dharti) and mother; both are perceived as being in need of protection; both are loved and admired; both are respected; there a willingness to die for the honour of each. The irony is that while the trope of mother-as-nation is so powerful in nationalist thought, actual mothers and women are unequal, lesser citizens with less rights in the nation-state's structure of power. The discriminatory laws about women in Pakistan bear ample testimony to that.

Nevertheless, the symbolic appropriation of woman as mother into the nation-state carries immense emotional investment. Women's primary entry point into the nation-state is as mothers, as producers of strong, brave sons ready to fight to death for the sacred land. It has been argued that "family play[s] such a central role in the nation's public imaginings that motherhood could be viewed as a national service." The idea of motherhood as a national service is explicitly present in Pakistan's educational policies in which the stated aim of female education is to produce good, moral motherhood for the benefit of the family, nation and State.

The fact that the symbolism of motherhood is intensely emotionally evocative can be gauged from the reaction to the US State Attorney's mindless and foolish remark regarding how easily Pakistanis would sell their mothers. It is a well-known fact that women are exchanged, bought and sold in some form or another in all societies, including American society. The remark was thoughtless and insensitive, but the reaction reveals the intensely threatened self which relies on moral motherhood to reproduce a nation of valiant sons. As Syed Talat Hussain observed:

> *"Mothers are the hub of most family activity and even when they do not enjoy financial freedom and when they are confined to their homes, they enjoy incredible power and clout over the whole family. They run this basic unit of the society and command a position on the scale of honour that cannot be compared with any other relationship...Pakistanis do take their mothers very seriously."*

In the quotation above, Hussain recognises the confinement and lack of financial power Pakistani suffer but refers to their clout in the family. The family is the basic unit of society, as well as the pillar of the State, and it is within the family that the nation can reproduce itself, its sons and future mothers. It is the family, therefore, that exercises the greatest control over female sexuality in the name of the purity of the nation. Women's sexuality can find legitimate expression only in national service through the family; it is otherwise denied, controlled and hidden behind the chadar and chardivari, the personalised boundaries placed around the woman, equivalent to the boundaries, frontiers, and borders of the state, all of which are under the protection of the son/mujahid or other male member.

The figure of the mother appears in nationalistic poetry and war songs as the bearer of brave sons, the sacrificing brave mother who suffers in silence, the proud mother who bore the shaheed and who salutes him. Women in war songs praise male valour and the fact that the lover, or husband, or son, is a soldier. They praise his war exploits, urge him on and promise eternal love in life or in death. The following song was extremely popular during the 1965 war with India and brought tears to the eyes of all who heard it. In this song, the mother of a soldier who has just been killed in battle, is the speaker:

Ik Jinay Jamia si, o teri maan ay
dooji teri maan ay, zameen jida naan ay
lay ke meray kolon onay tenu godi pa lia
sadqay main jawan teray, maan kehn walia
hoyon tu shaheed, khat aya teray naan da
puchday nay lok lal si o keri maan da
rab di janab wich sir main jhuka lia
sadqay main jawan teray, maan kehn walia
teray jeaan putran da des Pakistan ay
meray jiaan maanwaan noon jinan utay maan ay
sadqay main jawan teray, maan kehn walia
The one who gave you birth is your mother

The land is also your mother
it has taken you from my loving embrace
and placed you in her own lap
May you have my life, Oh you who calls me Mother
When you were killed in battle
the news came in a letter
the people asked 'who is the proud mother of this soldier'
I bowed my head in obedience to God's will
May you have my life, Oh you who calls me Mother
Pakistan is the land of sons like you
of whom mothers like me are proud
May you have my life, Oh you who calls me Mother

Here the various elements of nationalism are all woven together; the sacrificing but proud mother, the connection between the mother's lap and the land/grave, the soldier as the son of the soil who was killed defending the honour of the motherland. Another extremely popular song during the 1965 war had the following words:

Ay rah-e-haq kay shaheedo, wafa ki tasweero
watan ki betian, maaien salaam kehti hain
Oh, martyrs in the path of righteousness
pictures of faith the daughters and mothers of the land salute you

The women of the nation are cast as those who praise, applaud and eulogise the young males who fight in battle. The glory, the greatness and the eternal life belongs to the men; the women are in the background urging, encouraging, praising and supporting. An essentially passive role is carved out for them to participate vicariously in the masculine exploits of war. Giving birth to such sons, or having such brave men as lovers is the greatest honour that a woman can receive. In a lighter vein, the lover/fighter is praised for his position in the army by a doting beloved who sings: Mera mahi chail chabeela, hai ni karnail ni, jernail ni (My lively lover is a colonel, a general).

Songs like this one became so popular during the war of 1965 that the singer Noor Jehan, who sang these at the front to entertain the jawaans, herself became a kind of icon of the eulogising, doting, loving woman/mother.

Nationalistic poetry and songs, which connect the whole enterprise with the honour of mothers/sisters and one's inner sanctum, enable the gory reality of war to be forgotten. The glory attached to martyrdom and bravery in battle, the playfulness in the song above, all mask the sordid reality of war-the mangled and charred bodies, the brutalisation, the violence, the excruciating pain, the needless wastage of precious life, the human degradation and misery, all for state expansion and economic gain. When religion is added on to the protection of state and nation, the emotional investment doubles.

In the creation of the war mind-set, it is not only young men who are conditioned to be the defenders of the faith, the motherland and nation; women are similarly conditioned to believe that they need defending by strong male protectors and that, as mothers, they must raise strong sons. Women are taught to be convinced of their own 'inherent weakness' from childhood and it is in opposition to this 'weakness' that male 'strength' is constructed. Hence, as mentioned earlier, gender ideology lies at the heart of the production of nationalist and militaristic thought. This kind of complementary construction of masculinity and femininity enables warlike nationalism to be imbibed by the whole population, which feels empowered by a sense of participation in the State's nationalist triumphs.

Women not only participate in the imagery of violence and war by creating and upholding it, they constitute the bodies on which the narrative of gendered violence is written. War imagery gets divided into masculine and feminine, for example, being defeated is equal to being feminine and winning is equal to being masculine. A very popular song during the 1965 war had the following verse:

Uj Hinduan jang di gal cheri
ukh hoi hairaan hairaanian di
Maharaj, ay khed talwar di ay
jang khed naien hondi zenaniaan di

Today, the Hindus have stirred up war

Surprise itself is surprised

Maharaj, this is a game of the sword

War is not the play of women

In this song not only is war referred to in terms of a game and play which removes attention from its horrors, the clear message is that war is not the play of women. In other words, war is a masculine pursuit, the implication being that it requires strength, valour and bravery which women lack. It is a manly enterprise, and Hindus, who are here equated with women, are too weak to fight.

The feminisation of Hindus is commonplace in Pakistan. It is indicated in common sayings like "the banya is a vegetable eater, he cannot fight". In textbooks, Hindus are frequently presented as weak, timid, non-warlike and effeminate, in contrast to Muslims who are represented as hypermasculine. It has been noted that the "difference between male and female human beings is exaggerated in warlike societies." With Pakistan's massive defence spending, and the preponderance of warlike imagery, it can safely be considered a warlike society.

Pakistani war songs not only reflect this hypermasculinity but exaggerate the imagery of blood, gore, death, weapons and pain. A very popular song during the 1965 war went:

jis rah se Aye ga us rah pe maarain gay pani bhi no maangay ga yoon nasha utarain gay

Whichever direction you come from we will kill you there

You will not even have the time to ask for a drink of water

So completely will we erase your intoxication with war

The enemy becomes a soldier who is dying in battle and cannot even ask for a drink of water. The humanity of a dying soldier is erased; he is merely the 'enemy' and has no existence as a person. His pain is obliterated, his sorrow a matter of scorn. The whole song is designed to show the immense power and prowess of the Pakistan army which is represented as capable of inflicting exemplary defeat on India. In the process, the army jawaan is also created as heartless and inhuman. Strength is equated with cruelty.

The idea of being unrelenting towards the enemy is emphasised in other songs as well, possibly as a way of keeping up the spirits of the jawaans. Another very popular song, also from the 1965 war days, is the following:

Rakh jigra tey ho ja hun tagra mit jaye kufr da jhagra bala ji hun thar ragra deyo ragra aena noon deyo ragra

Don't lose heart and become strong

The infidels must be eliminated give them a severe bashing give them a bashing, give them a bashing

The conflict is presented as that between Islam and kufr, which is not unusual. National war is couched in religious terms in order to increase emotional investment in it and exploit people's religious feelings. The aggressive impulses within human beings, meant for survival purposes, are here harnessed to the national cause in which manhood can be proved by a repeated bashing of the enemy.

In Pakistan, children have always been indoctrinated in the discourse of war, bloodshed, fighting and manhood. In a song which emerged early on after Partition:

Aao bacho sair karain tum ko Pakistan ki

Jis ki khatir hum ne di qurbani lakhon jan ki

Yeh dekho yeh Sindh jehan zalim Dahir ka tola tha yehin Muhammad Bin Qasim Allah-o-Akbar bola tha tuti hui talwaron mein kya bijli thi kya shola tha ginti ke kuch ghazi thay lakhon ka lashkar tola tha

Come children, we will take you on a journey around Pakistan the country for which we sacrificed millions of lives

See, this is Sindh where the cruel Dahir had a band of men this is where Muhammad Bin Qasim pronounced Allah-o-Akbar there was lightening and fire in their broken swords there were only a handful of ghazis and millions of the enemy

By associating victory, power, glory and fire with a hero and in turn associating the hero with religion, children, who all grow up listening to this song, are infused with the desire to become like the historically reconstructed heroes. The same message of martyrdom, war, death and fighting turns up in virtually every history and social science textbook. Aggressive impulses are directed towards a real or imagined enemy, within and without, so that legitimacy can be provided for organised state violence. As the song moves around the newly independent state of Pakistan it comes to Bengal. Praise is lavished on the beauty of the province, on its jute as a golden fibre and its ability to withstand floods and cyclones. The last line is: yehan ka bacha bacha upni qaum pe marne wala hai (Every child of this land is willing to die for the nation). This is highly ironic given that in 1971 many Bengalis did die for the nation, but the nation was not Pakistan; it was Bangladesh. They died fighting against Pakistan.

The nation is a fictional construct and at any moment in time, its boundaries can shift re-determining who is excluded and who is included. In 1947 East Bengal was part of the nation, a part much derided by Ayub Khan and other West Pakistani leaders. In 1971, Bengalis became outsiders, enemies of the nation. This shows how the homogenising process of the nation-state is replete with violence and how tentative the identity of any nation-state is; nevertheless, people are expected to lay down their lives for this precarious and contested entity.

In the last part of the same song, the masculinity and strength of the men of the Frontier Province is established.

> *yeh ilaqa sarhad ka hai, sub ki nirali shaan yehan bandooqon ke saye me bachay hotain hain jawaan yehan thokar main zalzalay yehan hain muthi main toofan yehan sar pe kafan baandhay phirta hai dekho har aik Pathan yehan Qaum kahe to abhi laga dain bazi yeh sab jaan ki*
>
> This is the Frontier region, everyone has a unique glory *children grow up in the shadow of the gun it has withstood many Earthquakes and Storms every Pathan wears a kafan on his head at all times If the nation desires, they are all willing to die*

Children are told here of how Pathans grow up in the shadow of a gun and are ever ready to die for the nation. The emphasis on the word jawaan repeatedly does not simply mean youth, but virility, power, strength and valour.

A recent incident shows how pervasive the evocative power of battle, conquest and glory, and masculinity have become. The Wills World Cup Cricket Championship in 1996 was described almost entirely in terms of war. The cricket grounds were referred to as a battlefield, the cricketers as warriors, coke bottles as missiles and winning and losing became a matter of life and death. In this kind of cricket nationalism, gender imagery was once again employed; the defeated Pakistani team was sent a set of bangles signifying that losing to arch-enemy, India, meant they must be feminine. Similarly, Wasim Akram was accused of losing the 'battle' against India because he wears an earring.

The concern about maintaining gender identities is evident in a news item entitled 'No long hair for Sahiwal boys', which reported that the District Administration in Sahiwal had decided to launch a campaign against young men with long hair and earrings. The City Magistrate started a campaign in which he took barbers with him to give haircuts to any offending boys and remove their earrings on the spot. This is a telling example of the State's nationalist anxiety manifesting itself in the possible loss of masculinity--if we don't have 'masculine' men, our nation will be weakened.

It is through a consistent reinforcement of the imagery of power, masculinity, strength, blood, death and war, that a masculine and powerful nation is evoked. Along with the imagery of strong and brave men, a concomitant imagery of weak women/ mothers in need of protection, is maintained. In order to buttress this imagery further, a permanent sense of threat and impending doom is maintained by means of the myth that India wants to devour Pakistan as it never accepted its existence.

WOMEN'S BODIES AS ARENAS OF VIOLENT STRUGGLE

An important part of nationalism in S. Asia has been the way women and their sexuality are treated as the symbol of culture, tradition and home. In a situation of national conflict this leads to the women of the enemy being forced into a similar symbolic role. This is why while violence during communal, ethnic and international conflicts is directed against everyone, women are violated in a sexually-specific way, that is, they are raped. Not only are they raped, their bodies are marked in particular ways that are meant as reminders of their being women, the honour of the community/nation.

The use of women in this way marked the moment of independence for India and Pakistan. The most horrifying tales of torture and insane violence during the Partition of 1947 have been recorded by writers like Saadat Hasan Manto in stories like Thanda Gosht (Frozen Flesh) and Siyah Hashiyeh (Black Frames). Similarly, Krishan Chandar in his story Ghaddar (Traitor), recorded the specific kinds of sexual violence against women of opposing communities. There are terrible instances of this in the more recent history of Pakistan. According to one estimate, the Pakistan army raped two hundred thousand women during the army action in East Pakistan in 1970.

Writing on the Partition of 1947, Veena Das comments that widespread violence against women of all religious communities was witnessed with more than hundred thousand women having been abducted from each of the two parts of Punjab alone. She argues that "the bodies of women became political signs, territories on which the political programmes of the rioting communities of men were inscribed." In her view, the desire to assert collective identity, whether of nation or of community, becomes transformed into "the desire to humiliate the men of other nations and communities through the violent appropriation of 'their' women." Women's own identities are transformed and subsumed in this process of state-formation and nation-building.

In their analysis of communal sexual violence during the Partition of India, and more recently in Bosnia, Ritu Menon and Kamla Bhasin find there are three specific features of the crimes against women, namely their brutality, their extreme sexual violence, and their collective nature. The range of explicit sexual violation includes "stripping; parading naked; mutilating and disfiguring; tattooing or branding the breasts and genitalia with triumphal slogans [including the phrases 'Pakistan

Zindabad!' and 'Jai Hind!'; amputating breasts; knifing open the womb; raping, of course; killing foetuses." Furthermore, violent sexual crimes were often committed against women of other communities in public places, such as the marketplace, usually in the presence of their male kin.

Given the symbolic role of women, the desecration of women becomes a matter of national shame and cultural/religious dishonour and must be avenged. Menon and Bhasin note that "one rumour guaranteed to provoke communal violence and reprisal during Partition, was that of large-scale raping of a community's women." Thus, just as the nation is narrated on women's bodies, the enemy inscribes its victory on the female body. The ultimate defeat that can be inflicted on the enemy is the pollution of its race through collective rape during war and other forms of conflict. Women's dishonour is the dishonour of the race, the nation and the country. It is the ultimate form of defiling, the defiling of one's mother. It is interesting to note that since so much emotion is evinced through the imagery of the mother, most forms of Punjabi abuse centre around the defiling of the mother, sister or daughter. This is usually considered the ultimate insult to be avenged with physical violence.

Menon and Bhasin quote Stasa Zajovic about ethnic cleansing in Bosnia: "when 'their' women are raped, it is experienced not as, and through, the women's pain, but as a male defeat: they were too feeble to protect their property." Menon and Bhasin conclude that the failure to protect women-as-property reflects on a man's masculinity--and, by extension, his community's honour. This is one reason why, in communal violence, a whole collectivity is involved.

Women's bodies are treated as territories to be conquered, claimed or marked by the assailant. The fact that so much of communal sexual violence took place in temples or gurudawaras means that it was the simultaneous violation of women and sacred space. As Menon and Bhasin assert, "In the context of Partition, it engraved the permanence of the division of India into India and Pakistan on the women of both religious communities, in the way that they became the respective countries, indelibly imprinted by the Other."

For Menon and Bhasin, then, the marking of the breasts and genitalia made permanent the sexual appropriation of the woman. This enabled the enemies to pollute the "biological national source of the family". In this way, women's reproductive power was appropriated to prevent the undesirable proliferation of the enemy's progeny. Thus, the female body itself could be made to appear as a traitor. Such violence constituted the "profaning of everything that was held to be of sacred and symbolic value to the Other."

It is clear that wherever identity and self are threatened by an Other, an outsider defined as an enemy, womenís bodies become the arena of the most violent forms of conflict. As global conflicts intensify, and males of weak and dependent countries feel threatened by global powers, the notion of womenís bodies as signifiers of nation, home, and honour is likely to increase. This increase can potentially manifest itself as nationalist anxiety and the response is most likely going to be further incarceration of women, greater emphasis on the veil and the chardivari, an enhanced desire to confine women to domestic tasks and motherhood. This is likely to be accompanied by an intensified glorification of motherhood and a more urgent need to protect motherhood against violation and impurity, even while increasing women's participation in the market due to economic imperatives. The double burden is, therefore, likely to increase along with the controls imposed on women's bodies. Women's bodies will not merely be the site of political, national and armed struggles; they will also become the major signifiers in economic struggles and market conflicts.

During the recent years, the indigenous Kashmiri struggle has been challenged by a number of potential hazards. The foremost threat to its continuation is a distinctive polarization on the basis of religion despite of the fact that the state of Jammu & Kashmir provides some of the clearest instances of shared religious identities in the world.

In truth, the Kashmir knot has assumed quite a different shape over the years from what it appeared at the time when the issue was taken up by the UNO in 1948. It is just not a dispute over a territory but a thorny political enigma and a perpetual threat to the peace in the region. Now, the issue is also linked to the future of a Nation. During the last few years the political tendency among Kashmiris gave heavy emphasis on religion. Whereas, the indigenous Kashmiri struggle when it started in 1989-1990 was provoked by the socio-economic factors and a growing sense of deprivation.

Though Kashmir issue played an important role to create an atmosphere of animosity between two neighboring countries, much of this rivalry was owing to the pre-independence environment of misconceptions and delusions. The Kashmiris as a people silently witnessed their exploitation in the years after partition. The succeeding years brought a misconception that Kashmiris were a people who could be traded. Another misconstruction was there that Kashmiris were a coward nation. Such a derogatory treatment increased the sense of resentment and bitterness among Kashmiris. Moreover, the political governments in both parts of Jammu & Kashmir set unhealthy socio-economic models which propagated dissatisfaction and mistrust among the masses.

On international scene the decade of 80s saw a remarkable change as oppressed societies around the world decided that it was time for a change. The winds of change swept across Eastern Europe and Central Asia. The Soviet empire disintegrated and the whole world got a new look. This was enough to give inspiration to the oppressed Kashmiris, who have been denied the right to self determination for half a century and who had been governed by corrupt rulers. Therefore they decided to take up arms against oppression and injustice.

In essence, the current uprising in Kashmir is a movement to assert an inborn right of human beings to live with dignity. Self respect and self esteem as a nation are the pith and marrow of this assertion. A nation can live without self rule but it can not survive without self assertion. This was the massive and spontaneous overflow of the popular feelings which transformed into an uprising.

But the last few years have seen a clear shifting of the ideological emphasis of this movement from a nationalistic character to a religious one. Some of the groups that were in the forefront of the armed insurgency in 1989 particularly the resistance elements advocating nationalism in Jammu and

Kashmir have receded into the background. In its larger perspective, it was a stringent blow on the resistance movement of Kashmiris to marginalize the nationalistic elements. Perhaps, those who wanted to cash in on Kashmir were not brave enough to devise some other reason to amass arsenal in the region. Therefore, a movement of self assertion was given a religious color. An eminent Indian bureaucrat Mr. Wajahat Habibullah asserts in his special report "the political economy of the Kashmir conflict "that "an ethnic conflict was given a religious color." During the past few decades there have been organized efforts to manipulate the indigenous movement of Kashmiri people by aggressive revivalist overtures.

The Kashmiris have over five thousand years old written history. They have evolved their own distinct cultural tradition and philosophy because of their peculiar disposition and natural bent. Throughout the ages they have remained peace loving and submissive.

Similarly, the story of aggression on life, culture and religion of the indigenous people of Kashmir has not its origin in the partition of India. It only added a new dimension to an age old tradition of invading the land of beauties. But, right from the genesis of Kashmir issue, there have been frequent though indistinct references by the historians, politicians and intellectuals to propose various solutions to this problem on the basis of Kashmiriat.

For instance, the state of Jammu and Kashmir presents a classic blend of linguistic and ethno-religious diversity. Historically, the entire state is composed of three geographical divisions. But as far as its ethnic disposition is concerned, the census report of 1941 provides an insight into the diversified nature of this peculiar piece of land on earth. The language situation in the State before independence is interestingly beautiful. The 1941 census listed Kashmiri, Dogri, Gujari, Rajasthani, Pahari, Balti, Ladakhi and Shina as the main languages spoken in the State. Among them Kashmiri commanded the largest number of speakers with Dogri at second and Gujari at third positions respectively.

Circumstantial evidence indicates that there have been an organized efforts and official patronage by the authoritarian and dictatorial elite on both sides of the divided state to suppress the growth of Kashmiri language and culture. Till now, the teaching of Kashmiri has not been introduced at school levels in both parts of the state. Not only that, no textbooks in Kashmiri are available even though a set of such books was prepared by experts.

If Sindhi and Pushto can be taught in schools, why not Kashmiri languages have been given such consideration? This is despite the general desire among Kashmiri masses to have Kashmiri languages as medium of instructions particularly at the primary and middle schools. In past, 83 per cent of the respondents of a survey in Kashmir valley showed their preference for use of Kashmiri as a medium of instruction at primary levels.

It is not a mere coincidence that all the names having Kashmiri identity have been changed and personalized. In this manner, the traditional and cultural heritage of Kashmir has been thrown into oblivion. The new generation of Kashmiris do not find themselves acquainted with the decencies of Kashmiri culture and civilization.

The polarization in the name of religious incongruity has played havoc to the Kashmiri fabric. Therefore, a true spirit of Kashmiriat can be restored only after giving rightful place to the indigenous Kashmiri tradition and culture. Due to unjust and unfair treatment of their identity, Kashmiris have come to feel discarded and deceived by the rest of the world. Much of this sentiment can be termed as general behavior of a people who has been mistreated and misunderstood anywhere in the world. In essence, Kashmiris are a peace loving nation whose opportunities to prosper have been curtailed due to misguided policies in the region since partition of the subcontinent.

To quote Salma Tasadduque Hussain, a former member of the Punjab Assembly (1946-58) and a social worker, "It gave great encouragement to women to see that they could find a place of honour with men like Quaid-i-Azam...."

In the meantime, at Jinnah's instance, the Muslim Women Students Federation (1941) and the Women National Guards (1942) were launched, in a concerted attempt to mobilize the womenfolk alongside the menfolk in the struggle for Pakistan.

All this signified the acceptance of an entirely new role for women, and the breaking down of the male-female segregation and stratification syndrome and, more important, of the male domination in vogue till then because of the patriarchal mindset and ethos, which had ruled the subcontinental Muslim societal structure for centuries.

Muslim Women During the general elections (1945-46) played a pivotal role. Women comprised almost one-third of the audiences in the election meetings in the Punjab, to quote Mian Mumtaz Daultana, the most dynamic Muslim League leader in the 1940s'. According to him, their role in getting the men voters to the polling booths was crucial, especially in the Punjab where the Unionist Ministry had put up all sorts of obstacles in the way of a favourable verdict on Pakistan.

More significant was the women's role in the burgeoning civil disobedience movement in the Punjab (January-February 1947) and in the NWFP (February-June 1947). Women took out processions in Lahore day after day for a whole month, undergoing all sorts of hazards, bravely facing teargas, lathi-charge, beatings, arrests, and imprisonment.

One of the prisoners, the intrepid Mumtaz Shah Nawaz, made a green flag out of her own dupatta, surreptitiously climbed up the jail building and hoisted it on top, shouting "Allah-o-Akbar" (God is great) and "Pakistan Zindabad".

Two weeks later, when a mammoth women's procession finally reached the imposing Punjab Secretariat building, the seat of Punjab bureaucracy, at the fag end of the Mall in Lahore, a 13-year-old girl, Fatima Sughra, suddenly climbed up the massive iron gate, pulled down the fluttering Union Jack, the living symbol of imperial power, and replaced it with the burgeoning green Muslim League flag, which she, too, had made out of her own dupatta. And all this in the presence of a strong police contingent.

No less striking was the women's performance in the NWFP, traditionally one of the subcontinent's most conservative areas. During the civil disobedience movement, the usually timid and traditionally home-bound Pakhtoon women plucked up courage to a point that they cast off their veil and organized public processions and demonstrations, in defiance of Section 144.

Like their compatriots in the Punjab, they also faced teargas, lathi charges, beatings, and even gunfire; they also scaled ladders and climbed up buildings to hoist the League flag at various public places. And on April 3, 1947, some 1,500 women resorted to picketing, for the first time in the NWFP history. More daring: they launched a secret organization called a "War Council", and ingeniously set up an underground radio station called Pakistan Broadcasting Radio Station, which continued to be on the air till Pakistan's emergence on August 14-15, 1947.

Thus, within a brief spell of ten years (1937-47), the apathetic and timid, homebound, purdah-clad, and superstition-prone Muslim women had been able to transform themselves radically into a pro-active, vocal, highly motivated and mobilized group, supremely conscious of their latent potentialities for political and social action. Indeed, the Pakistan movement had enabled them to prove their ability to organize, demonstrate, mobilize, court arrest, face persecution, lathi-charges, and teargas, as well as to raise funds and organize relief work in time of crises.

Thus, they had raised sizeable funds during the Bengal famine (1943-44) and the 1945-46 general elections, and for the victims of the communal holocausts in Calcutta and Bihar (1946). They had also organized extensive relief work over there, as well as for the seven million refugees that had poured into West Pakistan during the partition riots in 1947.

It's always crisis that catalytically helps to actualize the latent potential in a community no less than in an individual, and the Muslim crisis in 1937, when Muslim India had reached its nadir in their chequered history since 1857, had helped to cause this gigantic transformation in the mindset, ethos and behavioural patterns of both men and women.

It is an important fact that men gallantly went along with women in this emancipatory exercise-for the simple reason that the women could not have possibly donned this role without their full support. Thus Jinnah utilized the political mobilization route to put the male-female relationship on an even keel, and get women emancipated and empowered-to a point that it became routinized in Pakistan's national life.

Simultaneously, if only because of their role alongside their menfolk, they had won the right to vote, to receive education, and to own property. In their emergence as a vocal, pro-active group during the momentous 1937-47 decade, Jinnah had helped them the most. He also acknowledged their notable contribution in the freedom struggle.

Upon Pakistan's birth, therefore, he obviously felt that "In the great task of building the nation and maintaining its solidarity, the women have a valuable part to play---not only in their homes but by helping their less fortunate sisters outside."

And he saw to it that women were represented in the Pakistan Constituent Assembly, that they were included in the delegations to the UN and other international moots, and in the executive bodies of almost every organizational set up after Pakistan's birth. Again, it was he who had inspired his own sister, Fatima Jinnah, and Begum Ra'ana Liaquat Ali Khan, wife of Pakistan's first Prime Minister, to found several institutions and organizations for the educational uplift, economic amelioration and professional training of women in Pakistan's formative years.

Thus, a new matrix of socially acceptable behaviour on women's part was firmly laid, which, with the years, enabled women to work their way up into the upper echelons of the government, the professions, and the educational and political fields.

It was, again, Jinnah's benign influence that had emboldened Fatima Jinnah to contest against Field Marshal Mohammad Ayub Khan in the 1965 presidential election. Inter alia, her candidature had settled, once and for all, the thorny question whether or not a woman can be the head of an avowedly Muslim state, thus paving the way for Benazir Bhutto to become the first woman prime minister of a Muslim country, in 1988. Equally important, Fatima Jinnah was probably the first woman in the world to contest for the office of the president of a country.

In contesting the election in the most difficult circumstances, compounded by advanced and failing health, Fatima Jinnah had, in a sense, dramatized Jinnah's vision of Pakistan.

When asked, in 1942, by Geti Ara Bashir Ahmad, sister of Begum Shah Nawaz and daughter of Mian Mohammad Shafi, whether the "Foundations of our new State (would) be laid on conservatism or whether it would assume the shape of a progressive country", Jinnah had categorically said, "Tell your young girls, I am a progressive Muslim leader. I, therefore, take my sister along with me to backward areas like Balochistan and NWFP and she also attends the sessions of the All India Muslim League and other public meetings. Pakistan will be a progressive country in the building of which women will be seen working shoulder to shoulder with men in every department of life."

The author was Founder-Director of the Quaid-i-Azam Academy (1976-89), and authored "Jinnah: Studies in Interpretation" (1981), the only work to qualify for the President's Award for Best Books on Quaid-i-Azam.

A NIECE REMEMBERS

Gulshan Chandio, the grand niece of Quaid-i-Azam, remembers him fondly. The granddaughter of his sister Marium who was very close to him, Ms Chandio's memories of Mohammad Ali Jinnah and Fatima Jinnah remain vivid to this day.

"A day before Pakistan came into being we arrived at Karachi from Bombay and stayed at Central Hotel, now long demolished. My mother rang the Governor House and Jinnah's ADC informed them that they were invited to tea by the Quaid. He was extremely busy as they were preparing for Independence Day but he made time for us. Invited again on August 14 at the Governor House he came towards my mother to greet her. Such was his regard for his family."

While residing in Bombay she and her family were regular visitors of Mohammad Ali Jinnah. Gulshan remembers wearing a western dress to lunch with her mother to the Quaid's house. He asked her to wear a gharara and she happily agreed to it, wearing one when she next went to his house for lunch. Once she bought some jewellery and showed it to him and he advised her to buy one big thing rather than little sets, so she returned it the next day. A connoisseur of furniture he pointed out a shop where her parents could buy good furniture for her elder sister who was getting married.

Gulshan remembers the honesty, integrity and caring for each other in Jinnah's family. He didn't like his relatives using his name to achieve their ends. Gulshan's father firmly believed that Jinnah would be able to achieve the goal of creating Pakistan because of his honesty and principles. "Nehru and other leaders would come to visit him at his Bombay residence, he never went to them. People have misunderstood him saying he was distant, cold and arrogant but actually he was strong and principled," she says.

Gulshan recalls that Quaid-i-Azam encouraged women to step into different fields of life and he always encouraged Fatima Jinnah to take part in politics. She once accompanied Fatima Jinnah to a meeting arranged by the Muslim league in Bombay.

When Gulshan heard that Quaid-i-Azam had died she was very sad and wanted to come to Pakistan right away but her father did not allow it as he felt that it would have created problems for the family in India. She did, however, visit Pakistan a few weeks later and stayed with Fatima Jinnah. Flagstaff House, she said, was like a home to her.

After her marriage she came to Pakistan permanently in 1952, and grew very close to Fatima Jinnah who had moved to Mohatta Palace.

THE QUAID'S FAMILY LIFE

Mohammad Ali Jinnah's first marriage was with Emibai in 1892. He was 16 and she was 14. Only nikah was solemnized and the rukhsati was to take place later on. Shortly after the marriage, Jinnah left for England. When he returned, his child bride had died. Struck by the tragedy, Jinnah didn't marry for a long time. Years later in 1918, he married Ruttenbai Petit, daughter of Sir Dinshaw Petit.

Ruttie Jinnah, as she came to be known after her marriage, was a firebrand a revolutionary like her husband. She was at his side during his struggle, braving police brutality when Jinnah led a demonstration against Lord Willingdon (the

Bombay Governor). At a reception she greeted the viceroy in the native manner, the Viceroy told her: "In Rome, you must do as the Romans do", to which she retorted: "That is exactly what I did your excellency, in India, I have greeted you the Indian way".

Jinnah did not keep his wife under his shadow and in May 1919, she made her own speech protesting against the deportation of B.G. Horniman, Editor of the Bombay Chronicle. However, their marriage ran into difficulties. Why? We can perhaps gather a glimpse from her own words. She wrote to a mutual friend that "he has a habit of habitually overworking himself, and now that I am not there to bother and tease him, he will be worse than ever".

Jinnah could not give her the time she wanted. When she died, he opened his heart out to Kanji Dwarkadas, who wrote that Jinnah never recovered from this shock and lost his cheerful disposition forever.

Their only daughter, Dina Wadia, was born on August 14, 1919. She married a non-Muslim against her father's will; and for sometime there was estrangement. She phoned her father when he was attacked by an assassin in 1943. Later, she wrote to congratulate him on the achievement of Pakistan. She came to Pakistan on her father's funeral and then, in 2004, after many years.

A CONNOISSEUR WITH RICH AESTHETICS

While political aspects of the life of Mohammad Ali Jinnah have been well researched and documented, his personal life is still largely shrouded in mystery. Even less is known about his tastes and personal interests. For instance, most people are unaware of the fact that he was a collector of the most exquisite and classical carpets.

Azhar Samdani, a foreign trained economist who developed rare expertise for restoring damaged period carpets, described him as a 'connoisseur' with rich aesthetics and an eye for quality. His opinion is to be taken seriously because all the carpets of Quaid-e-Azam displayed in Mohatta Palace were restored by him.

Samdani's expertise led him to the Quaid's carpets that the Lahore-based economist inspected during a visit to Karachi. They were faded and frayed. He decided to undertake their restoration.

He spent over two years trying to convince concerned officials that the carpets could be revived but no one was interested. However, the then federal secretary culture awarded him the assignment.

Jinnah, according to Samdani, owned about 120 carpets; each of them expensive Bokhara or Iranian piece of the finest quality, every carpet numbered and signed M. A. Jinnah; however, only 17 pieces were left by then. The other over 100 carpets had apparently been either stolen or plundered by officials, or so callously neglected that there was just no trace of them. He selected 11 carpets for restoration; the others had reached a stage where nothing could be done about them.

It took him more than three years to complete the job. It was a challenging assignment because many carpets had 'only borders or corners intact that provided an idea of the carpet's design'. The carpets are now on display in Mohatta Palace.

WE'VE COME A NOT-SO-LONG WAY

It's become a common practise, when analyzing the state of the country's affairs, to say how disappointed the founders of this nation would be with the country's degeneration. Every year comes Jinnah's birth or death anniversary, every commentator writes how he would have bemoaned the collapse of virtually every state institution or public sector had he been alive. The same is true for the status of Pakistani women on whom Jinnah placed a great deal of hope when he envisioned a progressive nation, where men and women would equally share the burden of building a strong and secure future for their country. While women have made great strides in various fields, on a socio-political front, their situation is deplorable--and the onus of the blame lies with successive governments who did little to alleviate their lot.

It is particularly disappointing given that women made many contributions in the freedom movement and had remarkable female role models like Fatima Jinnah and Rana

Liaquat Ali Khan who inspired younger women to achieve the impossible. Then there was the women's movement, born as a reaction to draconian laws created by General Ziaul Haq that relegated them to second-class citizens, which dared to challenge the system. Women's groups in the 80s' galvanized support across the country to rise together against such discriminatory laws, and while they may not have met success in overturning these laws they were able to raise awareness and make their voices heard. The two Benazir Bhutto-led governments heralded new eras of promise but sadly did not translate into the necessary action that could have alleviated their plight.

While the two democratically elected governments of Bhutto and Nawaz Sharif had women in its assemblies, politics preceded women's issues which were always relegated to drawing room discussions. When it came to crimes against women, for example, the right speeches were always made but when it came to changing discriminatory laws, nothing was done.

Oddly enough, it was a military dictator's government which introduced the 33 per cent representation of women at local, provincial and federal governments that is bound to pave way for future generations of women. While this move, too, has not created any ripples as far as qualitative change is concerned, the mere fact that there are more women in parliament than ever before means that ultimately women's issues will be forced into the foreground--provided women parliamentarians are able to convince their male colleagues that their issues merit substantial consideration. As such, there is no powerful women's pressure group or lobby that can challenge the status quo. Nonetheless, one lives on hope.

Changing laws is only part of the solution, for according to the Constitution and Islam, women and men are accorded equal rights but rarely are those instances implemented. For real change to occur, society has to be integrated into a debate whereby men are taught on the ills that customs like honour-related crimes bring upon communities. It is a woman like Mukhtaran Mai who has initiated that debate by challenging the system. She symbolizes the very woman that Jinnah would have been proud of. She represents the perennial hope that can brighten the country's future.

A MAN OF PRINCIPLES

Till today, we have not tired of making M. A. Jinnah's personality elusive, creating a singular facet to introduce him only as a politician whose vision for this country has become a victim of self-interpretation. Historians have written about Jinnah's politics, his statesmanship, often condescending mention is made of how Anglicized the country's founder was. Not much is known, neither has the trouble been taken through academic research, to delayer and depoliticize the man who gave us an independent country on the world atlas.

Talk on Jinnah mostly revolves around the kind of republic he envisioned, Islamic or secular running high on debate is a deliberate attempt to diffuse his perspective on what his position was on women and their role in Pakistan's progress. The three most important women in his life, his sister, Fatima Jinnah, wife Ruttie and daughter Dina Jinnah are usually mentioned in stereotypes to under-emphasize their importance. Fatima Jinnah is forced to a somewhat higher level than the other two because she was his official companion, consort and confidante till the very end of life. The other two have become a series of disjointed historical anecdotes, not to be analyzed for fear of drawing out Jinnah's human side as a distressed father and an estranged husband.

Absent in the brief historical mention of his wife and daughter is Jinnah's unobtrusive and non-interfering self as a husband and a father. We fail to notice how a fiercely arrogant and unbending politician was an unimposing man. He did not confine his sister to become his domestic appendage nor did he ever force his wife and daughter to stay with him to gain political mileage.

A man whose goal was to get an independent state believed first and foremost in independence of mind and action. His wife Rattie left for Paris when his objective became bigger than familial considerations and his daughter went to stay with her maternal grandparents. Jinnah did not summon legal or moral prohibition to prove a patriarchal point. Jinnah's firm non-distinction between a man and a woman was obvious on many occasions.

Sarojini Naidu, the first woman president of the Indian National Congress and a nationalist poet, saw Jinnah "as a symbol of everything attractive about modern India", (Mohammad Ali Jinnah--ambassador of Hindu-Muslim unity by J. Ahmed 1966). If Jinnah were an inflexible, dogmatic man given in to confer specific roles to women, a political force of Naidu's stature would not have put down her praise in writing for him.

Sharing her views on Jinnah's liberalism, Tahira Mazhar Ali, daughter of Sir Sikandar Hayat Khan, leader of the Unionist Party and prime minister of the Punjab in 1937, now in her early 80s remembers the founder of Pakistan not only as a fastidious and extremely well-dressed man but also as an articulate person. "He used to come to visit my father quite often in Lahore. He wanted women to participate actively in politics just as the men. He drew no boundaries, restricting women to their houses. He encouraged women's movement for Pakistan and their role as equal partners," recalls Mrs Tahira Mazhar Ali.

As a 14-year-old Tahira Mazhar Ali bicycled her way to the Mamdot Palace in Lahore where he was staying to show him the pamphlet she was carrying for the Communist Party in which it had declared its support for an independent Pakistan. "I told the chowkidar at the Mamdot Villa to inform Jinnah that Tahira was there. He immediately asked me in and was amused to see a young girl carrying the Communist Party's pamphlet. Not once did he make me feel inadequate or try to patronize me because of my age. He was very civil and nice and when I asked him if I was going to be able to meet my friends in India after partition his reply was very comforting. He said that I need not worry because I'll be able to see my friends just as he was going to regularly visit his home in Bombay. That's what he said! I remember it only too well! He was an upright, honest and fair person and not a conservative man against the progress of women as some would like us to believe," asserted Mrs Mazhar Ali.

Support of Mrs Tahira Mazhar Ali's claim of how balanced Jinnah was can be found in Professor Akbar S. Ahmed's Jinnah, Pakistan, and Islamic Identity, (1997). In the book, Professor

Ahmed wrote about an incident related by Yahya Bakhtiar, a senator from Balochistan and a former Attorney General of Pakistan, which showed Jinnah's non-compromising stance on the freedom of women. "..... in those days not even British male politicians encouraged their womenfolk to take a public role as Jinnah did. After Pakistan had been created he asked Fatima Jinnah to sit beside him on the stage at the Sibi Darbar, the grand annual gathering of Baloch and Pukhtun chiefs and leaders at Sibi. He was making a point: Muslim women must take their place in history. The Sibi Darbar broke all precedents......"

After giving up dentistry to help her brother in creating a homeland for the Muslims, Ms Jinnah attended the League session in 1937 and all the annual sessions from 1940 onwards. "Her life was centred around her brother and she was all the time concerned about his health," comments Mrs Sarwat Ahsan, daughter of Syed Muratib Ali. "My father was close to Jinnah and he would often come to Nashaiman, our house on the Davis Road in Lahore," says the 81-year-old Begum Sarwat who was a good friend of Fatima Jinnah.

Fortunate enough to have met Jinnah at the age of 17, Begum Sarwat makes an effort to invoke her first impression of the great leader. "He had invited my father and my brothers over for dinner at his house on Malabar Hill in Bombay. I also went because Fatima Jinnah was my friend. I can't really remember what he and my father talked about, but I do remember Fatima by her brother's side all the time. He treated her like a friend, somebody he could talk to and with whom he could discuss important issues," recollects Begum Sarwar. "Fatima and I never discussed his wife and daughter, but she always spoke about how he encouraged her to be with him."

Merging Jinnah's politics with his person, the matter of his slant towards women cannot be left to mere speculation. In a country built to protect an individual's freedoms and beliefs, his reaction to the existence of discriminatory laws against women despite his categorical statements favouring their equal status would have been shocking. He would have been clear on that score because Jinnah did not separate practice from preaching.

JINNAH AND WOMEN'S EMANCIPATION

Jinnah himself had always taken his sister, Fatima Jinnah, to Muslim Leaque sessions, and wherever she went with him, she walked beside him and not behind him-heralding a message loud and clear, for everyone within reach: the elevating message of gender equality, writes Sharif al Mujahid

All said and done, Quaid-i-Azam Mohammad Ali Jinnah was a liberal, par excellence. To quote Hector Bolitho who had interviewed some two hundred persons who knew Jinnah personally, during 1952-54, "Jinnah told Dr K. M. Ashraf that during the last two years (1894-96) in London his time was 'utilized for further independent studies for the political career' he had already 'had in mind'."

Jinnah also said, "Fortune smiled on me, and I happened to meet several important English liberals with whose help I came to understand the doctrine of liberalism. The liberalism of Lord Morley was then in full sway. I grasped that liberalism, which became part of my life and thrilled me very much."

It is obvious that his fascination for liberalism led Jinnah to subscribe to democratic ethos, and these, in turn, inexorably led him to become, perhaps, the foremost spokesman for civic freedoms and human rights in the Central Indian Legislature, of which he was a member for some thirty years. Even when his opponents were involved, he consistently espoused the cause of the aggrieved and pled for conceding or restoring them their basic, inalienable rights.

And as a corollary to his liberal ethos and this consuming concern with human rights was his passion for reversing the "wretched" condition of women, who stood marginalized not only in the pre-modern East but also in the modern West, in the decades before and after the advent of the twentieth century.

Thus, to quote Miss Agatha Harrison, one of the speakers at a memorial meeting for Jinnah at Coxton Hall, London, on September 14, 1948, "When Jinnah was a student in London, (1892-96), the Suffragette Movement was gathering momentum; but we had very few sympathizers and supporters. He always came to our meetings and spoke in defence of vote for women. Even then he was not afraid of championing an unpopular cause." Jinnah's belief that women should be extended the opportunities available to men at various stages in their lives was amply reflected in his careful handling of the schooling and career orientation of Fatima Jinnah; his youngest sister and ward.

Much against the family and the community traditions, she had been sent to the Bandhara Convent School (1902), and then to the St. Patrick School (1906), both in Bombay, where she did her Senior Cambridge (1913), and, still later, to Dr Ahmad Dental College, Calcutta (1919-22), to study dentistry. There she stayed at a hostel, although her sister, Maryam, along with her family, was living in Calcutta.

Upon graduation, Fatima opened a dental clinic on Abdur Rahman Street in Bombay, in 1923, and simultaneously worked at the nearby Dhobi Talau Municipal Clinic on a voluntary basis. All this was, of course, something of a rare phenomenon even for cosmopolitan and modernized Bombay. But it was made possible; only because Jinnah believed that the women have an inalienable right to carve out for themselves a career.

During his long parliamentary career (1910-47), Jinnah stood against every sort of discrimination against women and other unprivileged classes. Thus, he stoutly supported Bhupendranath Basu's Special Marriage Amendment Bill (1912), which provided for legal cover to marriages falling outside the Hindu and Muslim laws, although it caused consternation among Muslims-to a point that he felt that he could no more claim to represent them in the Imperial Council and, hence, decided to sit out in the 1913 elections. Likewise he had materially helped in the passage of the Sarda Act (1935), prohibiting child marriage.

However, Jinnah's major role in the emancipation of Muslim women came in the mid-1930s when he began to reorganize and revitalize the moribund All India Muslim League (AIML), the most authoritative Muslim political organization since its inception in 1906.

Till then, the Muslim women were mere shrouded, silent creatures, confined to the four walls of their homes, steeped in dogma and superstition and denied the fruits of modern education, health care and a career. Mohammad Ali Jinnah was the foremost Muslim to raise his authoritative voice against the pathetic conditions to which the Muslim women had been consigned for a long time, and against discrimination of all sorts.

He boldly and consistently espoused the women's cause and wished to see them as equal partners often in all walks of life. No wonder, he declared in Aligarh on March 10, 1940: "No nation can rise to the height of glory unless your women are side by side with you. We are victims of evil customs. It is a crime against humanity that our women are shut up within the four walls of the houses as prisoners. I do not mean that we should imitate the evils of western life. But let us try to raise the status of our women according to our own Islamic ideas and standards. There is no sanction anywhere for the deplorable conditions in which our women have to live. You should take your women along with you as comrades in every sphere of life..."

When Begum Shah Nawaz told the AIML Council at Lucknow in October 1937 that she had set up a Punjab Muslim Women's League, Jinnah stood up and said that he did not believe in separate men and women's organizations, but in their working together from the primary League upwards. He instructed the provincial Leagues to include two women members in their respective quotas of membership in the AIML Council.

Thus, adequate women representation came to be secured and ensured. Jinnah also nominated Begum Mohammad Ali to the AIML apex body, the Working Committee, which position she held till her death in 1944.

In December 1938, at the AIML session at Patna, Jinnah appointed a Central Women's Committee with Fatima Jinnah as convener, for the specific purpose of drafting a programme for the social, economic and cultural uplift of women.

When the question of purdah (veil) was raised by a section at Patna, Jinnah intervened to emphasize that "It is absolutely essential for us to give every opportunity to our women to participate in our struggle for life and death. Women can do a good deal within their homes, even in purdah." On another occasion, Jinnah asserted, "No nation can make any progress without the co-operation of women. If women support their men as they did in the days of the prophet of Islam (PBUH) we should soon realize our goal."

Besides political mobilization, the Central Women's Committee addressed itself to social problems encountered by the community, and organized social work. Thus, it passed several resolutions concerning housewives' problems and food shortages, as well as on more fundamental issues such as women's inheritance. In subsequent years, the committee would hold separate sessions after the AIML annual sessions.

Separate arrangements were also made for women participants in the AIML sessions, while the more prominent among them sat on the dais. And with the years, their participation increased to a point that some 5,000 women attended the AIML session at Karachi, in December 1943.

Jinnah himself had always taken his sister, Fatima, to these sessions, and wherever she went with him, she walked beside him and not behind him-heralding a message loud and clear, for everyone within reach: the ennobling message of gender equality. And although it was politically risky to take her along to traditional and tribal areas such as the NWFP and Balochistan, especially when he was striving to gather them on the AIML platform, he did it with impunity since he would not compromise on a principle he had believed in so passionately since his student days.

3

CONFLICT PREVENTION AND RESOLUTION

DRAFT RESOLUTION

1. Conflict is a gendered activity: women and men have different access to resources, power and decision-making before, during and after conflicts. The experience of women and men in situations of tensions, war, and post-conflict reconstruction is significantly different. Approximately 80% of today's civilian casualties are women and 80% of all refugees and internally displaced people worldwide are women and children. As noted in the Platform for Action of the Fourth United Nations World Conference on Women, "while entire communities suffer the consequences of armed conflict and terrorism, women and girls are particularly affected because of their status in society as well as their sex".
2. Women are thus caught in a vicious paradox: while, on the one hand, they are the main civilian victims of conflicts, they are, on the other hand, often powerless to prevent them, excluded from the negotiating tables when it comes to their resolution and marginalised in the post-conflict reconstruction and reconciliation efforts. The general exclusion of women from decision-making positions prior to, during and following violent conflict, reinforces their victimisation.
3. The Parliamentary Assembly considers that women can play a particularly important role in the prevention and resolution of conflicts and appreciates the positive contribution women can make in post-conflict reconstruction and peace consolidation. Empowering women in

conflict situations would help prevent gender-based violence such as the abominable crimes of rape, forced pregnancy, sexual slavery and others. These crimes constitute grave breaches of the Geneva Conventions and their Protocols and should be prosecuted as such.

4. The Assembly recalls the adoption in October 2000 by the United Nations Security Council of Resolution 1325 on women, peace and security, in which it urges the member states to ensure increased representation of women at all decision-making levels in national, regional and international institutions and mechanisms for the prevention, management and resolution of conflicts.
5. It also recalls the European Parliament Resolution on the participation of women in peaceful resolution of conflict and the Resolution on "the roles of women and men in conflict prevention, peace building and post-conflict democratic processes-a gender perspective", adopted by the 5th European Ministerial Conference on Equality between Women and Men in January 2003, both of which encourage the integration of a gender perspective in all activities aimed at conflict prevention and resolution.
6. Notwithstanding resolutions, appeals and recommendations of international fora and the pressure of non-governmental organisations, Europe has so far failed to ensure women's full and equal participation in conflict prevention, peace operations and post-conflict peace-building. In particular, women are often marginalised or excluded from negotiation and diplomacy aimed at ending armed conflicts, as was the case in peace talks in Kosovo, the Southern Caucasus and recently in Afghanistan and Iraq.
7. The maintenance and promotion of international peace and security cannot be realised without fully understanding the impact of armed conflict on women and without appropriate measures being taken to ensure their empowerment and security. Women's equal participation in the peace process is an essential condition for establishing lasting peace. Women also

bring alternative perspectives to conflict prevention at the grass-roots and community levels. Practical steps and initiatives should be taken by the European countries to advance the role of women in all aspects of conflict prevention and post conflict peace-building.

8. Therefore, the Assembly calls on the government and parliaments of the member states of the Council of Europe to:

General Measures

a. ensure that their national legislation is compatible with the Statute of the International Criminal Court as a matter of priority, with particular attention given to the substantive and procedural provisions regarding crimes against women;

b. include in national legal systems, where it has not yet been done, provisions penalising all forms of violence against women in conflict and post-conflict situations;

c. support women's participation in peace-building and post-conflict reconstruction by strengthening women's representation in local, national and international bodies for the regulation of conflicts;

d. provide sustained funding to women's non-governmental organisations dealing with peace issues;

e. encourage research focused on women and their peace-building activities and the impact they have on peace processes and make the results widely known and used in designing domestic and regional policies;

f. increase public awareness of the importance of gender mainstreaming in peace-support operations and provide gender training at an early stage in the training of military personnel so that respect for women becomes a matter of course and a female-friendly atmosphere prevails in the army;

g. introduce education on human rights, peace and gender equality in school curricula at all levels;

h. increase the access of women to media and communication technologies so that gender perspectives, women's expertise and women's media can influence public discourse and decision-making on peace and security;

i. support the training of editors and journalists to eliminate gender bias in reporting and investigative journalism before, during and after conflict situations and to promote gender equality and perspectives;

j. involve women and their organisations in peace negotiations at all levels (for example, round tables);

In the Field of Conflict Prevention

a. empower local women and women's groups in situations where conflict is brewing and to support their strategies aimed at avoiding armed conflict;

b. encourage the appointment of women to regional, national and international posts relating to conflict prevention;

c. increase the percentage of women in delegations to national, regional and international meetings concerned with peace and security, as well as in formal peace negotiations;

d. include "education in peace" in all curricula beginning from primary school level up to the level of professional training in order to develop a spirit of and respect for peace in society;

In the Resolution of Conflicts

a. facilitate the input of women's peace groups and organisations into key peace conferences at all levels through systematic consultation with them, ensuring that their problems and priorities are reflected in the official peace process;

b. include gender experts and expertise in all levels and aspects of peace operations, including in technical surveys, the design of concepts of operation, training, staffing and programmes;

c. take necessary measures to train women as mediators to be involved in peace missions, conflict resolution and peace support operations;

d. provide safe personal security to women by police forces, protecting them from all forms of sexual and domestic violence;

e. ensure that actions against trafficking in women in conflict affected areas form part of gender sensitive peace and security initiatives;

f. give the opportunity to refugee and internally displaced women to play a key role in camp planning, management and decision-making so that women's interests are taken into account in all aspects, especially resource distribution, security and protection;

g. grant at least temporary refugee status to women who have been raped or have been subjected to other forms of sexual violence during armed conflict;

h. involve civil society in the design and implementation of humanitarian assistance programmes;

In Post-conflict Situations

a. establish macroeconomic policies in post-conflict reconstruction that prioritise the public provision of food, water, sanitation, health and energy, the key sectors of the life of people and communities in which women provide unpaid work;

b. introduce measures that give local women priority in recruitment during emergencies and post-conflict reconstruction;

c. adopt affirmative measures to guarantee women's socio-economic rights including employment, property ownership and inheritance during post-conflict reconstruction;

d. provide physical and mental health services for women recovering from war injuries and trauma, including specialist support for women who are caring for children conceived as a result of rape and for those who have been ostracised from communities and families as a consequence of rape;

e. ensure special legal and social support to women in order to aid their reporting and prosecuting of perpetrators of war crimes and human rights abuses committed during and after conflict;

f. conduct a gender budget analysis of humanitarian assistance and post-conflict reconstruction to ensure that women benefit directly from resources mobilised through multilateral and bilateral donors;

g. grant at least a temporary residence permit to women who have been raped or have been subjected to other forms of sexual violence following armed conflict.

DRAFT RECOMMENDATION

1. The Parliamentary Assembly refers to its Resolution ... (2004) on the role played by women in the prevention and resolution of conflicts and in post-conflict reconstruction and reconciliation. It considers that, given the effect of conflict on women who are the main civilian victims, they should be empowered and made part of conflict management initiatives and should be involved in preventive diplomacy, conflict resolution, peace-making and post-conflict peace-building debates and activities at all levels.

2. The Assembly welcomes the Resolution on "the roles of women and men in conflict prevention, peace building and post-conflict democratic processes-a gender perspective", adopted by the 5th European Ministerial Conference on Equality between Women and Men, which encourages the integration of a gender perspective in all activities aimed at conflict prevention and resolution.

3. The Assembly considers that the Committee of Ministers should implement and build on this resolution, and therefore recommends that the Committee of Ministers:

   i. encourage and support multicultural, trans-border and regional women's initiatives for preventing and resolving conflicts, including the creation of women-only political parties;

   ii. call upon the international community, the United States of America and Europe to ensure ample women's leadership and participation in all discussions and activities regarding democratic transition and reconstruction in Afghanistan and Iraq;

iii. recommend that the Congress of Local and Regional Authorities of the Council of Europe support women's organisations and grassroots' groups working at the local level on issues of peace and security and give the Congress the financial means of doing so;

iv. include the issue of the promotion of women's participation in decision-making, in particular in relation to conflict situations, as one of the topics of the Third Summit of the Heads of State and Government of the Council of Europe;

v. take all necessary measures to ensure the personal security of applicants to the European Court of Human Rights, especially women applicants and their families.

EXPLANATORY MEMORANDUM BY MRS CLIVETI, RAPPORTEUSE

1. Despite the many United Nations and European Parliament resolutions, which called for women's needs to be given more serious attention in policies relating to conflict and peace, women remain marginalized from peace-building activities.
2. Women are practically excluded from official negotiations and diplomacy aimed at peaceful regulation of conflicts as well as from the decision-making on the post-conflict reconstruction process.
3. Conflict is a gendered activity and women and men have different access to resources (including power and decision-making) during conflicts. The experience of women and men in situations of tensions, war, and post-conflict reconstruction is significantly different. Approximately 80% of today's civilian casualties are women and 80% of all refugees and internally displaced people worldwide are women and children (UNHCR). As noted in the Platform for Action of the Fourth UN World Conference on Women, "while entire communities

suffer the consequences of armed conflict and terrorism, women and girls are particularly affected because of their status in society as well as their sex".

4. Despite a number of laws to protect women in conflict situations, including international humanitarian law, human rights law and refugee law, women continue to suffer, because these laws are frequently not respected or disregarded by the parties to the conflict.
5. Therefore, it is very important to develop a gender analysis of peace-building policy and implementation.
6. Peace-building looks beyond conflict regulation to the areas of social, economic and political life that constitute the original causes of conflict-and by extension the conditions underlying the many manifestations of violence and discrimination women face during the conflict and in post-conflict situations.
7. The peace-building process comprises several stages including conflict prevention, conflict resolution and post-conflict peace-building and reconstruction. Sustainable peace requires the full participation of women at each of the stages of the peace process.
8. The gender dimension of conflict resolution is a complex problem and can be divided into several components: legal protection of women's rights; violence against women; humanitarian assistance; refugee women and internally displaced women; participation of women in political and decision-making processes; participation of women in war operations.
9. Each of these elements constitutes a separate problem of women's rights, but in the context of the present report the task will be to find replies to the most urgent questions arising from these problems.
10. Conflict prevention comprises measures taken and efforts made to prevent the breakdown of peaceful conditions. It aims to prevent existing tensions escalating into violence and to contain the spread of conflict when it occurs. This may include measures to prevent the collapse of the social fabric and resulting fragmentation

of the society. Preventive action is an area where women, in countries or regions with strong civil societies, could make a mark by expressing their views on conflict through their direct participation in the negotiations between the parties to the conflict.

11. Women are often the first who detect the signs of potential conflict, but because they have no direct access to the decision-making positions, they have few opportunities to inform on the necessity of preventive actions.
12. It is internationally recognised that deadly conflicts could be prevented by addressing the root causes and investing in development. Many women's non-governmental organisations have taken concrete steps towards establishing systems of early warning and response. Those systems monitor potential crisis situations, collect information and generate analyses that can be used in generating conflict prevention actions.
13. Gender-sensitive indicators should be regarded as an important part of early warning-system analyses. Recent research has shown that the status of women in a country is associated with the country's level of stability. Those countries, where the percentage of women in parliament is low and the rates of violence against women are very high, are considered as countries at risk of conflict. Such violations of women's rights as rape, trafficking, domestic violence and military-related prostitution could also be regarded as indicators in these early warning systems.
14. The fact-finding missions of international organisations to areas of potential conflict should thus incorporate gender expertise and consultations with local women's organisations. Such regional organisations as the European Platform for conflict Prevention and Transformation, which is a network of 150 European NGOs that are involved in the prevention and /or resolution of conflicts in the international arena could also be of great help to conflict prevention missions.
15. The increase in military spending should also be considered as one of the major factors that influence the

destabilisation of world security. According to the World Bank, the reduction of global military spending would significantly improve the world economy and environmental conditions. Just one quarter of the world's approximately 839 billion dollars on military spending would allow nations to provide decent housing, health and education to their citizens.

16. Women play a particular role in the prevention of conflicts, as they are the main bearers of tradition and carry a special responsibility as educators of the young generation. As educators, women should be aware of the positive and negative influence they may have on their children's behaviour towards "the other" in the transmission of values and attitudes.

17. Education for peace should be developed in the society as one of the major and permanent measures aimed at conflict prevention. The training of present and future generations of children as peacemakers should be considered as a very important task for the public education systems. The educational policies should be developed, both at the formal and non-formal levels, in order to integrate the respect for human rights, the practice of democracy, the promotion of peace and intercultural understanding into mainstream education. Those policies should include training programmes for professionals, involved in educational activities, mass-media and decision-making.

WOMEN FACING WAR

Legal Protection of Women's Rights

18. As it was stated in the Vienna declaration and Programme of Action "violations of the human rights of women in situations of armed conflict are violations of the fundamental principles of international human rights and humanitarian law".

19. International humanitarian law has accorded women general protection equal to that of men, but it also recognizes in the four Geneva Conventions (of 12 August 1949) for the Protection of War Victims and their two

Additional Protocols (of 8 June 1977) the need to give women special protection according to their specific needs. In fact, international humanitarian law addresses women in terms of their relationship with others and not as individuals in their own right. For example, half of the provisions of the Geneva Conventions focusing on women deal with women as mothers.

20. Article 14, paragraph 2 of the Third Geneva Convention relative to the Treatment of Prisoners of War stipulates, "women shall be treated with all regard due to their sex". This provision refers to the conditions of detention for women in prisoners of war camps, e.g. the obligation to provide for separate dormitories for women and men and for separate sanitary convenience.

21. The Fourth Geneva Convention relative to the Protection of Civilian Persons in Time of War and its Additional Protocol No. 1 state that " women shall be especially protected against any attack on their honour, in particular against rape, enforced prostitution or any form of indecent assault". The problem is that such provisions have only a protective nature and do not outlaw the acts of violence.

22. Here, the main question is how can existing legal mechanisms protect women's rights?

23. The adoption of the Rome Statute of the International Criminal Court and its entry into force on 1 July 2002 is a step in that direction. It provides that rape, sexual slavery, enforced prostitution, forced pregnancy, enforced sterilisation or any other form of sexual violence of comparable gravity are crimes against humanity when committed as part of a widespread or systematic attack directed against any civilian population.

24. One of the most severe possible consequences of war is the taking of women as hostages. In 1995 the Republic of Azerbaijan initiated the adoption of the resolution "Release of women and children taken hostages, including those subsequently imprisoned, during armed conflict" by the UN Commission on the Status of Women. Since 1995, this resolution has been adopted by

consensus at each session of the Commission. But the measures undertaken by the international community regarding this issue remain ineffective.

Violence Against Women

25. Sexual violence against women has become a weapon of war, harking back to the cruel acts of antiquity. The number of women raped in the former Yugoslavia is put at between 20 000 and 50 000. The statistics can only be approximate since not all the victims are still alive and most will never talk of their ordeal.
26. In many conflicts women have been systematically targeted for sexual violence-sometimes with the broader objective of ethnic cleansing. A lot of women were killed, most often after rape or other forms of sexual abuse. There have been terrible cases of violence against women, including pregnant women having their foetus extracted before being murdered.
27. Women are raped as a way to humiliate them and/or their male relatives, who are often forced to watch the assault. In societies where ethnicity is inherited through the male line, "enemy" women are raped and forced to bear children.
28. Although progress has been made in broadening war crime definitions to include sexual violence committed against women, thereby increasing possibilities of prosecuting such crimes, the effective implementation of war crimes legislation is still limited.
29. Women victims have limited access to real justice and local authorities including peace-building missions often do not care about the punishment of perpetrators of violence. The police, military and judiciary should be specially trained to protect women and guarantee their legal rights. In Bosnia and Herzegovina local police created special teams to ensure privacy and protection for women who bring charges of violence committed against them.
30. Victims and survivors of sexual violence and rape are not being given adequate physical and psychological

care. Many women are afraid of speaking of their experiences of violence for the simple fear of ostracism by their community.

31. Violence during the conflict is inextricably linked to an increase in violence after the conflict, particularly in the form of domestic violence, when women are abused by their husbands, who return home after the war and are faced with a situation of disillusion and unemployment. Domestic violence is also considered to be prevalent in refugee camps.

32. It is very important to combat gender bias within the judiciary-the very institution that determines how equality is achieved in society. Support services and programmes should be provided to ensure that legal aid is available and that women witnesses and complaints are treated fairly.

33. The introduction of a quota system in the security sector would increase women's presence in all areas of police work that challenge security priorities and would mean that crimes against women will be taken more seriously.

Refugee Women and Internally Displaced Women

34. The forced displacement of civilians has became a direct objective of some conflicts. Many women who suffered from sexual violence, terror, or intimidation were forced to leave their homes and become refugees or internally displaced persons.

35. Refugee and internally displaced women suffer from a lack of protection. In camps, sexual and gender-based violence is an every-day reality-and it is also a cause of the spread of sexually transmitted diseases and of HIV/AIDS.

36. The specific needs of women are not taken into account in many camps for displaced persons. For example, pregnant women need greater access to health services and larger food rations. Women are also particularly concerned about their children's education and often have to find means to pay for clothes and books.

37. According to international law, the government of the country in which refugees or internally displaced persons are living should protect their human rights and provide them with humanitarian assistance. Some states refuse access to humanitarian agencies to their country under the pretext of the protection of state sovereignty. The Secretary General of the United Nations, Mr Kofi Annan, has challenged the governments of the world to reject the narrow interpretation of sovereignty that has prevented the international community from providing assistance unless a government asks for it.
38. The UNHCR has adopted guidelines on the protection of Refugee Women and on the Prevention of and Response to Sexual Violence against Refugees; nevertheless the norms provided in these documents are not respected by some states.
39. Women often try to escape the life in refugee camps by asking for asylum in another country. The Geneva Convention established principles for asylum, such as not forcing someone to return to a territory where he or she can be persecuted. But the definition of persecution does not take into consideration gender-based persecution. Very often women and children are imprisoned while they go through the legal process of applying for asylum status.
40. Many states make it harder for women and children to receive asylum status. The majority of staff working with asylum-seekers are men who have little understanding of the specific problems of women. Some countries do not provide an individual residence status to women and children, but only to the head of the family.
41. Special gender training should be provided for those organisations which are dealing with refugees and asylum-seekers.
42. However, this is a very difficult problem to tackle by state-by-state as the movement of refugees spreads out to other countries. The European community should try and find solution to the post-conflict regulation of the situation of returnees, in majority women and children.

Widowhood and Missing Persons Issue

43. War separates men from women and children. Many women continue to act as heads of the families after the conflicts have ended, as their husbands have died or disappeared. They have to cope with the difficulty of providing for the immediate livelihood of their families, and at the same time they suffer from not knowing the destiny of their husbands, fathers or sons.

44. Women often try to find out the fate of their missing male relatives. Humanitarian law recognizes the need and right of families to obtain information about missing persons. The International Committee of the Red Cross endeavours to find information about missing persons in relation to armed conflicts, but very often parties to an armed conflict do not provide the necessary information.

45. However, the issue of "the missing persons" has mobilised a lot of women in order to present their concerns to the authorities in different countries. In February 2003, the ICRC convened a landmark international conference on this issue, which reaffirmed that the families of missing persons needed material, financial, psychological and legal support. It directed particular attention to women and children who may find themselves in the situation of acute destitution and distress.

46. Governments, international and national non-governmental organisations should take measures to address the needs of these families and collect information on the fate of missing people.

Humanitarian Assistance

47. Women are rarely consulted or included in the management of humanitarian aid; therefore, very often they cannot even benefit from it.

48. The Inter-Agency Standing Committee on Humanitarian Affairs (IASC)-the group of agencies that are involved in humanitarian situations-does not include UNIFEM. Currently the agencies most concerned with women's issues have little input into many of the humanitarian policies developed by the United Nations.

49. As an example, Human Rights Watch reported that in the former Yugoslavia, women had been deliberately excluded from the assistance donor governments and international agencies poured into reconstruction efforts. The focus on assistance to demobilised soldiers significantly decreased women's opportunities for employment.
50. Women need to be included in the planning, implementation and evaluation of the activities of humanitarian agencies and the distribution of assistance. Such involvement of women can afford them better protection and assistance as specific concerns related to women can be raised and addressed throughout the programme life cycle.
51. In war and conflict situations the nutritional and health needs of women, including their reproductive and sexual health needs, and of pregnant and nursing mothers and their infants are often neglected. Reproductive health care is important for the physical and psychological well-being of men and women and should be available even in crisis situations.
52. The work of humanitarian agencies in the field can promote gender-sensitive measures, which should include monitoring of all forms of violence against women and providing counselling, legal, medical and other forms of material support to the victims of violence; giving women more control over the design and distribution of food aid in order to ensure that food and other forms of assistance benefit the most vulnerable; ensuring vocational training, income-generating skills and access to educational institutions and ensuring that women have opportunities for involvement in development and reconstruction projects, and access to credit, particularly micro-credit.

Participation of Women in Peace-keeping Operations

53. From the middle of the nineties women have been participating in peacekeeping missions. The results of the UN study "Mainstreaming a Gender Perspective in Multidimensional Peace Operations" proved that

women's participation in UN missions empowered local women and inspired them to organise towards a democratic society in which they could exercise their rights equally with men.

54. Despite these facts, women taking part in peace operations are still few. In general, women occupy lower-level positions in the peacekeeping arena. Professional women and female military officers are largely absent from senior peacekeeping management levels. Only 12,6% of staff involved in UN peace-keeping operations are women. Most of them participate only in civilian missions.

55. The Secretary General of the UN, Kofi Annan recommended a 50% participation of women in field missions and a European Parliament resolution called for a 40% representation of women on all reconciliation, peace-keeping, peace-enforcement, peace-building, and conflict prevention posts, including fact-finding and observer missions.

56. Women's participation has the capacity to expand the debate a little further, so that it may encompass more diverse subjects, including those, which may be more relevant to what is happening to women, children and communities.

57. Women are frequently less hierarchical in dealing with local communities and listen more, thereby having better insights into the root causes of conflict. Local women are more likely to confide in women peacekeepers about matters such as rape and sexual violence.

58. Women's participation in all aspects of the mission helps to break down traditional views and stereotypes of women in local communities, especially when women peacekeepers serve in a broad spectrum of activities of the mission. This has a spin off effect for the participation of local women in decision-making positions in the post-conflict phase.

59. The increase in female peacekeepers will influence the behaviour of their male counterparts and could improve the image of the peacekeeping operations.

60. Another contentious issue is the role women play as combatants. This phenomenon of "female combatants" raises several problems. Is it a progressive gender development or it is an inevitable necessity? How can women's interests be ensured during combat and the demobilisation and reintegration process? The Committee might want to draw up a motion for a resolution on this issue, as I cannot deal with it at length in this report.

Media and Women in War

61. The media coverage of the role of women in war is rather one-sided, women are often portrayed as victims rather than fighters against war. Journalists prefer to interview rape victims and rarely consider women newsworthy in their varied roles in the peacekeeping and conflict processes.
62. The war coverage by female correspondents has changed significantly the accent of field reports. While male correspondents tend to focus on conflict and the positions of the parties of it, women look at the impact of the conflict on people's lives.
63. Women journalists have the courage to criticize the hate messages spread by the media as part of war propaganda.
64. Women war correspondents face some threats that men do not, they are in danger of gender-based violence and often compromise their health in ways men never do.
65. The appearance of women correspondents in the field pushes women to use the mass-media to document their human rights violations and to promote peace-building, like in Bosnia, where women are using talk-shows on Resolution Radio to teach conflict-resolution skills.
66. Women should be present in the media both as producers of media information and as subjects of it. Only in this way the role of women in peace building will be known.
67. Conflict resolution is the process of building bridges between hostile communities, working to clarify issues which represent points of confrontation between them

and creating new opportunities for developing renewed relationships based upon a process of peaceful change and grassroots reconciliation. The focus of this is often on men, for example, as church or community leaders. However, creating initiatives to bring women together in discussion can bring greater vibrancy and legitimacy to a peace process.

Participation of Women in Political and Decision-making Processes

68. Women are not innocent and some of them participate directly or indirectly in conflicts by backing military efforts. Once a war is over those women also pay no attention to the needs and interests of their sisters who suffered during the conflict. Men, however, are just as guilty of such behaviour, but are still virtually guaranteed seats at the negotiating tables.
69. Women's participation in formal peace negotiations has faced strong opposition. There were no women present at the Dayton Accords, which ended the conflict in Bosnia, and just one woman was at the negotiating table in Rambouillet, prior to the NATO bombing campaign. The "gender task force" initially set up within the Stability Pact for South-Eastern Europe has disappeared from the list of new future priorities despite achieving positive results, notably in Macedonia.
70. They also are main victims of war and should have a right to voice their fears and concerns, their needs and demands.
71. If women, who are 50 percent of the world's population, made up 50 percent of any negotiating body, whether it be at the local, national, or international level, there would be a 50:50 chance of peaceful resolution of disputes and conflicts.1 Excluding the majority population from decision-making structures counters all basic principles of democracy and human rights.

Peace-building Activities of Women Organisations

72. According to an inventory compiled by the Council of Europe Steering Committee for Equality between

Women and Men (CDEG), over 200 peace-building movements have emerged in recent years.

73. Many are obviously in areas of conflict (Cyprus, Northern Ireland, Armenia, Russia, Azerbaijan Macedonia, Croatia and so on) but there are others in border regions, for example in Italy, Germany, Austria, Bulgaria, Montenegro, Scandinavian countries and all Union member states.

74. Women are socialized into wanting and supporting peace in a more concrete and conclusive framework. Due to their socialisation, women's role in building conditions for peace has been proven in history and women have a wealth of experience still waiting to be utilised and legitimised, not only in Europe but worldwide.

75. There are many different types of women's organisations, which have contributed to peace-building. Some of them have developed the capacity to work openly to protect and extend human rights; others have concentrated their activities on humanitarian assistance and social care. Finally there are those women's organisations that work to facilitate women's participation in war-crimes tribunals and post-conflict reconciliation processes. Many of these organisations attempt to build bridges between groups of women who might be separated by their ethnic, regional or political identities.

76. Women's organisations could achieve many important goals in peace-building: to increase women's participation in public, political processes and civil society in general, to increase the number of women who become leaders in peace-building, to reinforce efforts to challenge masculine cultures in institutions and society itself.

77. In 1996, the women of Northern Ireland formed the Northern Ireland Women's Coalition and fought the elections for the right to be represented at peace negotiations. As a result, two of its representatives were at the negotiating table and signed the peace agreement of 10 April 1998. Although the agreement is proving difficult to implement at present, the women of Northern Ireland are not giving up hope and are working to

overcome the obstacles. Two of them have been elected to the Northern Irish parliament and, thanks to the European programme supporting the peace process, many women have been able to become more involved and show their potential.

78. In the mid-nineties a group of women representing both Turkish and Greek communities of Cyprus was formed to work towards resolving the conflict. Now, there are around sixty joint groups keen to break down the barriers through the exchange of personal histories and experiences. In 1998 the international Eco-Peace Village was created on their initiative in Psematismenos to train young people and women in conflict-prevention and conflict resolution.

79. The Committee of mothers of Russian soldiers, founded by Valentina Melnikova, provides hope to thousands of Russian mothers trying to help their children who suffer ill-treatment or refuse to take part in the war in Chechnya, which makes them "war criminals" in the eyes of military justice.

80. Many of these organisations face problems in their continuing survival. Such problems include a lack of funding, marginalisation and stigmatisation by powerful governmental and non-governmental organisations, and also direct physical harassment from security forces, which is especially likely in post-conflict situations.

81. But the allocation of funds to women's organisations will not be sufficient for the promotion of women's role in development. It should be complemented by large-scale gender awareness policies.

POST-CONFLICT PEACE-BUILDING AND RECONSTRUCTION

82. Post-conflict peace-building work is the employment of measures which consolidate peaceful relations and societal institutions in order to contribute to the creation of an environment which deters the emergence or the escalation of tensions which may lead to violent conflicts. To achieve this, the root causes of violence need to be

identified and eradicated. This may involve a radical upheaval of existing structures. It is vital that this process is gendered. Sustainable, positive peace can only be achieved through democracy, egalitarianism and the protection of human rights. It is therefore essential that women's rights are acknowledged and safe-guarded. In this way peace-building does more than simply returning a society to its pre-conflict state.

83. Post-conflict reconstruction can be divided into three components: political reconstruction, which focuses on peace-building activities and the process of democratisation; economic reconstruction, which looks primarily at developments within agriculture and formal and informal economic sectors and social reconstruction, where the focus is shifted to the rehabilitation of the social sector and to social integration.

84. Post-conflict reconstruction also involves dealing with the damage caused by war. Women have particular needs in this process which are different from those of men and therefore are often overlooked. For example, the provision of psychological or physical health services or legal support in order to prosecute in cases of rape or other war crimes, is often lacking.

85. The political reconstruction of the country after the conflict usually includes free and fair elections, decentralisation of government institutions and mechanisms for increased participation of people in political decision-making.

86. Women face many obstacles in exercising their right to vote. Women often have limited political experience and consider politics as a male domain. Many often women just ignore the participation in elections. Nevertheless, local women's organisations encourage women to take part in elections, demanding equal representation in democratic institutions.

87. It should be taken into account that during the war women assume the role and full responsibilities of heads-of-households, and maintain social order. In post-war

situations, women act as peace activists and re-builders. But their interests are often ignored by men who develop and implement post-conflict reconstruction programmes.

88. The most recent developments in Iraq have shown that women were significantly underrepresented in bilateral and multilateral efforts to structure and manage the transition to democracy and reconstruction, although they comprise 55% of the country's population.

89. As a result of over a decade of intermittent conflict, widows and women heading households have long assumed a great deal of responsibility for managing families and communities in Iraq. Their role and expertise ought to be recognised in fostering the transition to a pluralistic, democratic society.

90. If women manage to find legal jobs, the terms and conditions are usually discriminatory, with less pay than men receive and longer working hours. They suffer employment discrimination and shoulder the double burden of caring for families while holding down a full-time job.

91. Excluding women from post-conflict planning and decision-making in reconstruction is a loss of immense resources, and understanding of a society's most critical social and economic capital and their needs.

92. Women are generally marginalised in formal sector training and employment, either because they lack formal qualifications or because they lack social support to assist with domestic tasks. Another reason is that male employment is given a higher priority.

93. Women generally put great emphasis on the rehabilitation and development of the social services sector, as this dimension of the post-war reconstruction task falls within their area of responsibility and authority. Therefore, they often take initiatives to improve existing facilities. In difficult conditions they do the best to re-establish children's education, to build up primary health care services, and to help the victims of violence and psycho-social distress.

94. As an example, in Bosnia and Herzegovina Medica-Zenica has established an education centre for traumatised women and girls whose education was interrupted during the war. They are offered individual counselling and the opportunity to complete their high school education or a vocational skills-training course.

95. Structural adjustment policies that reduce the government's ability to provide health care, education, water, transportation, energy, housing and sanitation mostly affect women's lives, since they influence the sectors in which women provide the majority of their unpaid labour.

96. Regarding social integration after the conflict, women stress the importance of social networks and organisations that link individual women with others who share their experiences and position. Such networks may improve women's situation in many respects, in terms of security, bargaining power, respect, self-confidence and so forth.

97. As an example, on the initiative of the non-governmental organisation "Transeuropéennes" a network of women's and human rights protection organisations was created to implement "Peacemaking activities of women across borders", which gave women the possibility to confront the reality of recent wars, to reflect on the question of responsibility and to work together against patriarchal and community pressures in order to build peace.

98. Supporting women's participation in reconstruction and reconciliation means giving women access to the rooms where decisions are made. Only with local, regional, national and international political support women's efforts can be accepted in the formal peace process.

99. The mainstreaming of gender has to take place in all policy contexts associated with post-conflict rehabilitation, development and peace-building. Investing in women may be one of the most effective means for real, sustainable development and peace-building.

CONCLUSIONS AND RECOMMENDATIONS

International Efforts to Promote Women's Involvement in Conflict Solution

100. The international community has started to recognise the positive contributions women can make in preventing conflicts and consolidating peace. Back in 1995 the United Nations 4th World Conference on Women in Beijing devoted an entire section of its Platform of Action to women and armed conflict. Six specific objectives were laid down to strengthen women's participation in the resolution of conflicts and the decision-making process. The platform also emphasizes the protection of women in war zones and refugee camps.

101. The role of women in conflict prevention, conflict resolution and post-conflict peace-building has been emphasized in the final document of the 23rd Special Session of the UN General Assembly "Women 2000: Gender Equality, Development and Peace for the Twenty-First Century".

102. In October 2000, the Security Council adopted Resolution 1325 on women, peace and security, which calls for: the participation of women in decision-making and peace processes; gender perspectives and training in peacekeeping; the protection of women; and gender mainstreaming in United Nations reporting systems and programmatic implementation mechanisms.

103. Resolution 1325 provided a tool for women that called for gender sensitivity in all UN missions including peacekeeping. For women to participate equally at all negotiating tables and for the protection of women and girls during armed conflict. This resolution is binding international law that for the first time officially endorses the inclusion of civil society groups, notably women, in peace processes and the implementation of peace agreements.

104. In order to ensure the implementation of this resolution, the Secretary General of the United Nations, Mr Kofi Annan established a task force on women, peace and

security which comprises representatives from 15 UN entities.

105. In November 2000, the European Parliament adopted its resolution on the participation of women in peaceful resolution of conflict, in which it had invited European Union member states to ensure increased representation of women at all decision-making levels, by recruiting and training more women for diplomatic service.

106. The Committee on Women's Rights and Equal Opportunities of the European Parliament prepared the report on Gender related Aspects of the Prevention and Resolution of Armed Conflicts.

107. In the conclusions of the G8 summit organised in July 2001 it had been stressed that "women brought alternative perspectives to conflict prevention at the grass-roots and community levels. Creative and innovative ways to better draw on the talents women brought to preventing conflict and sustaining peace should be encouraged and practical steps and strategies should be identified to advance the role of women in conflict and post conflict peace building."

108. A coalition of NGOs, headed by International Alert, launched an international campaign to promote women's participation in peace-building.

109. These instruments indicate a growing recognition that in conflict situations women are more than victims requiring the protection of the international community, but they can be equally present at the negotiation tables as peace-makers.

110. The Council of Europe organised the 5th European Ministerial Conference on Equality between Women and Men in Skopje on 22 and 23 January 2003. The main theme of the conference was: "Democratisation, conflict prevention and peace building: the perspectives and the roles of women".

111. The ministers adopted a Resolution2 that, among other things, calls on governments to promote the full participation of women at all levels of decision-making

and to encourage the integration of a gender perspective in all activities aimed at conflict prevention and resolution. The ministers also adopted a Declaration and Programme of Action3 outlining Council of Europe priorities in the field of equality for the coming years.

Recommendations

112. In order to ensure the effectiveness of peace-support operations, the principles of gender equality must be mainstreamed at all levels, thus ensuring the participation of women and men as equal partners and beneficiaries in all aspects of the peace process-from peace keeping, reconciliation and peace-building, towards a situation of political stability in which women and men play an equal part in the political, economic and social development of their country.

113. More focused research on women and their peace building activities and the impact women have on peace building and peace processes should be launched by each member state.

114. The governments should give women the opportunity to participate in peace-building and post-conflict reconstruction by strengthening women's representation in local, national and international bodies on the regulation of conflict.

115. Special attention should be paid to women-victims of war conflicts. Physical and mental health services for women recovering from war injuries and trauma should be provided, including specialist's support for women who are caring for children conceived as a result of rape and for those who have been ostracised from communities and families as a consequence of rape.

116. The police force should provide safe personal security of women, protecting them from all forms of sexual and domestic violence.

117. It is very important to give opportunity to refugee and internally displaced women to play a key role in camp planning, management and decision-making, so that women's interests are taken into account in all aspects,

especially resource distribution, security and protection. Women should also be involved in all aspects of repatriation and resettlement planning and implementation.

118. The specific needs, including protection, health and assistance, of women and girls affected by armed conflict should be assessed and addressed by humanitarian organisations.

119. It is important to create economic opportunities for women in post-conflict reconstruction.

120. Gender-sensitive training programmes for participants in peacekeeping missions, including military staff, police and humanitarian assistance personnel should be financed by member-countries.

121. Capacity building, training and the creation of women's forums are essential to supporting women's participation in post-conflict reconstruction.

122. The relevant state institutions in co-operation with NGOs should develop special programmes to train women as mediators in order to prepare them to the work in peace building and conflict resolution missions and peace support operations.

123. The governments should encourage research into gender issues, conflict prevention and mediation by women and make the results widely known and used in designing domestic and regional policies.

124. It is important to encourage the appointment of women to national and international posts relating to the conflict-prevention sphere.

125. Governments should provide support to women's NGOs involved in peace-building, conflict prevention and related activities and facilitate the input of women's organisations into key peace conferences and other decision-making bodies.

126. All possible means should be employed to increase public awareness of the importance of gender mainstreaming in peace-support operations. In this connection, the media should play a significant role.

127. The media should take measures to eradicated hate speech and violence messages in audiovisual programmes and press articles.

128. It is important to increase the access for women to media and communication technologies, so that gender perspectives, women's expertise and women's media can influence public discourse and decision-making on peace and security.

129. Non-governmental organisations working in peace building should try to share their practices with each other and to link with other strategic partners in order to maximise the effectiveness of their actions.

130. Multicultural, trans-border and regional women's initiatives for preventing and resolving conflicts should be promoted and disseminated by all possible means including through networking and information technology.

131. Conflict-prevention approaches to peace-building work should be mainstreamed into development and humanitarian aid work and development actors should ensure that a strategy of strengthening local capacities does not increase gender injustice.

GENERAL CONCLUSIONS

132. Women are often exposed to a high risk of rape and associated violence during and immediately after conflict. They bear the main burden of the care for survivors, which includes both adults and children. Therefore, there is a strong need for peace-building to incorporate policies that address women's specific health and economic needs.

133. Given the effect of conflicts on women, it should be recognised that women should play a significant role in conflict management. Women should be properly empowered and should be in the centre of conflict management initiatives.

134. Any peace-building process can only be effective embedded and sustained when there is a broad social

involvement in this task. Society as a whole must be involved in peace-building, developing the relationships of trust, mutual respect and tolerance needed to cement the blocks of peace agreements together. Non-governmental organisations can support and sustain women's efforts by pressing governments to increase the number of women at senior diplomatic positions, pressing for greater involvement and monitoring the actions of national and international negotiators in conflict zones, assuring that local civil society groups are integrated into all levels and aspects of conflict prevention, resolution and management.

135. The most direct way to support women's activity in peace-building is to support women's organisations. Peace-building and conflict-prevention are long-term processes that require follow-up. Thus, governments should provide sustainable support to women's organisations giving them the opportunity to develop their activities.

136. Keeping women's movements together, along with encouraging women parliamentarians to co-operate more with women's organisations is the only way to go if women wish to change politics, introduce new values such as peace, equality and justice and, finally, draw up a new political culture based on the principle of consensus and the refusal of all forms of exclusion.

4

Building a National Democratic Society

INTRODUCTION

South Africa has entered its Second Decade of Freedom with the strengthening of democracy and acceleration of the programme to improve the quality of life of all the people. Steadily, the dark night of white minority political domination is receding into a distant memory.

Yet we are only at the beginning of a long journey to a truly united, democratic and prosperous South Africa in which the value of all citizens is measured by their humanity, without regard to race, gender and social status.

The achievement of democracy in 1994 marked the birth of our country as an African nation on the southern tip of the continent. It provided South Africans with the opportunity to:

- set up a government based on the will of the people and on people-centred and people-driven principles;
- pursue economic growth, development and redistribution so as to achieve a better life for all;
- strengthen the ANC as a leader in the implementation of a practical programme of social change and a movement rooted among the people;
- build democracy, a culture of human rights and value system based on human solidarity; and
- work with African and global progressive forces to advance human development in our country, our continent and across the globe.

These tasks, which make up the pillars of our process of change, have to be undertaken in a global environment of contradictory tendencies.

The dominance of a capitalist system with minimal regulation, in a unipolar world, presents enormous challenges for social development and for global governance and security.

At the same time, programmes of progressive social change are finding pride of place on the agenda of many developing nations and some global institutions. Most African countries have successfully set out to resolve conflict, entrench democracy and reconstruct economies in a manner that benefits the people.

This environment provides a basis for the advancement of the National Democratic Revolution (NDR) in our country.

However, this cannot be assumed. It depends on the ability of progressive forces to promote the positive elements in both the global and domestic settings and to assert a progressive vision of the world we want to live in. For the ANC, this also means forging a corps of cadres unwaveringly committed to the cause of change, and the mobilisation of the majority of South Africans to act as one in pursuit of a better life for all.

WHERE WE COME FROM: STREAMS OF AN EMERGENT NATION

The South African nation is a product of many streams of history and culture, representing the origins, dispersal and re-integration of humanity over hundreds of thousands of years. Archaeological findings in various parts of the country and the rest of Africa have located South Africa and the continent at large as the cradle of humankind and early forms of human civilisation.

From the earliest manifestations of intellectual activity; the settlements of pastoral communities characterised by foundries, artisanship and trade across oceans; colonisation by Europeans; the slave trade and indentured labour-South Africa has emerged as one of the most diverse nations across the globe. This is our collective national heritage which we should continue to share and understand, the better to appreciate who we are as a nation.

Besides the African inter-communal co-operation and wars of nation-formation, the greatest impact on the evolution of the South African nation-state was made by European colonial settlement. On the one hand, colonialism interrupted internally-driven advancement of indigenous South African communities along the ladder of human development. It resulted in the subjugation of the African population, including the Khoi and the San who were subjected to genocidal campaigns, as well as Malay and Indian communities. On the other hand, the advanced industrial base of the colonial powers which made such subjugation possible, introduced into the South African geographic entity the application of advanced forms of economic production and trade.

The South African nation-state is a product of these interactions, characterised between 1652 and 1994 by ongoing and mostly violent conflict between the oppressors and the oppressed. Despite their heroism, the African people were defeated in a series of wars that took place over two-and-half centuries of colonial expansion. Part of the heroic resistance took the form of slave revolts in the Cape Colony. Besides the advanced productive forces at the disposal of the colonial powers, one of the central reasons for the defeat of indigenous communities was division and conflict among these communities themselves.

It speaks to South Africa's strategic geographic location and its vast endowments in mineral and other resources that this geographic entity experienced colonial intrusion earlier than most African societies. Further, the colonial designs of the imperial powers were applied more systematically; the European settlers fought intensely among themselves over the territory; and most of these settlers came to characterise South Africa as their home.

As such, what emerged in our country was Colonialism of a Special Type, with both the coloniser and the colonised located in a common territory and with a large European settler population. The deal between the descendants of Dutch settlers and the British imperial power at the end of the so-called Anglo-Boer War formalised, in 1910, South Africa's statehood, premised on the political oppression and social subordination and exclusion of the majority of the people. The African National Congress (ANC) was formed in 1912 in part as a response to this deal among the colonisers, as well as the defeat of the Bhambatha Rebellion of 1906 which marked the end of armed resistance against colonial occupation. It was also a product of new forms of African resistance across various parts of the country and the globe.

Starting off with petitions to the colonial powers, the ANC over the years developed ever more militant forms of struggle, and finally adopted armed struggle in 1961, a year after its banning. Combined with armed actions, the ANC and other resistance movements used international mobilisation, underground organisation and mass mobilisation to challenge colonialism and its apartheid derivative.

As a result of a generalised mass revolt, a situation was reached in the late 1980s in which the system of white minority domination could no longer be sustained. Yet at the same time, the liberation struggle at the head of which was the ANC had not as yet amassed sufficient strength to overthrow the apartheid regime. Conditions were created for a negotiations process which resulted in a settlement underpinned by non-racial democracy, with the first ever democratic elections held in April 1994.

South Africa's colonial experience was based on the intersection of class, race and patriarchal relations of power. These distinctive social and biological features have been used in human history to exclude, to repress and to stymie the progress of individuals and communities.

Across the globe, these practices represented and in the main still represent the exercise of raw power as opposed to human compassion; relations based on subjugation as opposed to human solidarity; greed and self-aggrandisement as opposed to shared prosperity; religion and other belief systems used as justification for hatred and war as opposed to spiritual and cultural advancement; and treatment of the world as a theatre for narrow self-interest as opposed to the collective well-being of humanity. Because the struggle against colonialism sought to eliminate most of the manifestations of these iniquitous social relations, it evolved to embrace the best in human civilisation and value systems. While the anti-colonial struggle could easily have been conducted as one against a racial group, it rose above these categories to embrace the principle of non-racialism: to see humanity as one and diversity as a source of strength. While all communities, including the oppressors and the oppressed, practiced discrimination against women, the struggle evolved to appreciate the real and potential role of women, and that their liberation from patriarchy was and should be an integral part of the new democracy.

While in the early years, the liberation movement evinced characteristics of elitism, it developed over the decades to appreciate the place and role of the working class and the poor both as a critical social force in production and trade and as a militant contingent against apartheid colonialism.

As such, the liberation struggle by oppressed communities, even in the midst of bitter confrontation, developed moral values of human compassion and solidarity far beyond the narrow confines of its opposition to the apartheid social system. It represented something good, not just something better than apartheid. It asserted the humanness of the human spirit-the search for societies at peace within and among themselves. It developed to advocate the use of human intelligence to advance collective social comfort and to preserve the endowments of our planet and outer space for the sustenance of current and future generations.

In this sense therefore, it is both an honour and a challenge for the ANC to claim the legacy of the liberation struggle, to occupy the high ground of its moral suasion and wield its compass.

VISION OF OUR COLLECTIVE EFFORT

If the progress we have made since 1994 constitutes only the beginning of a protracted process of change, what is it that we aim for! What kind of society do we seek to create? What is the character of the NDR?

Colonialism of a Special Type contained within itself contradictions that could not be resolved through reform. It had to be destroyed. As such, the system we seek to create will stand or fall on the basis of whether it is able to eliminate the main antagonisms of this system. A national democratic society constitutes the ideal state we aspire to as the ANC and the broad democratic movement. It should thus not be confused with tactical positions that the liberation movement may adopt from time to time, taking into account the balance of forces within our country and abroad. Circumstances in which we conduct social transformation will change all the time. And in the process of effecting such transformation, there will be successes and setbacks.

The liberation movement should avoid the temptation to crow over such successes in these early years as if we had already achieved our ultimate objective. Nor should we seek to justify mistakes and setbacks as unavoidable, pleading a fixed set of circumstances and thus leading us into the danger of redefining the ultimate objective.

This is where the line should be drawn between strategy-the ultimate goal; and tactics-the methods and actions that respond to changing immediate circumstances. Clearly, at all times we should develop tactics that are suitable for the specific conditions under which we operate. But such tactics should be informed by our commitment to the strategic goal.

What does this Mean in Actual Practice?

Our definition of Colonialism of a Special Type identifies three interrelated antagonistic contradictions: class, race and patriarchal oppression. These antagonisms found expression in national oppression based on race; class super-exploitation directed against Black workers on the basis of race; and triple oppression of women based on their race, their class and their gender.

The National Democratic Revolution is defined as such precisely because it seeks to abolish this combination of sources of social conflict. It has national and democratic tasks, and it should strive to realise:

- a united state based on the will of all the people, without regard race, sex, belief or geographic location;
- a dignified and improving quality of life among all the people by providing equal rights and opportunities to all citizens; and

- the restoration of the birthright of all South Africans regarding access to land and other resources.

The NDR seeks to build a society based on the best in human civilisation in terms of political and human freedoms, socio-economic rights, value systems and identity.

Such human civilisation should be reflected, firstly, in the constant improvement of the means to take advantage of our natural environment, turn it to collective human advantage and ensure its regeneration for future use. Secondly, it should find expression in the management of human relations based on political equality and social inclusivity. If there were to be any single measure of the civilising mission of the NDR, it would be how it treats the most vulnerable within its ranks.

One of the most critical acts of the NDR is the creation of a legitimate state which derives its authority from the people, through regular elections and continuing popular participation in the processes of governance. Mobilised around a clear vision of the kind of society we wish to become, the nation should act in partnership-each sector contributing to the realisation of the common good. The means should be put in place for citizens to exercise their human rights, and for the checks and balances necessary in a law-governed society. The democratic state should also have the organisational and technical capacity to realise its objectives.

As with any nation, South Africans will continue to have multiple identities based on class, gender, age, language, geographic location, religion and so on. In a national democratic society, such diversity should feed into an overarching national identity. In its own unique way, South Africa should emerge as a united African nation, adding to the diversity and identity of the continent and humanity at large.

The main content of the NDR is the liberation of Africans in particular and Blacks in general. At the same time it has the effect of liberating the white community from the false ideology of racial superiority and the insecurity attached to oppressing others. The hierarchy of disadvantage suffered under apartheid will naturally inform the magnitude of impact of the programmes of change and the attention paid particularly to those who occupied the lowest rungs on the apartheid social ladder. Preciscly because patriarchal oppression was embedded in the economic, social, religious, cultural, family and other relations in all communities, its eradication cannot be an assumed consequence of democracy. From the feminisation of poverty, physical and psychological abuse, undermining of self-confidence, to open and hidden forms of exclusion from positions of authority and power-all these manifestations of gender discrimination need to be eliminated. Critical in this regard is the creation of the material and cultural conditions that would allow the abilities of women to flourish and enrich the life of the nation.

A nation's success depends also on its ability to encourage, harness and incorporate into its endeavours the creativity, daring and energy of youth. This relates to such issues as access to social and economic opportunities, engendering activism around issues of development and values of community solidarity and creating the space for youth creativity to flourish.

Among the most vulnerable in society are children and people with disability: and a national democratic society should ensure their protection and continuous advancement.

Implementing these corrective measures requires more than just references to general political rights. A continuing element of democratic transformation should be a systematic programme to correct the historical injustice and affirm those deliberately excluded under apartheid-on the basis of race, class and gender. The need for such affirmative action will decline in the same measure as all centres of power and influence become broadly representative of the country's demographics. In the process, all inequalities that may persist or arise will need to be addressed.

Apartheid colonialism visited such devastating consequences on Black communities because it ordered the ownership and control of wealth in such a manner that these communities were deliberately excluded and neglected.

Therefore, fundamental to the destruction of apartheid is the eradication of apartheid production relations. This is more than just an issue of social justice. It is also about the fact that these relations had become a brake on the advancement of technology and competitiveness of the economy.

A national democratic society should be founded on a thriving economy the structure of which should reflect the natural endowments of the country and the creativity that a skilled population can offer. It should be an economy in which cutting edge technology, labour-absorbing industrial development, a thriving small business and co-operative sector, utilisation of information and communication technologies and efficient forms of production and management all combine to ensure national prosperity. This is conditional on ensuring that the brain and brawn of all of society are brought to bear on all economic activity. It requires de-racialisation of ownership and control of wealth (including land), management and the professions.

A thriving economy in a national democratic society requires as efficient a market as possible, shorn of the racial and gender exclusions that characterised apartheid colonialism, and freed from the barriers to entry and competition that the economy endured under colonial capitalism. It will also require a state able to use its capacities to direct national development through fiscal redistribution, utilisation of State-owned Enterprises and effective regulation.

A national democratic society will have a mixed economy, with state, co-operative and other forms of social ownership, and private capital. The balance between social and private ownership of investment resources will be determined on the balance of evidence in relation to national development needs and the concrete tasks of the NDR at any point in time.

In this regard, the state will relate to private owners of investment resources in the context of the national objective to build a better life for all. Through its various capacities the state will encourage socially-beneficial conduct on the part of private business. Similarly, through such capacities, it will ensure that these investors are able to make reasonable returns on their investments.

Social cohesion in a national democratic society will also depend on the extent to which the rights of those in the lower rungs of the socio-economic ladder are protected. Such a society should proceed from the obvious premise that workers' rights are human rights; and these rights should find expression in law-governed measures to ensure decent jobs, job security and a living wage. Through legislation and other means, the state should manage the environment for fair and balanced relations between employers and employees.

Particular attention in such a society should be paid to conditions of the poor in rural areas. This also applies the life circumstances of such groups as citizens in informal settlements as well as female-headed and single households.

A national democratic society should use the redistributive mechanism of the fiscus to provide a safety net for the poor. As such, built into its social policy should be a comprehensive social security system which includes various elements of the social wage such as social grants, free basic services, free education, free health care, subsidised public transport and basic accommodation.

A national democratic state should continually implement integrated anti-poverty programmes, ensuring that these programmes address not only social assistance, but also the sustainable integration of all communities into economic activity. This is critical in dealing with poverty in general, but also in addressing the condition of the majority of women.

All these measures are important for social cohesion. They should be supported by joint efforts among all sectors of society to strengthen community organisation and mobilisation around issues pertaining to sport, women's rights, youth interests, the battle against crime and so on. There also should be deliberate collective action to promote a positive role by the institution of the family. The public media also have a critical role to play in promoting social cohesion.

Critical elements of a value system based on human solidarity should include pride in social activism and respect for an honest day's work. They should include social dissuasion against conspicuous consumption, ostentatiousness and corruption. This is part of the ideological engagement that should be a permanent feature of the process of change, involving both the state and civil society.

Whether such common social decency is achievable under a market-based system in a globalised world is an issue on which society should continually engage its mind. Concrete practice, rather than mere theory, will help answer this question. What is clear though is that such was the symbiosis between political oppression and the apartheid capitalist system that, if decisive action is not taken to deal with economic subjugation and exclusion, the essence of apartheid will remain, with a few black men and women incorporated into the courtyard of privilege. The old fault-lines will persist, and social stability will be threatened.

A national democratic society is made up of various classes and strata. The NDR seeks to eradicate the specific relations of production that underpin the national and patriarchal oppression of the majority of South Africans. It does not eradicate capitalist relations of production in general. It should therefore be expected that in a national democratic society class contradictions and class struggle, particularly between the working class and the bourgeoisie, will play themselves out. As such, a national democratic state will be called upon to regulate the environment in which such contradictions manifest themselves, in the interest of national development.

In broad terms, the NDR seeks to ensure that every South African, especially the poor, experiences an improving quality of life. It seeks to bring together:

- the best traditions of a developmental state, represented by an efficient state that guides national economic development and mobilises domestic and foreign capital to achieve this goal; and
- the best traditions of social democracy, represented by popular democracy which places the needs of the poor and social issues such as health care, education and a social safety net at the top of the national agenda.

PROGRESS IN CHANGING SOCIETY

How far then have we moved up the road towards a national democratic society? In what ways has the balance of forces changed since the advent of democracy?

Our starting point in this regard is that revolutionary democrats shall not find social relations of the new order ripe and ready for harvesting at the point of transfer of power. A national democratic society is a conscious construct, dependent on conscious action by politically advanced sections of society.

A mere decade-and-a-few years after the democratic transition in 1994, the liberation movement can claim great progress towards a democratic and prosperous society.

But we are not satisfied with the current order of things.

It is possible in national liberation processes to mark time, tinkering with social relations under the veneer of formal political democracy. Yet as with all historical phenomena, to mark time is to move in reverse. The consequence is either gradual regression, with a self-satisfied elite unsighted; or a rapid collapse of social cohesion under the weight of poverty and lawlessness.

The political transition of the early 1990s was premised on a few basic principles: firstly, that the outcome of the negotiations process would not be a compromise between apartheid and democracy but would as rapidly as possible result in democratic majority rule. Secondly, the Interim Constitution prescribed the need for a multi-party government at national and provincial levels. Thirdly, it was considered necessary to ensure orderly management of the exit of senior functionaries of the apartheid state and gradual law-based transformation of state institutions such as the army, the police, intelligence agencies and the judiciary. Fourthly, changes in local government were introduced in stages, with fully-fledged democracy being achieved only in the year 2000.

During negotiations, representatives of the previous order sought an outcome that would leave many elements of the apartheid system intact. On the other hand, the liberation movement sued for democratic majority rule as understood throughout the world. The transitional measures were seen by the liberation movement as necessary compromises to ensure the broadest possible legitimacy of the new order and to use the advances made as a beach-head to a truly united, non-racial, non-sexist, democratic and prosperous society.

At the point of change of government in 1994, the state was manned at all senior levels by apartheid functionaries; the economy was almost totally in the hands of whites; many of the parties sought constitutional outcomes that would guarantee white privilege; and networks of apartheid and extreme right-wing destabilisation remained burrowed, or had multiple links, within the state.

How has the Situation Changed since Then?

South Africa enjoys a system of vibrant multi-party democracy, with a progressive Bill of Rights which recognises political, socio-economic and environmental rights and obligations, and with separation of powers among the executive, the judiciary and the legislatures. Beyond the formal processes of regular elections and legislatures, various forms of legislated and other forums ensure popular participation.

The Constitution enjoys the respect of the overwhelming majority of the population, and it is seen as the canvass upon which South Africans' freedom of spirit can find expression. While some within the ranks of those who were privileged under apartheid may harbour ill-feelings towards the process of change and evince racist attitudes, virtually all of them accept that their aims and views should be pursued within the constitutional and legal framework. While pockets of ethnic chauvinism and regionalism still manifest themselves and may take new forms under the new conditions, our society has made massive progress in ensuring a common national identity.

Over the years, state institutions have been transformed through doctrines that guide them as well as improvements in their racial and gender profiles. A state entity has emerged that enjoys such allegiance that only the most fanatical can dare frontally to challenge it. This is not to rule out continuing attempts by forces connected to the old apartheid order to undermine the state and the liberation movement through clandestine means, including all kinds of manipulation. These forces, however, do not constitute a critical threat to the democratic order.

Many short-comings remain in ensuring that all citizens are able in actual practice to exercise their rights; in the efficiency of the state; and in changing mindsets within various state institutions. However, as a broad canvass, the Constitution and the state system provide the requisite wherewithal to implement objectives of the NDR.

The achievement of democracy has opened up critical space for organisations of civil society to flourish. This finds expression in the growth and activism particularly of the labour movement and some community-based and other non-governmental organisations dealing with generic or single-issue campaigns. However, this 'social movement' has manifested contradictory features under democracy. This is partly due to the hemorrhaging of experienced cadreship, and tendencies towards mechanical oppositionism in relation to government or towards an exclusive focus on narrow self-interest. The question of the role of progressive trade unionism within the state, in relation to broader issues of providing services to citizens, the fight against corruption and revolutionary transformation of the state itself has not been adequately addressed.

While a battery of legislation and programmes has been put in place to transform the socio-economic dynamics of South African society, the changes in this sphere illustrate the distance that still has to be traversed to achieve national democracy.

The removal of the glass ceiling of apartheid has created space for many Blacks to rise into the middle and upper strata of society. It is in these middle sectors where the greatest dynamism in income mobility is to be found. However, the improvement in Black and female ownership and control of wealth and access to management and many professions is still limited, with overall proportions which are inversely related to the country's demographics. This is more starkly reflected in terms of land ownership. Even more critically, trends do indicate a persistence of the poverty trap-a form of marginalized Second Economy community excluded form the advanced First Economy mainstream-afflicting mainly Black people, especially women.

Major improvements have been registered at the turn of the Second Decade of Freedom in terms of the economy's rate of labour-absorption and generation of self-employment. But these have not matched the needs of society. At the same time, while the achievement of macroeconomic balances has released huge resources for social and economic expenditure by government, this has not translated into rates and quality of investment needed to deal with the legacy of apartheid.

Combined with this is the restructuring of the economy, which has resulted in higher levels of competitiveness and better access to world markets; but also in the ascendancy of the services sector which requires fewer, skilled jobs. A tendency has also developed in the period since 1994 for the informalisation of jobs, contracting out and utilisation of labour brokers affecting particular sectors of the economy. While the achievement of democracy has resulted in a better regime of workers' rights, this tendency has undermined the quality of jobs, job security and union activism in the affected sectors.

The period since 1994 has also seen other macrosocial trends that include:

- rapid rates of migration to areas with better economic potential, with resultant sprawls of informal settlements in the major cities and towns;
- greater self-assertion by the youth in taking advantage of professions now opened up and opportunities in the arts and other areas; but also marginalisation of millions of young people who do not have the skills required by the economy;
- better gender representation in the legislatures and other organs of state; but also slow progress in the private sector and serious manifestations of poverty and women abuse;
- better advocacy and access in relation to the rights of people with disability; but a huge legacy of marginalisation; and
- greater focus on the rights of children; but still unacceptable levels of child poverty and abuse.

The state has massively expanded access to welfare grants; and the social wage includes such elements for the poor as free and compulsory education, free health care, free basic services, and asset provision through the housing and land reform programmes. Steady progress has been made in the battle against crime. However, the reach of such programmes is still constrained by access to information, availability of resources and capacity of the state. The gradual reduction in life expectancy at the turn of the 21st Century is a matter of great concern; and it is influenced mainly by the impact of HIV and AIDS. At the same time, we need to address the challenge of crime, particularly unique features such as random violence, disrespect for human life, as well as women and child abuse. These are in part a consequence of social conditions, gender stereotypes and negative value systems such as greed.

The legitimacy of the state system is reflected partly in the growing number of South Africans of all colours who view their national identity as the primary form of self-identification. In the middle rungs of the socio-economic ladder, there is much inter-racial acculturation especially among the youth. But the majority of South Africans still remain separated by a wide chasm of income, skills, assets, spatial settlement patterns and access to opportunities. The majority of the poor are disproportionately Black and female.

Combined with this chasm and high levels of inequality is a value system within society that encourages greed, crass materialism and conspicuous consumption. These are tendencies that go beyond the necessary spirit of entrepreneurship, ambition, daring, competition and material reward that are inherent to a market-based system and perhaps to human development in general. Among the consequences of this value system are corruption in state institutions and corporate greed reflected in outrageous executive packages, short-termism in the conduct of business and private sector corruption.

Overall, since 1994, the balance of forces has shifted in favour of the forces of change. It provides the basis for speedier implementation of programmes to build a truly democratic and prosperous society. The legal and policy scaffolding for this is essentially in place. Most of society wants this to happen. At least in public discourse, except for a tiny minority, those apprehensive about change are concerned more with pace and scale rather than substance.

The critical questions therefore are: is society mobilised for faster progress! Does the liberation movement have the cadreship able not only to withstand the pull of negative values but also to lead society along the road towards a caring nation that a national democratic society should be!

DRIVERS OF CHANGE

Who then are the Drivers of Change?

The ANC seeks to mobilise all South Africans to contribute to the ongoing transformation of our country. In doing this, we strive to appeal to and foster a common sense of South Africanness and a shared responsibility for our common destiny among all citizens of South Africa, black and white.

Yet, any major historical process of social transformation has to be driven by a core of classes and strata that objectively stand to benefit from and have the capacity together to drive such change.

It should be emphasised, though, that the mere prospect of objective benefit does not necessarily translate into revolutionary consciousness and resolve to act in the collective interest. Nor does the fact of belonging to either side of the divide remove the possibility of individuals from these classes and strata aligning themselves with the antagonists.

It also stands to reason that the extent of receptiveness to ideas of change and commitment to take part in struggle would in broad terms depend on the role in the production process and the depth of subordination and exclusion. In other words, among the classes and strata suing for change, there will be concentric circles or a hierarchy of involvement.

Historically, the liberation movement characterised Africans in particular and Blacks in general as the motive forces of the NDR. These communities were, by law, defined outside of the political system except as servants of white minority domination. In class terms, they were made up of workers and the rural poor, the middle strata including small business operators, and real or aspirant capitalists.

The liberation movement defined the enemy, on the other hand, as the system of white minority domination with the white community being the beneficiaries and defenders of this system. These in turn were made up of workers, middle strata and capitalists. Monopoly capital was identified as the chief enemy of the NDR. It was also emphasised that apartheid was not in the long-term interest of the white community.

More than ten years into democracy, does this still apply? To answer this question we need to examine the strategic objectives of the NDR and changing socio-political dynamics under the new system.

As indicated earlier, the character of the NDR-in terms of the social contradictions that it seeks to resolve-remains the same. The progress made since the attainment of democracy is such that we are still some way from the ideal society of national democracy. The ownership and control of wealth and income, the poverty trap, access to opportunity and so on-are all in the main defined, as under apartheid, on the basis of race and gender.

As such, the central task in the current period is the eradication of the socio-economic legacy of apartheid; and this will remain so for many years to come. However, the establishment of a government based on the will of the people, progress in the transformation of the state, the codification of rights and implementation of progressive socio-economic programmes represent a major change in the socio-political environment.

Given all these factors, how then do we define the drivers of change today: which are the forces that the ANC relies on to achieve its objectives?

To the extent that the socio-economic legacy of apartheid continues to manifest in national terms, to that extent are Africans in particular and Blacks in general the motive forces of the NDR. Profound self-interest impels them to act in the collective interest to realise the strategic objectives of the NDR. They are the drivers of reconstruction and development. As in the past when they rose above the politics of race hatred, these communities do carry the responsibility of leading the process of nation-building and reconciliation too. Critical for them to play this role is the defence and consolidation of unity across ethnic and racial divides, to fight tribalism and racism whenever and wherever they rear their ugly head.

In class terms, these forces are made up of black workers: employed and unemployed, rural and urban. The early and extensive development of capitalism in South Africa led to the emergence of black workers as the majority in our society. They are located strategically at the heart of modern production and services. Because of and in addition to this, their sense of organisation and mobilisation locates them as the main motive force and the leader of the process of change.

Their tasks in this phase of the NDR include: advancing the struggle for quality jobs and job security; building class and national solidarity among all sectors of workers including causalised, informalised and unemployed workers; ensuring a strategic contribution by public sector workers to the transformation of the state and efficient provision of services to the population; directing the employment of institutional capital in which workers have a large stake towards developmental goals; and leading in the definition of a common vision and in implementing a common programme of action among all the motive forces and the nation as a whole. In addition to leading in mass struggles, the working class will continue to enjoy the confidence of the rest of the motive forces and advance its own interests if it is also able to wield the opportunities and instruments provided by democracy-both economic and political-to advance social transformation.

A significant part of the working class in our country are the rural poor, mostly unemployed, landless, engaged in self-employment through survivalist micro-entrepreneurial activity or farm-workers in insecure low-paying jobs. Land dispossession and marginalisation destroyed any semblance of an African peasantry in our country, reducing these rural areas into reserves for cheap labour. In addition to the strategic challenges that face workers in general, these rural masses face tasks that include: taking active part in defining and implementing strategies for rural development; enhancing the struggle for rural workers' rights; advancing the land reform programme; and mobilising for the optimal utilisation of agricultural land and other activities in the agricultural value chain.

As part of the motive forces, the black middle strata constitute a critical resource of the NDR. They include the intelligentsia, small business operators and professionals. Besides their varied identification with either of the main classes, these strata-especially the intelligentsia-not only provide professional skills, but also are critical in the determination of culture and value systems. They are called upon to play an active role in the provision of a variety of services to the population; in fostering a culture of searching for new and better ways of doing things; and in promoting progressive intellectual discourse through the media and other platforms.

The achievement of democracy in 1994 has seen the dramatic, if still exceedingly limited, emergence of the black capitalist group. This group is in most respects a product of democratic change, a direct creation of the NDR. The continued advancement of the revolution, particularly the necessary de-racialisation of ownership and control of wealth and income, is in their objective interest. In this sense they are part of the motive forces, with great potential to play a critical role in changing the structure of the South African economy: developing national forces of production in line with the character of the national democratic society including an extensive manufacturing base, research and development, local economic development, job-creation, skills development as well as national and continental economic integration.

However, because their rise is dependent in part on co-operation with elements of established white capital, they are susceptible to co-option into serving its narrow interests-and thus developing into a comprador bourgeoisie. Because their advancement is dependent on a variety of interventions and, as with all private capital, on opportunities provided by the state, they are constantly tempted to use corrupt means to advance their personal interests-and thus developing into a parasitic bureaucratic bourgeoisie. The liberation movement must combat these tendencies.

What about the Various Classes and Strata within the White Community?

Virtually all South Africans pay allegiance to the Constitution. Increasing numbers, including among the whites, entertain a sense of collective belonging to South Africa. It can be argued that most in the white community have come to realise that, indeed, non-racial democracy is in their immediate and long-term interest. This, combined with the social dynamics within the middle strata and acculturation referred to earlier, brings to the fore the question whether merely by dint of being white, this community still can be defined as antagonists of NDR!

In terms of practical experiences especially in the private sector, public discourse and voting patterns, it seems that many in the white community still have to realise that the poverty and inequality spawned by apartheid are not in their long-term interest, and that black people are as capable as anyone else to lead and exercise authority in all spheres of life.

But, unlike before, when antagonists across the apartheid divide were locked in mortal combat, engagement around issues of transformation in a democracy forms part of legitimate discourse and electoral politics. Those who continue to resist change within the constitutional framework are opponents in a democratic order. Their political and other organisations are legitimate expressions of a school of thought that should be challenged, but at the same time accepted as part of democratic engagement.

It behoves the liberation movement to persist in clarifying the long-term self-interest that the white community shares in ridding our society of the legacy of apartheid. Indeed, formal political democracy including the new human rights regime would be imperilled if conditions of abject poverty and massive inequality persist.

In this regard, the liberation movement must lead each of the classes and strata within the Black community in narrowing the racial chasm. This applies more so to the working class which, by reaching out across the racial divide within this class, should be the lightning rod to the emergence of inclusive nationhood. But it also does apply in large measure to the middle strata especially the intelligentsia, and the capitalist class.

The approach of the liberation movement to private capital, including monopoly capital, is informed by our understanding of the national democratic society as a market-based system that encourages competition, promotes labour-absorbing activity, discourages rent-seeking in the form of super-profits arising from monopoly control and other selfish advantages and so on.

The relationship between the national democratic state and private capital is one of unity and struggle. On the one hand, the democratic state has to create an environment conducive for private investments from which the investors can make reasonable returns, and through which employment and technological progress can be derived. On the other hand, through effective regulation, taxation and other means, the state seeks to ensure redistribution of income, to direct investments into areas which will help national development, to play a central role in providing public goods and broadly to ensure social responsibility.

Across all these class and national permutations are to be found women in their various capacities. As workers they bear the greatest burden of super-exploitation and poverty. As survivalist micro-entrepreneurs, they are called upon to provide use-values to working class communities under unbearable conditions. As middle strata and business-persons, they are compelled to hew their way through the jungle of male-dominated professions and environments. In the home, they carry the burden of nurturing families and are forced to reproduce relations of patriarchy. In challenging these anomalies along with progressive men, women form, in gender terms, the bedrock of the construction of a caring nation.

These then are the core, the real and the potential drivers of change in the National Democratic Revolution. Much clearer than before, the concentric circles of united action are taking shape, with Black workers at the core and Black communities broadly as the motive forces.

Unlike before, when white support for non-racial democracy and social transformation was an exception to the rule, large sections within this community accept at least the imperatives of the National Constitution. As such, tapering off towards the outer edges of the concentric circles of drivers of change is the balance of the nation's majority-made up of all races-steadily forging a social compact of common interest.

Across these circles the intertwining of Black and white interests is taking shape, with the definitions of the past starting to fade. As these circles intertwine and the currents across them flow into one another, so will the objectives of the NDR be reaching maturity. Common interests will increasingly be forged across the racial divide within the various social classes and strata. And so, other defining issues in pursuit of other strategic objectives may become the paramount driving forces for continuing change.

ORGANISATIONAL LEADER OF CHANGE

Given the vision of a national democratic society, what should be the character of the movement to lead social transformation?

To carry out the NDR in the current phase requires a progressive national liberation movement which:

- understands the interconnection between political and socio-economic challenges in our society;
- leads the motive forces of the NDR in pursuing their common aspirations and ensuring that their sectoral interests are linked to the strategic objective;
- masters the terrain of electoral contest, utilises political power to advance the objectives of the NDR and wields instruments of state in line with these ideals reflected in the National Constitution;
- organises and mobilises the motive forces and builds broader partnerships to drive the process of reconstruction and development, nation-building and reconciliation; and
- conducts itself, both in its internal practices and in relation to society at large, in line with the ideals represented by the NDR and acts as a microcosm of the future.

The African National Congress is such a movement. Over the years, it led the struggle of the people of South Africa for the achievement of democracy. In turn, during successive elections since 1994, it has resoundingly been returned to office.

The primary task of the ANC remains the mobilisation of all the classes and strata that objectively stand to benefit from the cause of social change. The dictum that the people are their own liberators remains as relevant today as it was during the days of anti-apartheid struggle. The dynamics within South African society, resulting in the concentric circles described earlier, impose on the ANC the responsibility more intensely to work among all sectors of the population and to ensure that they join the people's contract to change South Africa for the better. This includes all the class forces from within the white community, each of which can and should make a contribution to the construction of a better society.

The vision that the ANC pursues is informed by the morality of caring and human solidarity. The kind of democracy it pursues leans towards the poor; and it recognises the leading role of the working class in the project of social transformation. Recognising the reality of unequal gender relations, and the fact that the majority of the poor are African women, the ANC pursues gender equality in all practical respects.

In this context, the ANC is a disciplined force of the left, organised to conduct consistent struggle in pursuit of a caring society in which the well-being of the poor receives focussed and consistent attention. It seeks to put in place a combination of the best elements of a developmental state and social democracy. In this regard, the ANC contrasts its own positions with those of:

- national liberation struggles which stalled at the stage of formal political independence and achieved little in terms of changing colonial production relations and social conditions of the poor;
- neo-liberalism which worships the market above all else and advocates rampant unregulated capitalism and a minimalist approach to the role of the state and the public sphere in general; and
- ultra-leftism which advocates voluntaristic adventures including dangerous leaps towards a classless society ignoring the objective tasks in a national democratic revolution.

In order for it to exercise its vanguard role, the ANC puts a high premium on the involvement of its cadres in all centres of power. This includes the presence of ANC members and supporters in state institutions. It includes activism in the mass terrain of which structures of civil society are part. It includes the involvement of cadres in the intellectual and ideological terrain to help shape the value systems of society. This requires a cadre policy that encourages creativity in thought and in practice and eschews rigid dogma. In this regard, the ANC has a responsibility to promote progressive traditions within the intellectual community, including institutions such as universities and the media. Playing a vanguard role also means the presence of members and supporters of the ANC in business, the better to reshape production relations in line with the outlook of a national democratic society.

The activism of the ANC among the motive forces should be a responsibility of members and leaders alike. And wherever they are to be found, ANC cadres should act as the custodians of the principles of fundamental social change; winning respect among their peers and society at large through their exemplary conduct.

As a multi-class mass movement, the ANC is required to master the science and art of crafting long-and short-term common platforms to ensure that all the motive forces pull in the same direction. We do acknowledge that, at times, the narrow self-interest of a particular class or stratum or group may not necessarily coincide with that of other motive forces. In some instances, as with the working class and the bourgeoisie, these interests may even be contradictory.

However, guided by the ideals of the NDR, the ANC has to ensure that these forces appreciate the common strategic interest. It should strive to manage 'contradictions among the people' in such a manner that they do not undermine the long-term goal of national democratic transformation. In attending to these issues, the ANC should remain steadfast to principle, and guard against attempts by any force to turn it into a hostage of narrow sectoral interest.

Our approach to all these responsibilities derives from the understanding that a national democratic society has to be systematically constructed. It is not found ready-made at the point of transfer of political power. Nor can it emerge spontaneously through the agency of the 'hidden hand' of the market. What this means is that members of the ANC should continually improve their capacity-both political and technical-to act as the most advanced elements of society.

As such, the ANC cannot conduct itself as an ordinary electoral party. It cannot behave like a shapeless jelly-fish with a political form that is fashioned hither and thither by the multiple contradictory forces of sea-waves. There should be clear value systems that attach to being a member and a leader of the ANC, informed by the strategic objectives that we pursue.

In essence, the ANC is faced with two options: either to act as a party of the present, an electoral machine blinded by short-term interest, satisfied with current social reality and merely giving stewardship to its sustenance. Or it can become a party of the future, using political power and harnessing the organisational and intellectual resources of society to attain the vision of a national democratic society.

This arises in even bolder relief given the new terrain in which we operate. In actual fact, the world of the ANC changed drastically at the point of the 1994 democratic breakthrough. On the one hand, a new critical instrument of struggle, state power, one of the prime prizes of resistance, was attained. On the other, this instrument of power and status can impact in negative ways on a revolutionary movement.

Many leaders and cadres of the movement are found in positions of massive influence in the executive, the legislatures and state institutions. By breaking the glass ceiling of apartheid, the liberation movement opened up enticing opportunities for its cadres in business and the professions. Even within the trade union movement and students', youth, women's and other mass democratic organisations, unprecedented opportunities for individual material gain have opened up. All this creates a problem of 'social distance' between these cadres of the movement and ordinary members and supporters, the majority of whom are working class and poor.

Political incumbency also presents a myriad of problems in the management of relations within the organisation. Patronage, arrogance of power, bureaucratic indifference, corruption and other ills arise, undermining the lofty core values of the organisation: to serve the people!

How the ANC negotiates this minefield will determine its future survival as a principled leader of the process of fundamental change. A number of principles need to be observed in dealing with this challenge.

Firstly, the critical importance of political power as an instrument to address the ills of colonialism needs to be fully appreciated. In this regard, politics and public service need to be treated as a calling with requisite moral status, in which any of the motive forces can take part, either as a profession or as time-bound service.

Secondly, the ANC should give strategic leadership to those of its cadres in institutions of government, through Conferences, Councils and Branch General Meetings. In this respect, it needs to act as the ultimate strategic centre of power for its members.

Thirdly, in order to ensure that its strategic mandate is carried out, the ANC needs massively to strengthen its monitoring and evaluation capacity. This will ensure that cadres deployed in various capacities are able to improve their work in meeting set objectives. At the same time, these cadres should have sufficient space to exercise initiative within the strategic mandate rather than being subjected to micro-management.

Fourthly, systems of information-sharing within leadership structures and across the organisation should afford those outside of government sufficient data to make strategic interventions. In the same measure, all cadres should apply themselves seriously to governance issues, practically to add strategic value to the work of government.

Lastly, in its conduct in relation to the state, the ANC should be guided by its own principles, and act within the framework of the National Constitution and relevant legislation. In this regard, it should manage the state as an organ of the people as a whole rather than a party political instrument.

Within the ANC, the Women's League (ANCWL) is tasked with the responsibility of helping the ANC to broaden its mass base, as it champions the aspirations of a section of our society which over the decades, has been oppressed and exploited as "a nation", as a class and as women. It should continue to be the voice of ANC women members, but it should also be at the cutting edge of the Broad Women's Movement, spearheading gender transformation and the advancement of a women's agenda.

In a similar vein, the ANC Youth League (ANCYL) is a critical tool of South Africa's youth in pursuit of a better life for all. It should continue to function as an organisational and political preparatory school of young activists of our movement, informed by our strategic and tactical positions. The organisational autonomy of the ANCYL always provides organisational vibrancy and the youthful political debate imperative to a revolutionary organisation. It should continually broaden its base and deepen its political and organisational strength. It must strive to galvanise, and place itself at the centre of, the broadest spectrum of youth organisations for reconstruction and development.

Historically, the three streams of the national liberation struggle in our country-the revolutionary democratic, the socialist and the trade union movements-have found common cause in pursuit of the objectives of the NDR as commonly understood. The ANC will continue to work for strategic unity among all components of this Tripartite Alliance, in pursuit of a national democratic society.

In line with its responsibility to lead the motive forces of change, the ANC will continue to encourage the formation of, and to work within, progressive civil society: organisations of communities, students, youth, women, people with disability, traditional leaders, business and other non-governmental and community-based organisations. It will also continue to reach out to religious and other institutions to ensure common approaches to challenges of transformation. The ANC will conduct such mass work taking into account the dynamic changes taking place in the social structure and varied lifestyles of South African society.

The character and strength of the ANC must continue to reside in and derive from its mass base. As the leading force in government, the ANC should continually improve its capacity and skill to wield and transform the instruments of power.

THE GLOBAL BALANCE

The ANC was formed and it evolved as part of progressive forces across the globe in the fight against colonialism, racism, poverty, underdevelopment and gender-discrimination. It drank and continues to drink from the well of these progressive global experiences. The strategic objectives of our National Democratic Revolution reflect some of the best values in human civilisation.

Today, the system of capitalism holds sway across the world; and it is underpinned by the unique dominance of one 'hyper-power'. This situation of unipolarity also has secondary multi-polar features reflected in geopolitical blocs among developed and developing countries, and the historical resurgence of China, India and Russia as centres of growth and development. This world-wide system of capitalism is characterised by globalisation, which has seen impressive advances in the development and utilisation of technology, integration of production and management processes across oceans, massive trade in financial instruments and expansion of trade in goods and services.

But beyond this its technical expression, globalisation has also been shaped by the agenda of dominant global forces. These include transnational corporations controlling trillions of Rand of humanity's wealth, alliances around one 'hyper-power' whose dominance is reminiscent of empires of a bygone era, and cultural domination reflected in trends towards homogenisation of media content and the arts. A critical consequence of all this is the undermining of the system of global governance.

At the political level, unilateralism and militarism have reared their ugly head on a scale hardly witnessed in recent history. In intellectual and policy discourse, notions of empire and benevolent colonialism find respectable articulation. In many respects, the current global balance is evocative of the situation in previous eras of dominant empires and colonialism when brute force became the currency of geo-political intercourse.

In a situation in which an exploitative socio-economic system rules the waves, the danger should not be underestimated of widening wars of conquest and other more sophisticated means of subversion in search of resources, markets and geo-political advantage. This imperils sovereignty of smaller and weaker nations. Attached to this phenomenon is the assertion of shallow and populist ideologies such as the so-called 'clash of civilisations', which seeks to justify political crusades of blood and gore. By-products of this mindset include racial profiling and the undermining of the rule of law both in domestic and global conduct.

The growing threat of terrorism on a global scale forms an indistinguishable part of this phenomenon. Masked as resistance against imperialism, terrorism-which is the deliberate targeting of civilians in violent conflict-is as inhuman and right-wing as unilateralism and militarism. The two phenomena feed one another. They are two sides of the same coin. Indeed, though some of the elements engaged in such actions may plead conditions of cultural alienation, poverty and unemployment, many of them were formed, trained and armed by the very imperialist forces they claim to be fighting.

However, these dangers manifest themselves in a period in which humanity is keenly aware of the disastrous consequences of war and the dehumanisation that can result from warped ideologies of race hatred and religious intolerance. Ordinary citizens across the globe are finding various ways of resisting the encroachment of the rapacious licence of empire. Through mass mobilisation and progressive political parties, and through the power of the vote, continuous processes of self-correction do assert themselves.

At the socio-economic level, the wonder of technology including computing and nano-technology continues to broaden the horizons of human civilisation and create possibilities that only a few decades ago existed only in the wildest of human imagination. It is the irony of our age that such possibilities for the resolution of problems of health, environmental degradation as well as poverty and under-development are appropriated for the benefit of a few, and are seen to impress mainly in the shock and awe of war.

Technological advancement has created a global economic system that increasingly works as 'a unit in real time on a planetary scale'. The advantages of this are limitless.

On the other hand, these opportunities can be abused through financial systems in which paper money begets paper money: with new ingenious ways found to extract so-called shareholder value that has little bearing on actual production. This also creates an environment for a pervasive short-termism that can hold back the development of productive forces. Related to this is the growing tendency to sustain and justify staggering packages and astonishing lifestyles of corporate executives and so-called celebrities, with levels of inequality that are reminiscent of the eras of slavery and feudalism.

Globalisation also impels the search for the lowest in human deprivation to locate production and extract maximum returns, with developing countries encouraged to bid one another lower on a catwalk of mutual beggaring. Combined with this is the utilisation of economic power to rip open frontiers of protectionism among the weak, while doing the opposite in developed countries. All these developments and others such as unregulated capital flows that include complex derivatives and private equity takeovers negatively impact the sovereignty of developing countries.

These are some of the fundamental shortcomings of a rampant and poorly regulated market-based system. This system perpetuates under-development and deepens inequality within and among nations. It fuels corruption on a massive scale. It also results in the careless exploitation of natural resources, endangering the long-term survival of the human species. The wanton destruction of the environment, the threat to biodiversity and the danger of global warming are all a grave challenge that should receive priority attention. In addition, this system entrenches patriarchy, including the vicious exploitation of female labour, degenerate trafficking in women and children and poor representation of women in global positions of authority.

Parallel to these short-comings has been the widening access to modern technology and foreign markets across the globe. Nations which organise and position themselves to take advantage of this are advancing at a rapid pace. New economic growth centres are emerging-in Asia-and Africa is poised to join the trend.

It is a measure of the changing global economic balance that the fastest growing regions of the world are located in developing countries. Their share of global production has increased dramatically, with profound implications for global economics and politics. In various parts of the 'developing world', including Latin America, there is a growing assertion of national and collective sovereignty and a progressive developmental agenda. As a consequence, the voice of the South is growing stronger by the day. Both from the point of view of their common historical experiences and common current interests, countries of the South need to strengthen co-operation among themselves.

Globalisation also means growing inter-dependence among nations, reflected among others in production and trade, financial flows, environmental challenges, health issues and migration which includes a brain drain from developing countries. Further, improved platforms of mass communication help lay bare the advances in human comfort and thus the unfairness of massive global inequality.

The global mass movements around these and other issues attest to the impact of these factors on global human consciousness and conscience. Progressive parties, workers' and women's organisations, popular campaigns around local development issues, associations of professionals and movements of people with disability, indigenous communities, the homeless and so on-all have resolved to challenge the negative effects of globalisation.

It is in part a result of these trends that the United Nations Organisation (UN) has put high on its agenda the notion of human security as encompassing issues of poverty and underdevelopment. Whatever their limitations, initiatives such as the UN Millennium Development Goals, the programme for sustainable development, and the development round in global trade negotiations do reflect the positive impact of a progressive global paradigm. At the same time, the voices calling for democratisation of the UN and other multilateral institutions and the restructuring of the global exercise of power are growing.

Africa has the best possibility in this milieu to emerge from an era of political and social decline. It can on a massive scale turn adversity into opportunity. A new spirit is abroad on the continent, and the people of Africa are determined to use their newly-harnessed energy, pride and self-assertiveness to chart their own course of development and extricate themselves from the lowest rungs of human development.

Most of the conflicts on the continent have been resolved. Democracy is spreading. Economic growth is accelerating. And there is a collective determination to turn Africa into one of the centres of rapid industrialisation and social development.

While historical experiences of subjugation have much to do with Africa's current position, it is Africans themselves partnered by others, who can bring about the renaissance of their nations and continent. The most immediate challenges in this regard consist in the development of infrastructure for economic activity and social services, the deepening of democracy and mass participation and improved public service. Also crucial are regional integration and assertion of national and collective sovereignty in relation to global partners.

The ANC forms part of the global forces-including governments, political parties and civil society organisations in developing and developed countries-campaigning for a humane and equitable world order. In its history it has gained from and contributed to a culture of human solidarity across the globe. It is informed in its international work by values of internationalism, promotion of human rights against all abuses and violations, and support for national liberation. We remain committed to these principles, and we will continue to build and strengthen progressive networks across the globe to see to the emergence of an equitable and humane world order.

Our standpoint on these matters is both a matter of profound self-interest and an issue about the humanity of our own outlook. We will continue to build alliances and work with other progressive parties, organisations and individuals, in Africa and further afield, in pursuit of these ideals.

STEPS TOWARDS THE VISION

What then are the main steps that we need to take, in the current phase, to bring us closer to the ideal of a national democratic society?

The answer to this question is informed by the character of the NDR, actual practical experience since 1994 and our reading of the current balance of forces. In broad terms, the practical measures towards a national democratic society are contained in the Reconstruction and Development Programme (RDP) adopted by the ANC, the Tripartite Alliance and the broad mass democratic movement in the run-up to the first democratic elections. This was further updated and elaborated in Election Manifestos during subsequent elections.

What we outline hereunder are the main emphases in the work of the ANC government in the coming decade.

Constitution and Governance

The National Constitution sets out the framework within which to manage social relations. Some of the basic principles include: multi-party democracy; the doctrine and practice of separation of powers in a constitutional democracy; equal human rights and access to opportunity; freedom of speech and of the media; equality of all before the law; respect for the rights of linguistic, religious and cultural communities; social equity and practical corrective action against racial, gender and other forms of discrimination.

In order to ensure popular involvement in the processes of change, the ANC will continue to build partnerships across society. Practically, the ANC will strengthen institutions and practices of popular participation and encourage efforts to build an enduring people's contract-for each sector to contribute to the common objective.

There will be continuing work to improve the legitimacy of the democratic state, encourage national identity and the role of the state as an instrument of social cohesion. Informed by this legitimacy, the state will also ensure that its collective national authority as regulator of social relations is respected, in the context of rule of law.

The ANC will consistently improve the role played by legislative organs of government as tribunes of the people, and as platforms to monitor and advance the programme of change. It will continue to promote the transformation of the judiciary and to consolidate the legitimacy of this important arm of the state in a constitutional democracy. Informed by the doctrine of separation of powers, the ANC will encourage mutual respect among the three arms of the state-the legislature, the executive and the judiciary-in dealing with matters of common interest.

Building a Developmental State

The first attribute of a developmental state in our conditions should be its strategic capacity: popular legitimacy deriving from its democratic nature and approach of people-centred and people-driven change. In this regard, it should be able to lead in the definition of a common national agenda and in mobilising all of society to take part in their implementation.

The second attribute should be its organisational capacity: ensuring that its structures and systems facilitate realisation of a set agenda. As such, issues of macro-organisation of the state will continue to receive attention. These include permutations among policy and implementation organs within each sphere, allocation of responsibilities across the spheres, effective inter-governmental relations and stability of the management system. The third attribute should be its technical capacity: the ability to translate broad objectives into programmes and projects and to ensure their implementation. This depends among others on the proper training, orientation and leadership of the public service, and on acquiring and retaining skilled personnel. The ongoing transformation of the state is meant to ensure that these capacities are attained; and the process of identifying weaknesses and correcting them will be intensified. This includes engendering new doctrines, culture and practices as well as ensuring that state institutions reflect the demographics of the country, including appropriate representation of women and people with disability.

This applies to the public service in its totality as well as specialised institutions such as the judiciary, the police, intelligence agencies and the defence force. All these organs should serve the people in an efficient and impartial manner.

Accelerated and Shared Growth

Central to the country's economic challenges in the current phase is to build an integrated and growing economy from which all South Africans can benefit. The ANC will continue to strive for macro-economic balances that support sustainable growth and development. This applies to such indicators as the budget deficit, inflation and interest rates. In other words these balances shall not be treated as things-in-themselves, but as requirements that ensure higher rates of growth, labour-absorption and poverty-reduction.

Government action will be guided by an industrial strategy and a corresponding programme which continually identifies and addresses constraints to investment. This will help build an economy that is characterised by high levels of manufacturing activity, modern services, expanding trade, cutting edge technology and a vibrant small business and co-operative sector. State and private capital as well as resources and capacities in the hands of communities will be mobilised for this purpose. During various periods, specific industries will be identified for concerted joint action by all economic partners.

To ensure that benefits of growth are shared by all, there will be focus on creating decent jobs and ensuring an improving quality of life for workers. Government will implement programmes to eliminate economic dualism and exclusion. These include skills development, specific attention to industries that lend themselves to involvement by marginalized communities, access to micro-credit and small business assistance, land reform, public works projects and promotion of sustainable livelihoods at community and household levels.

The government will intensify broad-based programmes to empower those previously excluded from mainstream economic activity, including women. To ensure balanced and sustainable spatial development, systematic analysis will be conducted of economic potential and incidence of poverty in various geographic areas, and the three spheres of government will integrate their development plans to address these issues.

Macrosocial Tasks-meeting Social Needs

The central objective of social policy should be to preserve and develop human resources and ensure social cohesion.

To achieve this objective, the ANC government will continuously improve service to society, through enhanced public infrastructure, efficient systems and requisite personnel. We approach these issues proceeding from the premise that the state has a critical role to play in providing public goods such as health, education, housing, public transport, education and social security.

The ANC will implement a comprehensive social security system which brings together initiatives such as free basic services for the poor, passenger transport subsidy, social grants, expansion of the asset base of the poor through housing, small business and land reform programmes as well as private retirement savings, unemployment and accident insurance and medical aids. Government will align and integrate the various programmes-economic and social-directed at eradicating poverty with the aim of ensuring effectiveness and better monitoring and evaluation. Given the reality of feminisation of poverty, central focus in this regard will be paid to the conditions of women, especially in rural, 'township' and informal settlements.

Central to the preservation of human resources is the issue of the nation's health profile and causes of death. The ANC government will strive massively to reduce cases of TB, diabetes, malnutrition, maternal deaths and malaria, as well as violent crime and road accidents. Over and above this, the impact of the pandemic of HIV and AIDS requires a massive joint effort of the state and all sectors of society so as to reverse and finally eradicate it. Government will intensify its implementation of the comprehensive strategy against this pandemic and mobilise all sectors and all citizens to play their role.

The ANC government will implement a comprehensive human development strategy which includes: improvement of the general education system; intensification of education in mathematics and natural sciences; promotion of social sciences that help build social cohesion; expansion of the nation's artisanship base; improving throughput and research in the universities; and an effective adult basic education programme.

Specific programmes of redress such as land restitution and follow up to the recommendations of the Truth and Reconciliation Commission will continue.

The ANC government will consolidate partnerships across society to strengthen social cohesion and ensure that our nation achieves the moral values of a caring society. It will contribute to the improvement of structures of civil society including sports, women's and youth bodies; the media; and the institution of the family.

Safety and Security

The national struggle for freedom was the critical overarching vehicle to bring about peace, security and stability to our society. In dealing with issues of crime, the ANC proceeds from the premise that a rising quality of life also means improvement in the safety and security of citizens in their homes and environs where they live, work and engage in extramural activity. Three principles are critical in addressing the challenge of crime, especially its uniquely random and violent nature in our country.

The first of these is that the battle against crime cannot be separated from the war on want. In the main, incidents of contact crime such as murder, grievous bodily harm and rape occur among acquaintances in poor communities where living and entertainment environments do not allow for decent family and social life.

Secondly, specific mindsets and historical conditions drive elements of the crime problem. These are the proliferation of firearms in the hands of civilians, greed and conspicuous consumption, the psychology of patriarchal gender power relations and attitudes towards weaker members of society especially children.

Thirdly, the networks of crime have grown in their reach and sophistication across national boundaries. These include syndicates that deal with money laundering, human smuggling as well as drug trafficking and abuse.

The overall programme of national democratic transformation will gradually eliminate some of the conditions that breed social crime. So shall our contribution to creating an environment of peace, stability, economic growth and social development in Southern Africa and the rest of the continent.

Critically, focus must be placed on mobilising society to make life difficult for criminals in our midst. This should include an overhaul of gender and family relations and intolerance of abuse within communities. The transformation of institutions dealing with crime, including integrated efficiency is also critical. This applies to management, expansion of personnel, utilisation of latest technology, enhanced intelligence capacity, commitment to work with the people and eradication of corruption within the 'criminal justice system'. It also applies to the efficient regulation of the private security industry to ensure that its varicus capacities, integrity of its recruitment practices and employees' conditions of service are in line with the requirements of what is otherwise an important part of our nation's security establishment.

Government will continue to expand and deepen co-operation among law-enforcement agencies in the region and further afield. At the same time we will enhance our systems of border control and improve the capacity of our defence force and intelligence agencies to secure the integrity of our nation-state. We will continue to pay attention to any remaining networks from apartheid's 'dirty war' some of which are an integral part of the criminal networks.

CONCLUSION

Contained in this outline of our Strategy and Tactics is the ANC's assessment of the environment in which we live and the immediate and long-term tasks that we face. It is our collective view of the theory of the South African revolution.

During the First Decade of Freedom, we were able to consolidate and deepen our democratic system and introduce critical programmes for social transformation. The progress we have made is commendable; and the decisive actions in the early years of the Second Decade of Freedom hold out the promise of faster progress towards our ideals. But we are only at the beginning of a protracted process of change.

The ANC celebrates the end of the first century of its existence wielding political power-a critical platform to improve the quality of life of South Africans and contribute to building a better world. The strategic task remains the same. But the environment in which it has to be pursued has changed significantly for the better.

In this phase of national democratic transformation, the ANC commits itself to intensifying its work around the five pillars of social transformation:

- the state,
- the economy,
- organisational work,
- ideological struggle, and
- international work.

We will undertake these tasks conscious of our responsibility as one of the battalions of the global army for progressive social change, a disciplined force of the left.

The ANC is confident that South Africans will persist in building an enduring national partnership further to change our country for the better. Working together with them, we shall spare neither strength nor courage, until the strategic objective has been attained.

5

ROLE OF WOMEN IN RURAL DEVELOPMENT

Here in this chapter I am giving a few personal experiences of mine and of a very renouned socialists working for women development.

The Conference welcomed the introductory statement of Mrs. Helvi Sipila, United Nations Assistant Secretary-General for Social Development ant Humanitarian Affairs and Secretary-General of the World Conference of International Women's Year (IWY) 1975. In reviewing sequential events during IWY and plans for future action at national, regional and international levels, including resolutions under consideration at the Thirtieth Session of the UN General Assembly, she stressed the importance of the commitment of Governments to implement measures recommended in the World Plan of Action for implementation of the objectives of International Women's Year.

The Conference expressed unanimous approval for the inclusion of this item on the Agenda of its Session and a number of countries indicated that it wee long overdue. It wee strongly urged that this issue be not dealt with in isolation, but be a continuing concern of FAO subject to systematic and periodic review.

The Conference discussed the role and status of rural women within the context of overall development at country, regional and international levels. Several delegates outlined accomplishments, problems and specific needs of rural women within their country's national development efforts. It noted FAO's current policy, programme and areas of competence and its projected collaboration with Member Governments, UN

Specialized and Other Agencies and Non-Governmental Organizational FAO's unique role and its constitutional responsibilities in this area were also recognized by a number of delegates.

Many delegates expressed support for the belief that the full integration of women into the rural development process required a multi-disciplinary approach, as their problems and conditions could not be considered in isolation. Modernization and transformation of the agricultural sector which would provide adequate rural infrastructure and services was considered to be a necessary pre-requisite for improving the lives of rural people and especially rural women. It was stressed, however, that unless rural women were actively involved in decision-making and in the planning and implementation of programmes for action, modernization could have adverse effects on their lives. Several delegates expressed justification for giving special attention to the provision of opportunities for rural women so that they would be capable of assuming equal responaibilities and taking advantage of equal rights open to them.

There was consensus that equal opportunity in education and training was important if rural women of developing countries were to participate effectively in the development process. The Conference stressed the need for more training to improve information, knowledge and skills in the areas of health, hygiene, nutrition, child care, household management, food storage, family budgeting, family planning and home based income producing activities. To enhance rural women's role as agricultural producers, the Conference expressed the need for more training opportunities in farm management, training in techniques and leadership for cooperatives and appropriate technical agricultural skills.

In view of the recognized relationship among the multiple roles of women particularly in agricultural production, nutrition, family and community life, the Conference strongly urged that all FAO unite and divisions seek ways to contribute to this effort within their regular programme of work and allocate more of the regular programme budget for this purpose. The Conference decided that there wee an immediate need for FAO to review, reorient and coordinate activities in its regular and field programmes in order to ensure that the involvement of women in the development process could be given the strongest possible support.

Several delegates requested the assistance of FAO in preparatory activities needed within their countries to plan and conduct realistic programmes for improving opportunities for women both as participants and beneficiaries of rural development.

The Conference welcomed the initiatives of the Home Economics and Social Programmes Service in promoting the full integration of women in rural development and agreed that this involvement should be continued and expanded and adequate resources be provided. Some delegates pointed out that the magnitude of the task seemed more than could be expected of the projected resources in the 1976-77 Programme of Work and Budget.

In order to extend the limited technical and financial resources available for measures to improve the conditions of rural women, the Conference strongly urged close collaboration in the planning and implementation of action programmes between and within countries, among UN Agencies, Bilateral Programmes and Non-Governmental Organizational Some delegates pointed out that FAO should increase its collaboration and joint activities with the UN Economic and Social Commission. It was also recognized that the Non-Governmental Organization had a significant role to play and should be involved in the planning and implementation of activities in collaboration with FAO. Particular mention wee made of the valuable contribution the Freedom from Hunger Campaign Action for Development (FFH/AD) could make due to its close association with local groups.

Several delegates inquired as to measures being taken to increase the proportion of women in professional positions in FAO, particularly in decision-making posts. The Conference wee assured that such measures were under active consideration, including special efforts to obtain more female candidates for professional posts, and that progress on this matter would be reported to the Council in accordance with paragraph 7 of the Council Resolution 2/66. It was urged that the issues related to the role of women in rural development should be incorporated in the deliberations of all FAO Regional Conferences.

Some delegates requested that FAO, together with the UN General Assembly, proclaim, within the framework of FFH/AD, a Rural Women's Year within the context of a United Nations Decade for 'Women and Development,' if and when SO decided upon by the UN General Assembly.

The Conference adopted the following resolutions.

Resolution 10/75.

ROLE OF WOMEN IN RURAL DEVELOPMENT

THE CONFERENCE,

Recalling Council Resolution 2/66 on "Integration of Women in Agricultural and Rural Development and Nutrition Policies",

Recalling Resolution VIII of the World Food Conference,

Recalling further the World Plan of Action adopted by the World Conference on International Women 'a Year.

1. Reaffirms the Council decision to:

   (a) Support the necessary approach to the development of food production, food availability and utilization and the improvement of the quality of rural family life through the full integration of women in rural development;

   (b) Request that the Director-General assure the integration of women in all FAO programmes and projects by directing all Departments and Divisions concerned with these activities to investigate, design, plan, implement and review, on a regular and systematic basis, all proposed projects and programmes in order to establish a measure of progress in assuring the important participation of women as equal partners with men in the total development process, it being understood that wherever possible women should be directly engaged in the planning, decision-making, implementation and evaluation of FAO projects end programmes;

(c) Declare that the policy of the Organization be directed towards bringing about the increased participation of women in professional positions in all its unite and that immediate action be taken to eliminate any differential treatment based upon sex;

(d) Express the intention to review periodically the progress mate in assuring participation of women in the development process and in achieving an increase in the number and improvement in the roles and status of women employees within all levels of the FAO staff, with due consideration given to the provisions of Article VIII of the FAO Constitution;

2. Invites all Member States of the United Nations and its specialized agencies to support measures ensuring that women share in the benefits of development in the rural sector, particularly through the recognition of their full legal equality and the adoption of measures implementing such equality:

3. Invites Governments of Member Nations to ensure that women participate on an equitable basis with men in the policy-making, planning and implementation process in all agriculture and rural development programmes, in particular those related to food and nutrition planning;

4. Requests the Director-General to ensure that:

(a) current programmes ant projects in nutrition, agriculture (including fisheries and forestry) and rural development be reviewed by all departments and divisions concerned with these activities with a view to arrive at the full integration of women, who should be provided with the benefit of education, training, extension, cooperative activities, credit marketing and other community facilities in order to enable them to participate fully in agricultural and rural development;

(b) plans, programme and sector analyses, and programme documents incorporate an impact statement of how such proposed programmes will affect women as participants and beneficiaries;

(c) matters relating to the role of women in rural development be included in the agendas of the Regional Conferences so that specific programmes may result;

5. Requests further that information on progress and projections on the integration of women in all FAO programmes be submitted periodically to the Council and Conference in such reports as the Review of Field Programmes and the Medium-Term Objectives. (Adopted 26 November 1975)

Policies and Programmes for Improving Human Nutrition

The Conference held a broad discussion on the increasing extent of malnutrition and its various causes; it noted the danger of possible further deterioration of the most needy population groups' food situation' resulting from poor harvests and from the adverse economic situation. It recognized that increased production and productivity was not by itself sufficient to improve nutrition, since maldistribution of food supply due to the insufficiency of distributory channels added to lack of purchasing power was at least as important as food shortfall in causing malnutrition.

The Conference recognized that, to reduce and if possible eliminate hunger and malnutrition in the coming decade, governments must clearly express their political will to cope with the problem and, by concerted action and a multidisciplinary type of operation, integrate food and nutrition objectives in development plans.

While particularly stressing the importance of food and nutrition planning with a view to a solution in the long term of the problem of world malnutrition and hunger, the Conference emphasized the need to continue and expand short-term actions undertaken to remedy nutritional deficiencies such as food aid programmes, nutritional education, and fortification of foods with special attention to the role of Vitamin A, and promotion of breast feeding.

The Conference expressed itself strongly in favour of the importance FAO gave to planning in the food and nutrition field, and affirmed that nutrition should be one of the fundamental objectives of the Organization's activities. The need to develop appropriate mechanisms for interdivisional cooperation in this respect was stressed. As some delegates expressed their concern over the reduction of resources available to the Food Policy and Nutrition Division, the Conference requested the Director-General to give all possible attention to the funds available to that Division to enable it to meet its increasing responsibilities stemming from the world food situation and to reach the objectives set by the World Food Conference.

The Conference underlined the need to define food and nutrition planning not only as a technical exercise but as a continuing process involving political decisions, and the need therefore to recognize that each country must be responsible for the development of its own food and nutrition planning. The emphasis should therefore be on building national capacity for food and nutrition analysis and planning. Same delegates stressed the need to undertake food and nutrition planning in all countries.

The Conference noted with satisfaction the efforts undertaken by the United Nations system in general and by FAO in particular, in conformity with the recommendations of the 1973 Conference and Resolution V of the World Food Conference, to assist countries to assess the magnitude and frequency of hunger and malnutrition, inter alia through preparation for the Global Nutrition Surveillance System, to develop their nutritional planning potential, and prepare programmes with a view to immediate action especially by continuing expansion of food aid programmes.

The Conference noted the progress achieved by organizations of the United Nations system and bilateral aid agencies in the area of coordination of initiatives in the nutrition field. It considered, in particular, that the ad hoc Committee on Food and Nutrition Policies, with membership open to all FAO Member Nations, should continue within the framework of its present terms of reference to play its role as a catalyst and coordinator of nutrition activities within FAO and with organizations of the United Nations system.

Several delegates pointed out the lack of basic data in many countries which limited the possibility of identifying and assessing malnutrition formulating programmes designed to combat it, and utilizing food and nutrition planning methods. Some delegates stressed the important role of women in improving nutritional levels and regretted the lack of reference to this in the document.

Some delegates emphasized the role of rural social and health workers in nutrition activities in rural areas, and also the need to stimulate community initiatives and mobilize human resources for the improvement of nutrition. FAO was requested to prepare policy guidelines for the establishment of primary services to provide a framework for their food and nutrition activities at local level, which would also link central and community level planning objectives.

Concerning FAO's activities in the fields of food standards, control and safety, the Conference stressed the importance of the Joint FAO/WHO Food Standards Programme (Codex Alimentarius) and the benefits to be derived from it. The Conference emphasized the need for FAO and WHO to give greater support to these activities in order to accelerate their tempo, and pointed out the particular need to provide increasing technical assistance and advice to developing countries in food legislation, training and strengthening of their food control infrastructure. The Conference expressed appreciation to UNEP for the financial aid being given to these activities.

The shortage of specialized nutrition personnel, in particular in the nutrition planning sector, wee mentioned by many delegates. The Conference requested FAO, with assistance provided by bilateral agencies, to organize international, regional and national seminars and training courses to train a new generation of nutritionists able to participate in the permanent planning process with the help of national organizations.

The Conference asked FAO to develop its competence in the intersectoral planning area in collaboration with the other organizations concerned and inter alia in association with the United Nations University. It also asked FAO to take the initiative in developing applied nutrition research, especially in the food and nutrition planning field.

Lastly, the Conference approved the Council's decision to hold a session of the ad hoc Committee on Food and Nutrition Policies in 1976 taking into account the proposals presented by some delegates concerning the agenda, and expressed the wish that more nutrition specialists, particularly from developing countries, should participate in meetings of the Committee and in those of the governing bodies of FAO.

Review of the World Fishery Situation

The Conference reviewed the present state of some mayor fishery problems, discussed opportunities offered by the development of fisheries on unconventional resources and by aquaculture, and also drew attention to the possible implications of the Third UN Conference on the Law of the Sea.

The Conference expressed its satisfaction at the clear and concise presentation of the basic problems and issues relating to fisheries in the document. There wee general agreement that FAO and in particular the Department of Fisheries had a mayor role to play in assisting developing countries in the development and rational management of fisheries. The assistance FAO had provided hitherto was acknowledged.

The Conference stressed the important and increasing contribution fisheries were making to food production and the supply of high quality animal protein, and the need to ensure that the fisheries sector received adequate recognition and assistance both nationally and internationally. It wee stressed that care should be taken to clearly identify fisheries as being an important part of agriculture when mayor policy matters were befog considered.

The importance of improving the statistical data and assessments of resource potentials in order to provide an adequate basis for development planning and rational management of heavily fished stocks which were in danger of depletion wee emphasized. Although coastal states were assuming greater responsibilities for management of resources in wider areas off their coasts, there was also an increasing need for further international collaboration and coordination. FAO's competence and work in this field was recognized as was the need to strengthen its capacity in this direction.

It was recognized that while more of the conventional stocks were being heavily, and in some instances even excessively, exploited, there was still potential for further development of fisheries on some conventional stocks, both through increase of the total harvest and through improved use of the catches.

The Conference noted that much of FAO's work in fisheries was carried out through its regional fishery bodies which provided opportunities for intergovernmental cooperation. It strongly endorsed the activities of the regional and interregional projects assisting some of these regional fishery bodies and noted that, with the support of the FAO Department of Fisheries, they already provided for decentralization of responsibilities and activities in a manner which was in any case well suited to fisheries and was possibly also applicable in other sectors. The regional bodies were, with this effective FAO support, actively promoting fishery development on a regional basis, coordinating development activities, promoting international collaboration and providing a focus to all assistance to fisheries in the regions. The Conference strongly supported the strengthening of these bodies and agreed that they should have increasing responsibility for stock assessment and management and also be fore for working out development strategies suited to each region. The importance of international collaboration was emphasized and the useful role of FAO and in particular the Committee on Fisheries (COFI) in promoting coordination among all regional fishery bodies including those established outside FAO was stressed. A suggestion was made that a special meeting of experts on Collaboration in International Fisheries be organized and that this matter be discussed by the Sub-Committee on the Development of Cooperation with International Organizations of COFI.

One delegate stressed that national jurisdictions should be fully respected whenever the regional and interregional projects undertook resource surveys.

The importance of better utilization of catches, the avoidance of waste through better handling and storage, and the utilization of species hitherto discarded at sea through better processing methods was emphasized. In this connexion the need for better distribution and marketing methods, especially in developing countries, was noted. The need to develop low cost and appropriate technologies in the developing countries was also pointed out. Attention was drawn to the need for better and more timely information on production and marketing and a suggestion was made for the issue of a bulletin on a regular basis

The Conference noted the vast untapped potential in unconventional species notably the Antarctic krill, various cephalopods and small pelagic fish. International cooperation was needed to develop these fisheries particularly in view of the special fishing and processing techniques involved. The Conference noted the competence of the signatories of the Antarctic Treaty for all matters concerning the ecosystem of Antarctica, particularly its equilibrium and preservation, and the adoption of measures for the preservation of the Antarctic environment and its natural resources by the contracting parties over the last decade. The Conference agreed that FAO should keep itself informed of the relevant activities undertaken under the Treaty and coordinate its own activities with them. One delegate felt it desirable that the Director-General submit a report to the next COFI session clarifying the issues involved and delineating the relations between FAO and the Antarctic Treaty countries in this field.

Much stress wee laid on the development of small scale fisheries, and the initiatives taken by FAO through regional and country projects was welcomed. Development of small-scale fisheries was central to the improvement of the social and economic life of rural communities and its problems had economic, social and cultural dimensions much wider than providing pure technology. The Conference noted with satisfaction the growing awareness of these dimensions at COFI, in FAO and the countries concerned. The Conference stressed FAO's role in this field and emphasized that it should pay greater attention to the problems of the small-scale fishermen.

The special role of training and its indispensability in any fisheries development programme were pointed out. Training of fisheries scientific and technical personnel in research, stock assessment, catching and processing technology, pollution control, marketing and statistics was specifically mentioned. It was suggested that it might be useful to commence training national scientific counterpart staff immediately after a project wee approved so that they would be familiar with the work when the international staff arrived and would be able to participate more fully in the project activities. The importance of providing training on the spot and in the appropriate environment and through regional research and training centres was also mentioned.

The great potential in the development of fisheries through aquaculture and FAO's development programmes in this field, particularly the Interregional Aquaculture Development and Training Project, were noted. The Conference looked forward to the World Conference on Aquaculture (Japan, 1976) and expressed the hope that it would lead to the development of aquaculture on a broad front.

It was pointed out that there was an urgent need to ensure adequately trained and qualified personnel in this field. Suggestions were made for the establishment of regional training and research centres, which would facilitate and promote aquaculture development. In view of its high returns and its wide and beneficial effects on large numbers of rural poor, it was agreed that aquaculture could be a suitable field for consideration for investment assistance from the proposed International Fund for Agricultural Development.

The Conference noted that greater attention should be paid to environmental and pollution problems in relation to fisheries, particularly those in inland waters and coastal areas, both in developed and developing countries.

The importance of these problems was emphasized and FAO was urged to take a more active part in this area and requested to collaborate closely with organizations and bodies dealing with this problem. In this connexion it was pointed out that conflicts in use of coastal zones were assuming a greater importance and the claims of fisheries were often being overlooked.

It wee necessary therefore to maintain close links with other bodies involved in coastal area development. A suggestion was also made that FAO should intervene in such situations in order to protect the living resources and that it should play an important role in coordinating these activities within the United Nations system.

The Conference commended COFI for recognizing the importance of the UN Conference on the Law of the Sea and for giving thought to the need to adapt to changing circumstances. Recognizing that the Committee, as the only worldwide policy-coordinating body for fisheries, and FAO would have an increased role to play in promoting international cooperation and accelerating the transfer of technology to developing countries in the fishery sector, the Conference noted that a Sub-Committee of COFI would meet in March 1976 to consider these matters and suggest specific action.

Review of the World Forestry Situation

The Conference considered document C 7520 which contained a review of the current forestry and forest industries situation and set out the four main lines of action which FAO proposed to follow in this field.

The Conference expressed its satisfaction with the content and presentation of this document, and agreed with the general thrust of the policy set out in it, which wee to concentrate on tropical forestry, on the harmonization of forestry with food production and general rural development, on development of pulp and paper industries, and on promotion of trade in forest, products.

The Conference agreed that high priority should be assigned to work in tropical forestry The importance of these forests, both directly and indirectly, in connexion with the production of food, the development of rural economies and as a source of raw material for a wide range of important industries wee stressed.

The Conference expressed its approval of the "Tropical Forest Cover Monitoring Programme" being developed by FAO and UNEP in order to obtain the data needed to provide the framework for accessibility and land suitability investigations. In this connexion, the importance was stressed of ensuring and strengthening collaboration with national institutions which had long experience in tropical forestry.

Attention was drawn to the importance of tropical forests in-the regulation of water yields for agriculture and in the protection of agricultural soils, and to the consequences for agriculture, in the form of floods and droughts, of the abuse or the removal of the forests where it performed these functions. The Conference noted with approval the proposed increased efforts that would be made by FAO to identify ecologically critical watersheds and zones and to assist in initiating suitable management systems for these areas, at the request of the national institutions concerned.

The Conference also emphasized the more direct contribution that forestry could make to food production through agri-silvicultural systems that combined the production of both wood and food. While recognizing the complexities and problems involved, it was noted that a number of successful systems had been developed, appropriate to a range of different situations. Bearing in mind the size of the population in developing countries who lived in the forest zones and practiced shifting cultivation, and the low productivity of the latter system, the Conference endorsed the proposal to devote increased resources and attention in the coming biennium to the study and promotion of suitable agri-silvicultural systems in countries where these systems had been tested and accepted by the populations concerned.

It was also noted that agri-silviculture was an important component in harmonizing forestry with rural development. Forestry could create Job opportunities and help bring money into the economy in the rural areas both directly through forestry activities, and through wildlife, recreation and tourism activities, and through small forest-based industrial and craft activities. It was noted that in order to develop forestry in a rural context it was necessary to associate the people concerned with the forestry activity.

The role of communication and extension services in enhancing awareness and changing attitudes was underlined, as was the experience of agriculture in this respect. The importance of forest harvesting operations in creating rural employment was also recognized. Some delegates suggested that logging and transport wee the weakest link in the forestry production process, and that this subject should be studied by the Committee on Forestry.

The Conference noted with approval the priority attached to activities in the various fields related to rural development in the coming biennium. Attention was drawn to the fact that wood continued to be the main domestic source of energy for the rural populations of most developing countries.

It was noted that the drain on the forest cover that resulted wee particularly severe and destructive in arid and semiarid zones such as the Sahel, and the need in this and other areas for establishing fuelwood plantations was acknowledged. The scope for more efficient use of wood for energy in the form of charcoal wee noted. It wee also suggested that attention should be paid to investigating and developing alternative sources of energy, such as solar energy, to relieve the pressure on the forests.

The Conference expressed its satisfaction with the Pulp and Paper Industries Development Programme which FAO was implementing with the help of the UNDP and the World Bank in order to accelerate the process of identifying viable pulp and paper projects in developing countries.

Though supplies of pulp and paper were currently adequate, a renewed shortage was expected before the end of the decade which could badly affect developing countries. Noting both that very little use wee as yet made of the fibre of mixed tropical hardwoods for the manufacture of pulp and paper, and that research and development efforts in this industry had in the past been almost exclusively directed to the raw materials and market conditions of the developed countries, the Conference urged that the necessary effort be made to develop operational technologies and mill sizes appropriate to the forest base and situation of developing countries.

The need for training skills required for pulp ant paper manufacture was also stressed. In this connexion the recent Industry Cooperative Programme meeting with representatives of the pulp and paper industry and their positive attitude to this issue was noted.

Attention was also drawn to the need for research in the development of forestry in the tropics. Natural tropical forest ecosystems tended to be highly complex and much remained to be learnt about then.

To be competitive, productive forestry might often require the replacement of natural forests by man-made forests. The importance of choosing the correct genetic stock for this purpose was emphasized, and FAO's continuing work in this field was welcomed.

Some delegates pointed out the need to investigate indigenous as well as exotic species in making such choices, and the need for strong national research facilities and programmes in order to effect this. Certain delegates also drew attention to other areas of research requiring attention, including the need for further investigation into non-conventional use of forest products, such as the production of fodder for livestock and protein for human consumption.

The Conference underlined the great importance of forests as a renewable industrial raw material, and the particular potential in this respect of the tropical forest resources. Because of the selective utilization of the latter their potential was only being partially realized; huge quantities of tropical wood and wood fibre were being wasted or destroyed.

The Conference noted that much of this waste was associated with a pattern of trade which was primarily characterized by exports of unprocessed or partially processed forest products from developing countries.

The establishment or expansion of wood-based industries in the producing countries would not only permit a much fuller and more efficient use of the forest resource, but would allow more of the value added to accrue to the country of origin.

The Conference recognized the increasing role that trade wee likely to play in balancing the supply of, and demand for, forest products.

It also recognized that increased trade required more coordination and information intelligence at the international level, and that FAO was in a unique position to contribute to this, particularly since marketing of tropical wood and wood products was affected by resource utilization and development. However, the Conference emphasized the need to avoid duplication of effort with existing national and international institutions concerned with this trade.

In this connexion, attention was drawn to the continuing importance of FAO's regional and global timber trends studies. Particular mention was made of the recently completed study for Europe, and of the relevance of this and other FAO work in that region to the transfer of market and technological information to developing countries.

In this connexion, the Conference noted with regret the reduction in the resources made available by FAO to the Joint ECEFAO Timber Division and expressed the hope that this situation would be remedied in the Programme of Work of the next biennium.

The Conference stressed that the needed improvements and developments in forestry and forest industries in developing countries could only be achieved if they had strong national institutions. The Conference noted with approval FAO's continuing programmes to assist countries to improve their planning, administrative and research capabilities and to strengthen forestry education and training systems.

The Conference stressed the great importance of forestry to developing countries and agreed that FAO had a major role to play in this area. Noting the magnitude and range of the tasks that FAO was called upon to undertake in the forestry sector and the large size of its field programme responsibilities relative to its Regular Programme resources in this same sector, the Conference agreed that in future Programmes of Work and Budget of the Organization a more adequate share of resources should be made available for work in the field of forestry, forest industries and wildlife.

The Conference further expressed the view that, if possible, increased resources should be provided to the Forestry Department in the 1976-77 biennium.

The Conference then adopted the following resolution:

Resolution 1175.

Wildlife

THE CONFERENCE,

Considering the importance that should be given to forest conservation and management in the new world food strategy,

Considering the role of the forest in the general ecology of many regions of the world, particularly its influence on climate, soils, and the regulation of water regimes,

Considering the importance of the forest in recreation,

Considering the intimate connexion between fauna and flora, and

Considering the impact of fauna in the economic, tourist, cultural, social and scientific fields,

1. Recommends to the Director-General that special emphasis be placed on the conservation and management of wildlife and that appropriate financial and technical assistance be provided;
2. Requests the Director-General to exert every effort toward the rapid implementation of this Resolution.

6

Feminism and Politics

INTRODUCTION

The 1960s and 1970s saw the resurgence of feminism as a social movement in virtually every Western nation. In each, the movement adapted to the history, culture, and politics of the society (Bouchier 1984). This book focuses on how cultural traits and political institutions have shaped feminist movements in Britain, the United States, and Sweden. As Helga Hernes (1983:33) has pointed out, women in the state occupy similar roles regardless of national boundaries: they are citizens, consumers, clients, and employees. But they are also claimants in the arena of public policy, seeking to gain economic and political rewards and contesting for power and access. This study examines the mechanisms and impact of their role as political claimants helping to identify and influence policies that affect their lives as women.

The purpose of this inquiry is to demonstrate how differences in British, American, and Swedish feminism relate to systemic and cultural differences. A major hypothesis of this analysis is that such differences, in the respective "political opportunity structures" (that is, institutions, alignments, and ideology), have patterned the development, goals, and values of feminist activists in each nation. In turn, it will be argued, movement structure and systemic differences have affected and constrained opportunities for movement impact within each nation. While the feminist activists in the United States, the United Kingdom, and Sweden share many objectives, they differ significantly in their style of political activism, leadership orientation, and organizational values (Jenson 1983). These differences interact with contrasting political opportunities to shape the success of feminist claims. The analysis defines alternate meanings for the concept of movement success. How the role of women activists themselves shapes political alternatives is a central question of this study.

Other political scientists have questioned the view that autonomous women's groups organized to fight for political power and policy gains are more likely to succeed than groups integrated into prevailing institutions (Adams and Winston 1980). This study will argue, based on the British and American experience and with a briefer look at Sweden, that gender-based women's groups that are separate from institutionalized interests such as parties and unions are more likely to develop independent strategies and political agendas of their own choosing, thus permitting greater political impact. This analysis seeks to demonstrate that autonomous feminist movements play a major role in the achievement of significant social change. Otherwise, women are acted upon as objects of social policy but are not participants in their own destinies (Siim 1982:34).

The three countries studied here were selected because they are all postindustrial Western democracies, with policies that are superficially similar regarding women's rights. Each has legislation on abortion rights and labour force equality (Sweden was the last to adopt the latter), and each has set up an administrative commission on equal opportunities to monitor sex discrimination laws, albeit with very different powers. Although all three societies have experienced similar trends, their significance for feminist politics differs. For example, while in all three nations women have simultaneously been mobilized and incorporated as new participants into the political process and into the expanding tasks of the modern state, particularly as these relate to women, these developments have proceeded in different ways and with different impacts in each nation (Hernes 1982:7).

The participation of women in the labour force has increased dramatically in each society, as have family "pathologies," such as divorce and female-headed families (although these are not viewed as "pathologies" in Sweden). Paradoxically, Sweden, which is noted world-wide for the equality in its progressive social policies, has the highest level of sex segregation in the labour force as well as the highest percentage of part-time workers who are women. In all three societies women and men are concentrated in specific occupations. Women are further segregated into a far smaller number of occupations than are men. These occupations are lower-paying; many are in the public sector service area. In one study (Jonung 1984:54) an index of sex-based dissimilarity in employment reveals 70.7 for Sweden (282 occupations), 66.1 for Britain (223 occupations), and 65.1 for the United States (441 occupations). Another study has found Sweden to have a score of 60 percent, the United States 46.8 percent, and Britain 31.1 percent (apparently reflecting at least in part the fact that British men are less concentrated in a few occupations) (ibid.).

This study will focus on (1) the sociopolitical context in which each movement operates, (2) the organization and strategies utilized by each movement, and (3) the impact of each movement on the political process, public attitudes, and public policy. Within the context suggested, the study examines three Western countries that provide three different political models and therefore three different approaches to feminist politics.

To analyze the impact of women's movements on the political process and in helping to structure policy alternatives and outcomes, we will contrast three different models of women's participation and activism: 1) interest group feminism in the United States; 2) left-wing/ ideological feminism in the United Kingdom; and 3) state equality in Sweden.

Interest group feminism is characterized by a relatively open political system, a focus on equal rights and legal equality (although many demands may go beyond mere reformism), and the creation of lobbying groups that may have a mass membership or be staff dominated. Networking and inclusiveness typify the approach to different political orientations within the women's movement.

Ideological, or left-wing, feminism is characterized by insistence on ideological purity and a reluctance to work with groups espousing different viewpoints. This type of feminist politics is decentralized and locally based, largely lacking a national political presence and impact. Fragmentation as well as enthusiastic commitment to sectarian (feminist) views typify this model.

State equality is characterized by the absence of a visible and influential feminist movement. Instead, women are active via political parties and, to a lesser degree, trade unions (as is true to some extent in left-wing feminism, as an alternative to local political action). The state has tended to anticipate or co-opt women's concerns into public policy, even without significant pressure from women's groups. Policies related to women are generally discussed within the framework of "equality" or "family" policy.

In this analysis, movement development, effectiveness, and impact are seen as largely dependent on external factors such as political environment and available resources. Among the environmental variables that appear to be particularly significant are the current political complexion of government, the structure of the central administrative process, and the state of the economy (Whitely and Winyard 1983:10-11).

Examination of the structure of British politics, economics, and social life suggests a society highly traditional in its structure and values, a stagnant economy, and a centralized, secretive, and bureaucratically dominated system.

These factors contribute to a political setting in which feminists tend to be isolated from the formal political system, from feminists with different perspectives and women in general, and from potential allies. Ideological divisions, rooted in class and other conflicts, inhibit the formation of coalitions dedicated to resolving women's political and economic needs.

We focus on the role and structure of feminism in the nations studied by examining two wings of feminism. The first is the women's liberation movement, often characterized as the more radical, or "younger," branch of the movement.

Such groups in both the United States and Britain are distinguished by their emphasis on lifestyle change, provision of alternative services, and decentralization and anti-elitist values (Stacey and Price 1980:180). The second wing of feminism is that segment of the movement operating within the traditional policymaking structure. In the case of Britain, this segment participates in parties and unions that play a dominant role in the political system.

In the United States, women tend to be effective primarily as interest group activists, given the primacy of pressure groups in the American political arena (although we will examine the role of women in parties and unions for comparative purposes). These two sets of feminist activists are roughly analogous to "militant" and "reformist" branches of contemporary feminism, although many British feminists would decline the honor of inclusion in the reformist camp.

In Sweden, there is only one manifest face of feminism: that represented by women in parties and unions; the minute feminist movement is almost subterranean in character and visibility.

Among this study's major assumptions regarding the distinctions between the American, British, and Swedish systems are the importance in the United Kingdom and Sweden of centralized government and Parliament (called the Riksdag in Sweden) and the primacy of the administrative process.

Crucial variables affecting movement emergence and activism are the degree of corporatism/political centralization and pluralism.

Schmitter's (1984) well-known definition characterizes corporatism as interest representation in which constituent units are organized into a limited number of singular, noncompetitive, hierarchically ordered and functionally differentiated categories, recognized or licensed by the state and granted a deliberate representational monopoly within their respective categories.

Pluralism, in contrast, characterizes a society in which multiple, voluntary, competitive self-determined groups have access to state power. Table 1 makes the distinctions between the two approaches clearer.

The United States, where strong or strongly structured pluralism prevails, is found on the pluralist/dispersed side of the continuum, while Britain and Sweden are placed close to the corporatist/centralist side.

Table 1: Distinctions between Pluralism and Corporatism

Characteristic	Pluralism	Corporatism
Group unity/discipline	Low	High
Independence (economic)	High	Low
Character of state access	Open	Closed
Exclusivity of group participation	Unlimited	Limited
Character of state authority	Dispersed	Concentrated/ centralized
Consistency of issue resolution	Inconsistent	Consistent (planning)

In Table 2 we show how this structure may be supplemented to account for the organizational role of women's groups in the three nations studied.

The administrative process in the United Kingdom emphasizes ministerial responsibility and neutrality and operates behind closed doors, whereas in the United States there is far greater possibility for public scrutiny and intervention. British courts play a much more restricted role than their American counterparts.

Table 2: Structure and Potential Role of Women's Groups

Structure	Sweden	U.K.	U.S.
Strong labour unions	++	+	-
Strong political parties	++	+	-
Strong promotional interest groups (changed-oriented)	-	-	++
Women's section in parties/unions	++	+	-
Independent women's liberation group	-	++	+
Pluralist system	-	-	++
Politicized bureaucracy	+	-	++

Note:-= Limited; + = important; ++ = very important

The American party system is looser and less dominant in the political system; and because power is fragmented-both both in executive/legislative relations and in the federal structure-it is more accessible to interest groups of all types.

Swedish politics is usually characterized as a "consensual democracy" in which conflict and confrontation are customarily assiduously avoided. It resembles the British model of executive dominance and corporatism, although the political process incorporates a greater variety of groups.

The scope of government differs as well. In the United Kingdom the role of national government intervention in family and welfare policies (for example, the National Health Service) has been more firmly institutionalized, providing some support for British women in areas their American counterparts lack. Examples are child benefits (which are paid to mothers and were formerly called child tax allowances), maternity grants, and maternity allowances.

Welfare state benefits for women and children are greater in the United Kingdom than in the United States, including the non-means-tested child benefit of £5.25 per week, supplementary benefits, family income supplements, and rent rebates, although they are still far lower than those provided in most of the rest of industrialized Europe (the equivalent of $50 in British sterling, compared, for instance, with $93 in Hungary and $218 in France) (Norris 1984:43; Lewis 1985). After 1983, owing to a directive from the European Economic Community (EEC), married women on unemployment and sickness benefit could claim extra allowances for their children, although the new rights to Family Income Supplement and other benefits were significantly qualified by stringent requirements. The United Kingdom has lower pay benefits for maternity and stricter eligibility conditions than any other European country (Dex and Shaw 1986:5; Coote and Campbell 1987:90-91). In comparison with the United States, Britain has legislated more extensive maternity benefits, but many women do not meet the benefit conditions. In the United States nearly half of women employees are provided with paid or unpaid maternity leave-large corporations are most likely to provide such benefits (Dex and Shaw 1986:14; Kamerman, Kahn, and Kingston: 1983). Thus, despite the existence of statutory maternity benefits in Britain, more American women appear to get such support (albeit from the private sector) because there are fewer restrictions in the United States (Dex and Shaw 1986:14).

The British have the least day-care space available for children of working mothers (ibid.). American women are more likely to depend on paid and out-of-home child care than are their British sisters. British families tend to rely on family-based child care provided by husbands and grandmothers; few utilize institutional or nonfamily care (Employment Gazette, May 1984:209).

In the United States, antipathy to centralized state power and reluctance to intervene in the family have resulted in a system of categorical grants; policies are fragmented and lack coordination, providing meanstested support only for poor women who are (mainly) single parents. The United States is alone among these three nations (and the democratic West as a whole) in having no national insurance system for childbirth medical expenses, no children's allowances, and no statutory care benefits to cover pregnancy and childbirth. Civil/welfare rights activities in the 1960s did, however, expand the public sector's support of the poor.

In Sweden, a generous policy of support is available to parents (of either sex) for child care, housing, and other benefits to ease the burdens for working family members. In 1971, child allowances were $212 in Sweden, $62 in the United Kingdom, and $0 in the United States; the ratio has not changed much since then (Heidenheimer, Heclo, and Adams 1983:207). The Swedes have sought to develop social programs with a view to labour force and market control; the British have tried to universalize social benefits but at a low level; the Americans have kept state intervention to a minimum. While the Swedish welfare state has sought to develop a minimum level of well-being for each citizen, the United States, via the "residual welfare" model, prefers reliance on the private market and family to meet individual needs.

In the United States, universal social welfare is not seen as a desirable social good; instead, the society provides remedial solutions to politically identified social problems (Boneparth 1984:45; Hagtvet and Buding 1986:291). The concern of American policy is for the family as an institution but not for the individual member of the family (Boneparth 1984:46). Family policy often tends to be dealt with at the state, rather than the federal, level; resistance to federal public spending in recent years has reinforced this trend.

The institutionalization of the welfare state in Britain has to some degree altered the nature of the debate about such feminist issues as abortion, because of the presence of the National Health Service (NHS). Nonetheless, less than 50 percent of abortions are in fact performed by the NHS, a number that may be limited even further by cuts in the NHS under the Thatcher government (Greenwood and King 1981:180). And there is a great variation in the availability and cost of abortions throughout Britain. As in the United States, politics in recent years has been dominated by conservative interests who have sought to slash budgets and "reprivatize" numerous public sector functions, including those specifically related to women dependent on the state. Even in Sweden, concern over financing the extensive welfare state in an era of a shrinking economy has emerged as a significant political issue.

The emphasis to be placed here on externally caused distinctions among the feminist movements in the three nations should not obscure the many similarities, particularly in comparing the movements in the United States and Britain. Among these have been virtually simultaneous (parallel) historical developments, including the advent of the suffrage movement, the birth control movement, in which each country had a comparable leading figure-Stopes in the United Kingdom and Sanger in the United States (and Ottesen-Jensen in Sweden)-and the "renaissance" of feminism in the 1960s. In addition, the Seven Demands of the women's liberation movement in the United Kingdom (Feminist Anthology Collective 1981) are markedly similar to those advocated by the National Organization for Women (NOW) in the United States:

1. Equal pay.
2. Equal education and job opportunities.
3. Free contraception and abortion on demand.
4. Free 24-hour nurseries, under community control. (This demand, of course, goes further than the American one for day care.)
5. Legal and financial independence.

6. An end to discrimination against lesbians.
7. Freedom from intervention by the threat of violence or sexual coercion, regardless of marital status. An end to the laws, assumptions, and institutions that perpetuate male dominance and men's oppression of women.

It is significant that in Sweden a major statement, "Toward Equality," was adopted in 1969 by the dominant Social Democratic Party. Among its major and primarily economically oriented goals are a society in which rights, obligations, and work are no longer allocated according to sex." This manifesto calls for equality in working life: eradication of sex discrimination in recruitment, promotion, and wages; economic independence for married partners, with the two-wage-earner family as a model; uniform taxes for all; and parental leave (Qvist, Acker, and Lorwin 1984:265-66).

Analysis of public policy reveals similar trends. In the area of equal rights, the United Kingdom passed an Equal Pay Act (1970) and Sex Discrimination Act (1975), the latter establishing an Equal Opportunities Commission (EOC) to enforce the new laws. The Employment Protection Act of 1975 gave women a statutory right to paid maternity leave, protection from unfair dismissal during pregnancy, and a guaranteed maternity leave of 29 weeks. (However, as will be discussed later, these policies have been made more restrictive by the Thatcher administration, which has institutionalized stringent requirements concerning prior work for would-be recipients [Coote and Campbell 1987:93-94.]) With regard to violence and victimization of women and the right to self-determination, the Domestic Violence and Matrimonial Proceedings Act (1976) strengthened procedures by which women could obtain injunctions to restrain violent husbands, while the Sexual Offenses (Amendment) Act of 1976 provided better safeguards for a rape victim's privacy during trial (ibid., 37, 42). The 1967 Abortion Act authorized abortion up to 28 weeks of pregnancy in cases where two doctors agreed either that the life of the mother or other children would be at risk or that the baby was likely to be handicapped (Randall 1982:172).

In the United States, Title VII of the Civil Rights Act of 1964 and the establishment of the Equal Employment

Opportunity Commission (EEOC) provided equal employment protection for women. The 1978 Pregnancy Discrimination Act gave pregnant women equal access to insured maternity benefits.

Abortion rights in the United States were established largely via Supreme Court decisions (whereas in the United Kingdom they were enacted by legislation) and have been the subject of congressional action (primarily restrictive). Domestic-violence legislation (which involved funding for shelters, not procedural reform) was enacted in 1984 at the federal level, and additional funding for victims and shelter expansion, as well as improved police and judicial intervention, has been the subject of considerable legislative activity at the state level.

In Sweden, legislation permitting women to choose abortion freely up to the eighteenth week of pregnancy was passed in 1975 (although abortion after the twelfth week is subject to a special inquiry). After 1982, wife beating became open to public prosecution and, in March 1985, government grants were made available to aid some shelter activities. Equal opportunities legislation that prohibits sex-based discrimination in employment and requires employers to take steps to promote work equality was enacted into law in 1979. Despite the apparently similar nature of public policy related to women in the three nations, however, we will contend that the impact of such policy has depended in large measure on systemic factors and the strength of the organized feminist movement.

Social movements may be described as movements seeking to achieve social change through collective action. Directed groups (with more formal organizational structures) have formal leadership, definitive ideology, stated objectives, and specific programs. Nondirected movements stress a reshaping of perspectives and values through personal interaction (Hanmer 1977:92).

To a large extent, the most visible portion of the American feminist movement belongs to the "directed" category, at least in its formal leadership structure and definite programs of action. To a greater degree, British feminism is of a more "nondirected" nature, with greater emphasis on personal interaction, expression and articulation of feminist values, and the importance of internal democracy.

In addition, coalitional activities across issue and ideological lines are less well developed in the United Kingdom than in the United States. Hence, pressure group politics has not been the primary avenue for feminist involvement in Britain. However, the absence of formal, structured coalitional groups comparable to those in the United States should not obscure the existence of alternative groups actively involved in other aspects of political life.

As we have noted, in Sweden, feminist movement activity per se has been limited and women's organizations have tended to gravitate toward political parties. Some efforts to create all-party, gender-based groups have been made in recent years, and ad hoc activity has occurred around some women's issues (especially opposition to prostitution, pornography, and violence against women).

THE POLITICAL OPPORTUNITY STRUCTURE

This analysis rests on the premise that political structures provide the context for the development of social movement politics. Analysis of political structures includes the assessment of the significance of parties, pressure groups, the bureaucracy, the nature of state power, and the role of the judiciary. In addition, processes of socioeconomic change, including values and issue approaches, must be considered. External factors help structure the type of group mobilization that occurs as well as the character and success of a movement. Because British politics operate within a neocorporatist framework, large, economically labour-related pressure groups are primary actors in politics, although they are less well integrated into regimes dominated by the Conservative Party. There appears to be little support for Samuel Beer's view that British pressure groups are strong when promotional groups are considered. Most students of British politics agree that the nonorganized and lesser-organized are rarely consulted by policymakers (Richardson and Jordan 1979:45). Gender, rather than economic sources of influence, is inevitably rendered less important in such a system.

Richardson and Jordan (ibid., 122) have characterized the British political system in terms of strategies for group influence;

in their view, Whitehall is the primary target for influence; the legislative process comes second, and the public third. To a remarkable degree, the policy-making process is organized in an exclusive fashion (Ashford 1981:8). In fact, it may be suggested that the British political system tends to limit access for non-established, "promotional" groups, which seek social change. While producers-or key economic groups-may enjoy continued access to policy-making, based on sectional and economic roles and well-established relationships, the same is not true for groups, consumers, or others who may oppose them. A consequence of centralization and secrecy is to limit the role of "promotional" or attitude groups seeking change-they tend to be poor in size, finances, and the ability to obtain benefits (Christoph 1974:44; Blondel 1974).

Economic and technical problems are most often dealt with by a system that increasingly emphasizes executive dominance (Smith 1976:66-67). The role of Parliament is diminishing in comparison to the administrative sector. Whereas in the United States political power is diffused, in Britain it is highly centralized-in both the horizontal and the vertical structures of policy-making. (Grass-roots lobbying, common in the United States, has little impact in a system as centralized as that in Britain.) The administrative sector is characterized by limited public visibility and the absence of public scrutiny of decision-making (Pennock and Chapman 1969:11). The core of "politically neutral" permanent civil servants and the relatively small size and narrow social backgrounds of the political elite often present significant barriers to change-oriented policies (Ashford 1981; Sampson 1982). Cabinet meetings are secret, and closed doors are the rule in most administrative proceedings.

The system of "tripartism," which includes the government, the Confederation of British Industries (CBI), and unions, limits possibilities for other groups to influence politics (Beloff and Peele 1980:28). Pressure groups may present views but may have little impact on the legislative process or the cabinet (ibid., 238-39). Unlike the United States, where appointments to government, including administrative bodies, are often the product of "clientelism," or pressure group influence, in the United Kingdom such appointments are limited to "old boy" lists of the "Great and the Good." Confidentiality prevails, and there is virtually no opportunity for group activists to influence such processes. Traditional pressure group tactics are most successful for groups with high-level political or civil service contacts. (Less conventional forms of political activity, especially protest, may endanger opportunities to relate to government) (Grant 1984:134). The absence of alternative methods of access to the political process virtually forces promotional groups out of the system. The secret process of nomination and appointment is made by the civil service in consultation with the prime minister and "leading mandarins" (Ashford 1981:266). Little is publicly known about patronage politics. Policies are established behind the scenes-knowledge is hidden from Parliament and the people. The highly stratified administrative system means that many crucial steps in the policy-making process are unknown to ministers, the public, and groups interested in specific policies (ibid., 19). Ashford has argued that because, traditionally, civil servants and politicians have not engaged in conflict, the political system has never confronted and subordinated the bureaucracy (ibid.). The feedback and friction generated by implementation politics in the United States are almost entirely absent in Britain, owing to the primacy of appointed, not elected, officials.

Although parties are, by general consensus, declining in importance, they are major agents for the resolution of key political issues. Because of the significance of strong parties within Parliament, legislation of a controversial nature must enjoy government (party) support or at least sufficient neutrality to ensure that a private member's bill is given the time to introduce and nurture legislation. The final stages of the legislative process are less important than the negotiations that precede them (Beloff and Peele 1980:107).

British parties, more than those in the United States, tend to be parties of social integration rather than individual representation. Party policy does not seem to reflect group influence to the extent common in the United States, with the possible exception of the relationship between trade unions and the Labour Party (Christoph 1974:13). In the Conservative Party, the parliamentary structure plays a key role, and the organization is less federal than in the Labour Party. In Britain, where about 50 percent of workers are unionized (in contrast to less than 20 percent in the United States), trade unions play a dominant political role, particularly in the Labour Party. Ninety percent of total Labour Party membership and 85 percent of the funds are derived from unions (Punnett 1980:127). The tradition of class-based ideology, socialism, and a strong organized left involves many British feminists in Labour Party and trade movement politics.

The passage of legislation is determined by the parliamentary timetable, individual M.P.'s, and the ruling party (Pym 1974:114). Pressure groups may create a climate in which reform is possible but cannot make progress against a hostile government; they cannot dictate a bill's content or guarantee its passage, although they may generate a climate for reform and raise public consciousness about a special issue (ibid., 120). The individual M.P. has little say in drafting or amending bills in parliamentary politics (Ashford 1981:17), so lobbying must have different goals than in the United States. The House of Commons creates or prevents a climate of opinion favourable to legislation proposed by the government (Richardson and Jordan 1979). In the legislature, because of the absence of permanent standing committees, interest group relationships with specialized legislators are less common than in the United States, although contacts with M.P.'s are more frequent than with civil servants. The absence of regularly scheduled elections serves as an additional brake on opportunities for political pressure.

In Britain the courts define themselves as defenders more of the state and the general interest than of individual rights (Nelkin and Pollak 1981:52). The absence of distinct constitutional concepts and rules has limited the ability of courts to interpret (in contrast to applying) law. Judicial review in the American sense does not exist in the British system. Class action suits-such as those used to aid large groups in the United States-are limited or nonexistent. The system of administrative justice is a tangled web of appeals tribunals and administrative agencies with indirect and ambiguous relationships to the courts (Ashford 1981:40). Judicial recourse is limited by the role of industrial tribunals, which hear most discrimination-related cases. There is no general right of appeal from industrial tribunals.

New centers of power-including "quangos" such as the EOC (to be discussed later), which are largely oriented toward achieving social goals-are autonomous organizations, with advisory, executive, and policy-making functions not unlike those of American regulatory agencies. Because they are not subject to parliamentary control, they have created new loci of power, reducing the role of elected politicians even further (Beloff and Peele 1980:84). Quangos were initially viewed as mechanisms for inadequately represented interests to gain a voice in government in the postwar period, but because of the systemic constraints outlined, they have in fact been hard pressed to play such a role. Appointments to quangos are, as already noted, at the discretion of the ministers and civil service (Ashford 1981:39).

In Britain (and in the United States as well), local government may sometimes provide greater opportunities for political participation than the national arena (Beloff and Peele 1980:262) as there has been an increase in civic pressure-group activity concerned with the quality of life and services.

As noted earlier, the American party system is looser and less dominant in the political system, and the fragmented nature of power makes the system accessible to a wider variety of pressure groups. Politics is less "corporatist"; unions are less socialistic and less politically significant (Heclo 1974:18). Although in the United States there is no analogy to the strong labour union role linked to left and Labour Party politics in Britain, the Democratic Party most resembles the Labour Party in its organization as a party of groups rather than of individuals (Freeman 1987). The past decade has seen the further decline of political parties and the rise of single-issue pressure politics. The American political culture stresses incremental, nonradical change as well as compromise. With the step-up of federal policy on social and economic concerns in the 1960s, the number of interest groups involved in lobbying at the national level increased greatly. Citizen groups, in particular, expanded their activities, prompted in part by the social unrest of the time, which provided a powerful impetus for change. New regulatory legislation provided a route into the political process for hitherto excluded and unorganized groups. Jack Walker (1983) has shown that citizen groups, including women's groups, were able to gain patrons in the form of members (contributors), foundations, other groups, and/or government, which enabled them to organize and then maintain themselves as political activists.

The American process of interest group activity was given additional momentum with the passage of legislation on campaign finance reform, which helped to further institutionalize group formation in the electoral process in the 1970s and thereafter. In the United States, in contrast to Britain, decision-making is subject to considerable public scrutiny, in both legislative and bureaucratic politics, partly owing to the dispersed process of decision-making not only at the federal level but also at other levels of politics. Students of American public policy have pointed to policy networks, or "subgovernments" (Heclo 1980), that permit specialists in Congress, in the relevant administrative sector, and in pressure group organizations to play a dominant role in policy-making. While policy networks in many areas have given way to broader and more open and penetrable "issue networks" in the 1980s, this development only accentuates the significance of interest group actors in U.S. policy-making (ibid., 102). Interplay between several sets of political actors, both governmental and nongovernmental, is without parallel in the United Kingdom, at least as far as noneconomic groups are concerned.

To sum up, American politics is responsive to interest group demands if they are seen as legitimate, whereas the British government pays less heed to noneconomic-oriented group demands. (The Swedish government, to be discussed later, promotes-and to a degree controls-interest groups sympathetic to policies that are primarily economically based.)

A further aspect of movement politics in the constitutional/cultural setting is the role of third-party, or support, groups that may facilitate political access and provide needed assistance. Relationships with other reform/change-oriented groups may foster political consciousness and alliances that provide resources, access, and legitimacy for new movements (Parkin 1968). In the United Kingdom, movements such as the Campaign for Nuclear Disarmament (CND) helped set the stage for change-oriented politics in the 1950s and 1960s. The CND was probably the first major group to aim its strategies at the public-instead of only at decisionmakers-and in this way was a model for feminists who followed. However, the CND lacked a formal bureaucratic structure and formal membership, and although it was a major political presence and leading force in the mobilization of political consciousness for women, it was unable to provide a continuing institutional base on which emerging feminists could rely. In the 1960s numerous other social reform and environmental groups-including those successful in promoting pro-abortion policy and legalization of homosexuality, and opposing capital punishment-emerged politically, as did groups of university students.

Like their American counterparts, traditional women's groups in the United Kingdom survived the doldrums of the '40s and '50s and continue to have a mass membership base, although it is declining (Rogers 1983; Stott 1978; Randall 1982). While they do not identify with women's liberation, they do support some feminist demands and efforts to achieve them. But such British women's organizations as the Women's Institutes (WI), Townswomen's Guilds (TG), and National Council of Women (NCW) by and large eschew relations with socialist and radical feminists. They have felt little in common with a women's liberation movement perceived by the media and general public as antimale. Hence, the links to civil rights and other movements that provided resources and access for feminists in the United States are weak in the United Kingdom (Costain 1982; Gelb and Palley 1987), although there are important ties to such groups as the National Council for Civil Liberties (NCCL) and the Child Poverty Action Group (CPAG), as well as a historic relationship to the socialist left, as we shall see.

In the United States, feminists were able to learn from the example of black civil rights groups and to rely on support from traditional women's groups. More recently, feminists have developed relations with a variety of political allies who have broadened their resource base and opportunities for access to the political system.

A final basis for contrast is the area of funding. Economic resources for promotional groups are scarce in the United

Kingdom. In contrast, political scientists such as Jack Walker (1983) have stressed the crucial role played by patrons in the United States who contribute monetarily to both the formation and the maintenance of citizen-based promotional pressure groups, among them feminist groups.

In the United Kingdom, in contrast to the United States, there is relatively little money available for charitable gifts and little incentive for individual donors, who derive no direct financial benefit from contributions. Persons who wish to make annual payments to charities must sign a "covenant" for more than three years that obliges them to an annual payment (the charity receives the tax on earned income in lieu of the government; only individuals in the highest tax brackets are able to escape taxation up to £3,000). Apparently only a relatively few wealthy individuals are motivated to contribute in this manner. As in the United States, charitable status is not given to groups of a primarily political" nature, although some campaigning is usually considered permissible by the Charities Commission. The limited nature of charitable income available in the United Kingdom is evident from a study revealing that 81 percent of charities have annual incomes of less than £500 (Phillips 1982). Of the small number of charitable trusts, few contribute to feminist groups. In the main, only government agencies such as the EOC and the Manpower Services Commission (MSC) have provided any funds for feminist-related activity. Although American feminists are among the poorest of recipient groups, the infrastructure of contributors in the United States from both private and public sources supplies far more resources to emergent groups and movements than is the case in the United Kingdom.

American feminists have been able to rely on continuing, and in some periods even expanding, contributions from members, wealthy individuals, and foundations. For example, contributions increased in the post-1980 Reagan election period after the Equal Rights Amendment (ERA) failed to be ratified. Contributions have enabled groups to survive, and in some instances even expand, despite a very real decline in federal government support in the 1980s (Peterson and Walker 1986:7), although the fortunes of membership groups depend in part on issue visibility and changing political orientations. At the same time, lacking formal membership and funding, British feminist groups have tended to remain small and less bureaucratic, and thus further isolated from the centers of decision-making power.

THE ECONOMIC AND CULTURAL SETTING

In this analysis, economic and social factors, including values, attitudes toward change, and receptivity to new movements, are viewed as variables that influence the emergence and impact of new political claimants. Thus, they help provide the context in which movements such as feminism may emerge and flourish or, instead, fail to gain political strength and importance. Cultural differences, then, interact with political institutions and ideology to produce a climate in which opportunities for change are structured. In turn, the type of movement that develops and what we have called the "political opportunity structure" create systemic possibilities and/ or constraints that either promote or retard positive policy outcomes and political impact. The concept of political economy suggests the relationship between the state and the ways in which citizens pursue their private ends and satisfy their wants. In Robert Keohane's terms, if the rules of the game in a particular society allow or require actors in the economy to exert power over one another, then the "economy is political" (quoted in Levine 1986:5).

As noted earlier, British society is distinguished by its traditional structure and values. The British social structure, with its low educational attainment for women, norms of "good" motherhood and marriage, low wages, and a stratified labour market and class system, has greatly narrowed opportunities for political involvements (Hills 1981:13). The traditional family remains entrenched, to a degree unusual in Western society, with marriage rates high and divorce rates relatively low (Norris 1984:43). The rates for divorce continue to be lower in Britain than in the United States, although they have risen dramatically in recent years, as have the rates of out-of-wedlock births. The divorce rate is roughly half that in the United States (2.9 versus 5.3 per 1,000 persons). By 1987, 21 percent of live births were out-of-wedlock in the United Kingdom, in contrast with 20 percent in the United States and 45 percent in Sweden (Bianchi and Spahn 1986:74; Popenoe 1985-86; Population

Trends, Winter 1987:52). The link between female-headed families and poverty is blatantly apparent from an analysis of the data. In the United States, 17 percent of white families and over 50 percent of black families were headed by women in 1984, an increase from 8 percent and 33 percent, respectively, in 1970 (Bergmann 1986:229). Black and Hispanic female-headed families were especially likely to live in poverty. Nonetheless, while there are fewer single-parent families headed by women in the United Kingdom, their numbers doubled between 1961 and 1981, and over 60 percent of Supplementary Benefit recipients are women (Pierce 1980:84). Single parents received an extra £4.70 a week in Supplementary Benefits in 1987 (Social Welfare in Britain 1987:159).

Participation in the labour force by women, including married women with small children, has increased dramatically in Britain, the United States, and Sweden, as it has in virtually all Western countries. About 59 percent of British women are in the labour force, over 61 percent in the United States, and almost 80 percent in Sweden. Nonetheless, while in all three nations (and universally) women are concentrated in lower-paying, lower-status jobs, the situation in Britain appears to be worse than that in the United States and Sweden, at least partly because of Britain's serious economic recession, which has resulted in an even greater increase in unemployment for women than for men (although, as we shall see, the difference may be more apparent than real).

In the United States about 23 percent of women work part-time, limiting access to maternity leave, pensions, and job-training programs. In addition, part-time workers are usually first to be fired in cases of cutbacks and layoffs (UNESCO 1983). In Britain the part-time component (working 35 hours or less) of the labour force is especially large compared with that of other European nations (except Sweden) and the United States (Equality Ministry 1985:12). The most accurate assessment places the number of female part-time workers at about 42 percent in the United Kingdom, and rising steadily (the number is 46.2 percent in Sweden (International Labour Office Staff 1985:425, 459). Women often experience downward mobility when returning to work and are more likely to work at semiskilled or manual jobs. In 1982, 14.9 percent of British women were unemployed (in contrast with 9.4 percent in the United States [Edgell and Duke 1983:358] and about 4 percent in Sweden), although the unemployment figures for all countries appeared to be lower by the mid-1980s.

In the United Kingdom, several studies suggest that female unemployment is less than that of men because men have been disproportionately affected by the decline in manufacturing opportunities. (Thus, the statistics may reflect the ways in which unemployment data are gathered as much as actual statistical validity.)

There was a perceptible narrowing of wage differentials between men and women during the 1970s when, perhaps in response to the passage of the Equal Pay Act (to be discussed later), women's gross hourly earnings increased from 63 to 74 percent of men's from 1970 to 1977 (Phillips 1983:15). Nonetheless, even these figures reflect hourly wage rates for full-time employees over the age of 21, so they considerably exaggerate the scope of the gains made (Spare Rib, Sept. 1979:22). More recent evidence suggests a falling back to widened wage gaps based on gender (Coote and Campbell 1987:18; New York Times, Jan. 16, 1984:B10).

The backwardness of the economy has further constrained opportunities and value change for women in the class-ridden, elitist British society, reinforcing the concept of the "family wage," which entrenches the leading economic role of male breadwinners and limits opportunities for women in the labour force (Land 1983). At present the contracting nature of public-sector employment and concomitant reduction in education and social welfare subsidies have reinforced these tendencies (Rothwell 1980:161).

Norms of political efficacy are unusually low in the United Kingdom, no doubt owing to difficulties of access in a centralized bureaucratic state, suggesting that political participation in general is likely to be limited (Barnes and Kaase 1979). Participation and efficacy are related to high income and educational attainment, both of which are especially lacking for most British women (only one-twentieth of them-in contrast with one-fifth of American women-have college degrees).

Although the women in all three societies analyzed here are more likely to be clients of the state and workers for it than power wielders within it, this chapter has sought to suggest that opportunities for the British feminist movement are constrained by the values inherent in a traditional society, a declining economy, and a highly centralized, closed political system. In our further discussions we will explore the two wings of feminism by examining the structure of women's liberation and mainstream feminist activities in both Britain and the United States in order to develop a sense of how the "political opportunity structure" has affected movement strategy, style, and impact. We will then consider a different model, that posed by Sweden's "state equality," in which movement activism has tended to be absorbed by or incorporated in partisan and other institutions. In the conclusion, we will assess, within the comparative framework we have established, the meaning of movement "success" in each nation studied. Finally, we will evaluate autonomy versus integration as models for feminist aspirations.

7

Mobilizing Feminists: Social Movements and Political Activism

Social movements raise serious questions outside normal government channels, often concerning subjects that are not being treated as topics of public concern (Costain 1982:19). Such movements may be viewed along a continuum from unconventional, almost spontaneous, sometimes illegal activity to movement groups that seek more conventional political and legal change. Social movement organizations are the acting components of the movement, which may help turn grievances into programs (Lowi 1971). It is the hypothesis of this chapter that while American women's liberation groups have moved closer to an accommodation both to the political system and to the more "reformist" wing of the movement, largely because of an emphasis on coalition politics and pragmatic achievements (goals), no such tendencies are evident in the British movement. Rather, there has been little institutional transformation since the movement's inception in Britain, although constant activity is maintained and proliferation and fragmentation occur owing to conflicts regarding strategies and ideology (Banks 1981:227).

Feminist theory about the role of women in politics and society may be analyzed in several ways. One is to differentiate between "reformist" and "radical" feminists. Reformist feminists seek equality through freedom-they do not seek to overturn the prevailing system, although they may be in conflict with those elements of it that they see as oppressive and hostile to women's self-determination. Thus, the stated goal of NOW is "to bring women into full participation into the mainstream of American society in a truly equal partnership with men" (Bunch 1981:191;

Perrigo 1985:129). In contrast, "radical" feminists perceive society as rooted in inequality, based on patriarchy, or male domination, and often on racism and capitalism as well. In this perspective, the only way to alter women's oppression is to transform the ideology and institutions of existing society (Bunch 1981:190). A somewhat different approach to the disparate views within feminism may be found in the distinction between "radical revolutionary" and "socialist" feminism. Socialist feminists, rooted more firmly within Marxist theory, insist on the primacy of the class struggle and seek to redefine those aspects of Marxism that seem inadequate to alter women's oppression to meet the needs of contemporary feminists. Socialist feminists wish to develop a strategy to jointly attack male domination and capitalism and thus restructure male-female relationships.

A second group, the "radical" (revolutionary) feminists see the source of societal inequality in the institution of male domination, or "patriarchy," usually rooted in biological differences and roles. Both the family and the state are seen to embody systematic male power and domination. In this view, alliances with men are not possible, since men are always oppressors and society cannot be reformed. Women must form "separatist" groups, shun relations with men, and seek an end to male domination (Randall 1982:5). Revolutionary feminists have forcefully restated many traditional radical feminist positions, especially hostility to men (Spare Rib, May 1979:82). Their major points of attack are marriage, the family, control of reproduction, and violence against women.

Although in both the United States and Britain elements of these different views exist, in the United Kingdom what we have referred to as "reformist" feminism occupies a far more limited role than in the United States. And, although socialist feminism exists in the United States, it has tended to remain outside the mainstream of the feminist movement, given the historic American antipathy to leftist politics. In turn, because British feminism is linked by reasons of history and ideology to the left and socialism, it has tended to develop more theoretical perspectives on the relationship between these two ideological tendencies. As liberal feminists Betty Freidan and Gloria Steinem have tended to dominate aspects of the American feminist movement, so have the socialist feminists Sheila Rowbotham and Juliet Mitchell been major forces within the British movement. However, two significant differences ought to be noted. First, the contributions of the latter two are less related to movement activism than to an interest in theoretical reinterpretation. Second, Rowbotham and Mitchell are not viewed as "spokeswomen" for or by the British movement, which does not recognize movement "stars" in any role at all. Radical feminism, sparked by such writers as Shulamith Firestone and Kate Millett, had its origins in the United States, although it has now gained considerable support among British women's liberationists.

For some observers, "revolutionary feminism" has eclipsed other significant strands within the British movement. An article in the New Statesman (Heron 1983) deplored the tendency toward "political lesbianism" in the United Kingdom, suggesting that many feminists had entered a social and sexual stage that denigrated engagement with existing structures that could lead to change. The author decried a new prescriptive definition of feminism that limited options and rendered the British movement no longer open to all women who recognized the oppression of women as a social group and sought change. Whether a new and more exclusive era in British feminism has truly dawned is difficult to determine; but such commentary does suggest a vast chasm between socialist and some radical feminists in the United Kingdom.

A final element within feminism is "cultural" feminism. It may be animated by either socialist or radical feminism, but its major concern is less political than it is personal: that is, it seeks to change life-styles and modes of behavior.

It is only a partial exaggeration to suggest that the American civil rights movement played a role in the creation of second-wave American feminism comparable to that of the socialist left in Britain.

HISTORICAL BACKGROUND

The recent history of British and American feminist development reveals disparate organizational tendencies and styles. In the United States the New Left and the civil rights movement, each stressing different aspects of political equality, gave rise to the younger, or more "radical," branch of the feminist movement.

As women activists in these protest movements became aware of their secondary status, based on gender, they began to develop new, female-based groupings. Early on, these groups stressed consciousness-raising as a technique to develop greater self-and group awareness and, like their British counterparts, created localized, participatory projects, including day care, rape crisis centers, shelters for battered women, bookstores, and self-help health clinics. A second group of feminist activists formed around the national and state commissions on the status of women. These commissions created a focus and forum for a different set of women, older and of a more professional and media-oriented bent, to begin to contemplate the need for a feminist pressure group.

Their efforts were given additional impetus after the passage of the Civil Rights Act of 1964, which (almost by accident and certainly in the absence of any feminist pressure) was passed with the inclusion of Title VII, prohibiting sex discrimination in employment (Freeman 1975). The climate of expectations created by these two governmentally based actions, and the subsequent failure of the agency created by the Civil Rights Act, the EEOC, to enforce Title VII, led to the creation of NOW. Additional groups finally joined the Washington feminist lobby, including the Women's Equity Action League (WEAL), which initially rejected NOW's seemingly "radical" position on abortion rights; the National Women's Political Caucus (NWPC), focusing on recruiting and electing more women to political office and on legislative pressure; numerous groups concerned with single issues (abortion, health, education rights); and litigation groups.

THE BRITISH FEMINIST MOVEMENT

The British suffrage movement early demonstrated tendencies that persist in British feminism today. One was an early link between the Labour Party and constitutional feminists (Evans 1977:126). Another was militancy-perhaps related to the example of Irish nationalism, perhaps born of rage and disappointment when apparently close-at-hand victory failed.

Antisuffrage leaders and the Liberal Party served to isolate the movement and make it more sectarian and rigid (Evans 1977:197-98). However, although suffragists were interested in engaging public power in order to gain the vote, contemporary feminist advocates in Britain are not so sure.

As in the United States, the contemporary British feminist movement received its impetus from radical and New Left politics, especially the CND and anti-Vietnam campaigns (Randall 1982:152; Wilson 1980:184). In addition, working-class women in the 1960s organized as well: at Hull in 1968 for better conditions for their fishermen husbands and at Ford's auto machine works in Dagenham, where the demands for equal pay and equal work resulted in the creation of the short-lived Joint Action Committee for Women's Rights. This early effort at feminist militancy among working-class women seemed promising, but it has not proved as yet to be a significant element in British feminism, although in 1984-85 a new working-class women's movement, Women Against Pit Closures, emerged during the yearlong strike by the National Union of Miners (NUM) (Wandor 1972:96-97; Coote and Campbell 1987:179-81).

The revived movement in the United States provided the immediate spark for much women's liberation activity, which early on developed strength among socialist and university women. A London-based women's liberation workshop coordinated over 70-odd local groups and published a journal, Shrew (Randall 1982:152; Wandor 1972:96-97). A national women's liberation movement held its first conference at Oxford in 1970. The demands that emerged from the conference-24-hour child care, equal pay and education, free contraception, and abortion on demand-reflected a practical orientation, new to some movement activists.

Like the "younger," more radical branch of the American movement, the British movement lacked a coordinating structure other than national, regional, or issue-oriented conferences. The British movement developed numerous factions; one chart listed at least 14 different "tendencies" within the movement (Sebestyen 1979:16). Conflicts within the movement-largely between radical and socialist feminists-have since 1978 prevented the holding of a national conference. The conflicts have centered largely on the scrapping of the six demands listed in above in favour of the seventh demand against male violence (Randall 1982:5). Spare Rib, a monthly journalistic publication produced by a feminist collective, and the London-based Women's Research and Resources Center (WRRC) today provide the only comprehensive foci relating to different elements within the movement. (A Women's Place, also in London, is similarly run by a collective of women and operates a bookshop and reference facility, as well as publishing a weekly newsletter.) The once significant Women's Information, Reference and Enquiry Service (WIRES) has been severely circumscribed.

Despite the absence of a focal point, feminist activities in the United Kingdom continue energetically. Spare Rib and other publications advertise a host of feminist activities, and numerous groups are listed under "Women's Liberation" in the London and regional phone books. However, unlike the mass-membership equal rights focus of the visible American movement, the major locus of activity is the small group, which, eschewing formal rules and leadership, prefers to arrive at decisions by consensus. The movement's character is also defined by the proliferation of small groups, each with a single-issue orientation. Even more "traditional" women's groups, such as Women in the Media and the National Housewives Register (founded in the early 1960s by liberal-minded housewives), operate on the basis of principles of participatory democracy and minimization of hierarchy and rigid structure (Stott 1981).

It is possible that British women's experience with bureaucracy-in labour and leftist politics and, in the public sphere, in such areas as national health-has contributed to dislike of centralized, hierarchical power. However, though other British promotional groups began with a similarly diffuse structure, some, including the CPAG, have moved toward traditional interest-group organization. Often allied with feminist groups, the CPAG has developed a staff-dominated structure and a small membership as well, become more interested in fund-raising, and sought to develop a parliamentary lobby. These activities are in marked contrast to the deliberately antihierarchical structure maintained by feminist groups (Seyd 1976).

Feminists have developed legal groups, such as Rights of Women, day nurseries, shelters for battered women, and pro-abortion groups. National coordinating structures have evolved to focus on specific issues such as abortion and domestic violence, but their scope is limited. Women's Aid was established in London in 1972 by Erin Pizzey to counter domestic violence and, somewhat unique in British feminist experience, was able to attract government and charitable funding (Coote and Campbell 1987:141). Perhaps because it requires fewer resources than child care, domestic violence became a women's issue suitable for limited external support (Lovenduski 1986:79).

The Women's Aid movement broke away from its founder on ideological grounds and has proliferated-with 99 groups and 200 refugees in 1980. Member organizations operate on feminist principles, with an emphasis on autonomy and self-determination for women (ibid., 42). Local women support the National Women's Aid Federation (NWAF) through adherence to its aims and attendance at meetings (interview, NWAF, 1982). Within the national and half-dozen regional offices, jobs rotate every two to three years to provide varied experiences for all and prevent domination by one person.

Activists share in all work and there is no status distinction among the new staff members. Fund-raising is virtually nonexistent because of fear of creating strong central power, although resources from the national Department of Health and Social Services (DHSS) help pay staff salaries. While in the mid 1980s the London office of the NWAF was forced to close because of lack of funding, a newly modified collective structure has resumed national leadership in Bristol, England, as of 1988.

The NWAF's past activities helped create legislative reforms that gave increased protection to women against violent mates and imposed obligations on local authorities to rehouse victimized women. The NWAF also campaigned for more serious intervention by local police authorities (Perrigo 1985:135). (Women Against Rape, formed in 1976, has had some comparable success in raising consciousness and was in part responsible for the passage of the Sexual Offenses Act of 1976 making the rape victim's past sexual history irrelevant.)

A second organization that has developed a national structure is the National Abortion Campaign (NAC), launched in the spring of 1975 to defend the 1967 Abortion Act. It has a loosely organized mass base and operates from a socialist feminist perspective and on principles of participatory democracy (Marsh and Chambers 1981:1). The nonhierarchical, decentralized structure linking local groups claims a coalition of 400 organizations, with membership open to all who support its aims (interview, NAC, July 1982). In contrast to the operation of abortion rights groups in the United States, half the groups involved in NAC are trade union-related and receive some funding from the unions. Local groups are completely autonomous, deciding their own policy and method of campaigning. They have no elected officials or delegated structure. National policy is decided at the NAC annual conference and meetings are open to all members. An annual general meeting provides a forum for discussion of issues, although there is no mechanism for the resolution of conflicts on issues such as the role of racism and the broadening of the group's agenda to include types of reproductive freedom other than abortion. (In 1983, an organizational split between those who sought to focus on abortion as a single issue and advocates of broader reproductive rights divided NAC.) A national office provides backup resources and coordinates; a steering committee handles daily work. The staff is limited in policy-making authority, leaving most decision-making to annual and regional meetings. Volunteers are heavily relied on, particularly in the absence of funds to pay workers.

The contrast with most American pro-abortion groups is marked: U.S. organizations, such as the National Abortion Rights Action League (NARAL) and Planned Parenthood,

tend to be professionalized, hierarchical in structure, and reliant on-although not necessarily directly responsible to-a dues-paying, mass-membership constituency. Such groups may fit the model of reliance on a "conscience constituency" in which contributors supply movement resources without direct material benefit. Effective policy-making is in the hands of the full-time staff, as in the "funded social movement organizations" described by McCarthy and Zald (1977). Abortion rights groups lobby extensively to prevent progressive weakening of abortion legislation and, in marked contrast to the British experience, where courts have virtually no role in this policy area, have been active in litigating to preserve and strengthen abortion rights. NAC's strategy is largely extraparliamentary, emphasizing proselytizing through demonstrations and picketing (Marsh and Chambers 1981:48), influencing Parliament by showing M.P.'s that grass-roots support for abortion rights exists.

In the United Kingdom, even groups with a national focus are ambivalent about campaigning (lobbying) and the legislative process, although in fact the NWAF and NAC have intervened effectively in the political system. In 1975, NAC mobilized 20,000 supporters to defeat James White's antiabortion bill. It has collaborated with other sections of the pro-abortion lobby, including the Abortion Law Reform Association (ALRA), and with Labour Party women. NAC supporters have been active in unions and have gained support from the Trades Union Congress (TUC) for their efforts (Perrigo 1985:134). In July 1981, they held their first meeting with representatives from the trade union movement and Labour Party constituency parties in an effort to gain commitments for positive legislation on abortion. (After this meeting, a first attempt to enact legislation making abortion facilities mandatory under the NHS was introduced, and although it failed, it gained some media attention, perhaps setting the stage for further efforts [Spare Rib, Sept. 1981:106].) Because NAC's members are socialist feminists (drawn from the International Marxist Group), they have close ties to the Labour Party and trade union movement, particularly the National Union of Public Employees (NUPE) and the National and Local Government Officers' Association (NALGO) (Lovenduski 1986:80).

The potential of this alliance was evident in 1979 when a mass demonstration (some 100,000 people showed up), with major participation by the TUC, helped stop the Corrie bill, which threatened to reduce access to legal abortions. This was the largest union demonstration ever held in Britain for a noneconomic issue, and it demonstrated the mobilization potential inherent in the feminist movement. However, at the NAC National Congress in September 1983, a split developed over the organization's need to cover other areas of women's reproductive rights, including contraception and sterilization. A new group, the Women's Reproductive Rights Group, was formed as a result of this disagreement, further contributing to the proliferation of women's liberation groups (Perrigo 1985:134).

A second effort related to women's liberation, though not strictly part of it, has been the mobilization of Greenham Common women in protest against a cruise missile installation in Britain. Organized around feminist principles, and exclusively populated by women (and children), it has numbered some 30,000 women in rotating order. Utilizing principles of nonviolence, even when arrested and subject to police harassment and eviction attempts, these women have helped mobilize national consciousness about peace issues based on feminist ideology.

Other feminist groups, such as Rights of Women (ROW), exist in the field of law and have been active for the past decade. Their goal has been to provide legal advice to the women's movement, formulate legal policy, and campaign on issues of concern to women. They have produced informational material, discussion documents, parliamentary briefings, and responses to government publications in areas such as violence against women, rights of lesbians, and family law. Nonetheless, the movement lacks a professional campaigning body of women lawyers, partly owing to funding problems (Williscroft 1985:100). Another promotional group, the NCCL, has had a women's officer active since 1975 and has played an important role in movement politics.

A movement comparable to the liberal feminist structure in the United States (to be described in the next section) does not really exist in the United Kingdom. Nonetheless, while never dominant in the British feminist movement (and likely never to be), there are groups that seek to play a centrist, coordinating role. Among these are the Fawcett Society (with roots in the suffrage movement) and Women in the Media. The Fawcett Society remains a small group of only about 375 members, its efforts to develop a membership base in northeast England having failed. Women in the Media, organized in 1970, has engaged in active campaigning for equal pay and for legislation against sex discrimination. Other groups that do not identify with women's liberation. but do support many feminist demands and efforts to achieve them, are current manifestations of more traditional women's activities. Among them are the WI, with a membership base of 400,000; the TG, with 217,000; the British Federation of University Women, with 14,000; and the NCW, with 5,000 (Stott 1980). While these groups often support women's rights, by and large they eschew relationships with socialist and radical feminists.

Several new developments in Britain represent steps toward coalition building among different ideological groups in the women's community. In London in November 1980, a Women's Action Day involved some 67 organizations from a variety of women's perspectives and sought to discuss and develop common policies. A "women's agenda" was issued, dealing with issues of equal opportunity in law, education, work, politics, finances, the family, health, and the media. Groups represented included unions, NAC and ROW, traditional women's groups such as the NCW, and elements of the Liberal and Labour parties. With a grant from the EOC, the Women's Action Group (WAG) created a Lobby Pack with questions to be put to candidates for by-elections and parliamentary election (Pamela Robinson, Women in the Media, interview, Aug. 1982).

Aided by funds from the Greater London Council (GLC), a number of feminist groups purchased a new building to share cooperatively in London. The EOC and NCCL have also provided opportunities for discussion of specific feminist issues through conferences and forums and helped link trade unionists with other feminist activities. The GLC Women's Committee and other local women's committees (to be discussed presently) have also sought to end centrifugal politics by involving a variety of women's groups as policy participants and recipients. In 1986 a campaign to defend children's benefits against restrictive cuts by the Thatcher government engendered a national effort. Included within the alliance, consisting of over 60 organizations, were the National Federation of Women's Institutes, Women's Aid Federation, Fawcett Society, and Mother's Union. The future significance of such cooperative efforts remains unclear.

A fairly new political advocacy group-the 300 Group-has sought to increase the number of women in the House of Commons (as of 1986 6 percent were women, up significantly from the previous election). Like its American counterpart, the NWPC, it aims to recruit and train women candidates for political office. It has sought to build a dues-paying base, in 1982 having a membership of 3,000 and dues of £12 annually (interview, Abdela, July 1982). Now under new leadership, the 300 Group has a central staff and offices, indicating its ability to endure and grow even though it continues to encounter hostility from traditional party groups that resent external intrusion and from feminists who dislike its relatively centralized entrepreneurial style. Nonetheless, it has trained well over 1,500 women and helped them gain an interest and confidence in politics.

The focus of most British feminist groups, however, is interaction emphasizing value and life-style changes. Consciousness-raising is an important element (though perhaps to a lesser degree than in the United States), and values such as self-confidence, skill attainment, and self-esteem are promoted (Randall 1982:164). The democratic character of the movement provides flexibility and permits accommodation of all types of grass-roots activity, incorporating diverse elements. As Mansbridge (1980:278-89) has pointed out, small size allows intense interaction, and continued face-to-face contact may prevent elitism. Yet, the group process, rather than attainment of group ends, may develop as a major focus (Freeman 1975:103-46). Conformity to the group may be encouraged. The absence of recordkeeping and repetition of old issues may retard group development (Adlam 1980:94). An ahistorical perspective may cause repetition of past mistakes. Decision-making may be slowed and the real administrative and political skills of some may be underutilized or ignored (Mansbridge 1980:247). Individuals may become preoccupied with their own liberation and fail to seek more universal women's goals. And local, single-issue-oriented activity may reduce possibilities for national impact and comprehensive, as opposed to ad hoc, solutions to problems.

This analysis is consistent with Freeman's (1975:145) critique of movement structurelessness in the United States, in which she argues that the movement provided no coordinated or structured means of fitting local activity into other, existing projects. As she suggests, the consequence is that new groups form and dissolve at an accelerating rate, creating a great deal of consciousness and very little concerted action, failing to consolidate old gains while moving into new areas.

Finally, unaccountability to a constituency may create irresponsibility and unrealistic expectations. Inability to agree on goals and pool resources weakens opportunities for creation of alliances (Bouchier 1984:123). If, as suggested here, the women's movement in Britain is a "deliberately dispersed collection of groups, campaigns and political tendencies with no single ideology," the absence of coalitional structures prevents organization around multiple issues in a continuing fashion (ibid., 128-29, 218-23). The politics of personal experience, inward-looking and seeking redemptive life-styles, has often eclipsed the overtly "political." Women's liberation politics is fragmented, centered on single issues, and without networks in which different views may find expression and audience. The British emphasis on personal politics has often, though not always, resulted in reluctance to engage in the politics of the state (Barrett 1980:228, 245). Although feminist politics may serve as a model for other leftist groups in its emphasis on autonomy, flexibility, and democracy, the lack of a coordinating mechanism and national political presence presents a continuing challenge (Rowbotham 1979:90).

AMERICAN WOMEN'S LIBERATION

The structure of grass-roots, radical feminism in the United States is similar to that in Britain. However, even within this wing of feminist politics, recent developments have suggested somewhat different tendencies. For example, in shelters for battered women and in rape crisis centers, which emphasize the feminist ideology discussed earlier, professionals have often combined with feminist influences to provide services, negotiate with bureaucracies, write funding proposals, and develop more enduring organizational structures (Schechter 1982:38-39). While conflicts over the importance of service, self-determination, and politics continue to exist, there can be little doubt that such elements as networking, lobbying, and emphasis on legal changes are more evident in the American movement. Activists have mobilized around state legislation and legal change-and have often been less reluctant to engage with political and bureaucratic forces and to seek legitimacy than is true for their British counterparts. Structures have been modified as specialization has created more hierarchical organizations, including staffs and boards (ibid., 94-95). Schechter concludes that the need for government support has forced activists to modify practices and informal procedures. In some instances, "modified collectives" have sought a compromise between external imperatives and feminist principles (ibid., 100). From local coalitions, statewide and then federal efforts have been generated. There has been willingness to engage political authorities at all levels in order to gain resources and reform legal procedures.

Coalitions reflect a variety of influences-including traditional groups (like the YWCA), professional and service providers, radical feminists, and equal rights feminists from groups such as NOW-and emphasize the sharing of resources, access, and skills (ibid., 113, 148). To aid battered women, a National Coalition against Domestic Violence (NCADV) was created, which lobbied for passage of a Domestic Violence Act, built a large network of contacts, sought to build a dues-paying membership base, and wrote proposals to raise money from the federal government and private foundations. The coalition continues to monitor relevant public policy, disseminate information to state and local groups, and seek to retain a nonhierarchical, multiracial approach (interview, Mary Morrison, NCADV, October 1982).

In contrast to the British experience, change-oriented feminists have often been able to rely on government "insiders" to put forward issues and build government support for movement concerns (Schechter 1982). Hence, leadership and structure, engagement with political forces at all levels, and the need for coalition have been treated differently in the United States than in the United Kingdom. But, as an instance of congruence, women's liberation groups in both countries have tended to focus on single issues and do not necessarily coalesce with other movement activists in multiple-issue alignments. However, while in the United States a grass-roots women's movement still exists, it is less visible than formerly and has to a greater degree joined forces with the more "middle-class" reformist sector of the original movement.

In the United States, then, though a grass-roots movement continues to exist, having successfully helped shape a new policy agenda based on the alternative services it created at the state and local levels, the character of the movement has changed considerably. In addition to the pull toward coalitions and political engagement we have described, to some degree overlapping memberships and joint activities have altered this segment of the movement's role. These linkages have been strengthened by campaigns to save abortion rights and pass the ERA, which have tended to unite feminists of all ideologies.

In addition, NOW, although founded as a feminist pressure group from the top down, has sought to move further in the direction of feminist principles than might earlier have been expected. First, it has sought (though not always successfully) to break down traditional organizational roles, combining staff and elected positions and thus creating a more participatory structural setting. Second, it has moved to adopt more controversial issue orientations, in addition to its continued interest in equal rights. The organization first endorsed abortion on demand, at that time (1970) and still a controversial political and moral issue. It also acknowledged, in an even more controversial act, that sexual self-determination-lesbianism-was a legitimate part of the women's movement. It has continued to examine alternative life-styles and support alternate forms of sexuality, even as it ages in political terms, indicating that it has hardly become more conservative with time. Finally, galvanized by growing evidence of the costs and consequences of the "feminization of poverty," NOW has joined with other feminist groups (who have come together in such events as the 1977 conference in Houston for the International Women's Year) and has moved to a more radical view of ways to eradicate poverty, although it clearly remains within the American (slightly left-of-center) tradition. And as the major feminist mass-membership group, NOW, though not always successful, has sometimes been able to act as an umbrella group for different interests within the feminist movement (Randall 1982:235). As the most prominent feminist organization, NOW has to some degree eclipsed the more radical elements of the movement, because, given the American political system, its actions are more visible while its demands are viewed as both newsworthy and mildly radical. Though in many ways a traditional interest group, involved in electoral politics and campaign endorsements (to be described shortly), litigation, and lobbying, NOW's major significance for the movement continues to lie in its ability to focus public attention on key movement demands. It is able to do this through demonstrations, access to the media, and other social movement techniques.

But NOW does not operate alone in the political arena. Because the structure of American feminism has become specialized along issue and functional lines, groups such as NARAL in the area of abortion, WEAL on economic reform, and other organizations play a major role as well. In the area of domestic violence, the NCADV has become a leading voice. It may be argued that through the process, noted earlier, of coalition building and group mergers the movement has lost its radical edge and become limited by a turn toward more conventional politics. But the "legitimization" of American feminism as an interest group of political significance-at the same time as the movement has deepened its commitment to key feminist issues-suggests that considerable progress has been made from a feminist perspective.

The movement was strengthened by the creation of two types of women's groups: single-issue and multi-issue, or umbrella, groups. Single-issue groups dealing with abortion or domestic violence concentrate their resources and energy on one topic, keeping the issue before the public (Kolker 1983:212). Multi-issue organizations may have a broader range of contacts, a larger support base, and the ability to create coalitions.

Now and other feminist-oriented groups gained additional membership and support from contributors, especially during 1980-82, in response to conservative threats symbolized by the Reagan election of 1980 and the defeat of the ERA in 1982. Membership in NOW increased to 250,000 in 1983 but had decreased to 156,000 by 1986 (Bomafede 1986:2178). During this period, in addition to strengthening relations with the more radical sector of the feminist movement, NOW built stronger links to traditional women's groups, including the League of Women Voters, American Association of University Women, General Federation of Women's Clubs, and National Federation of Business and Professional Women. Although some of these older, established women's groups had early on shared resources and opportunities for access with their feminist sisters, as the movement moved into its second decade, they too became constituents of feminist-sponsored, issue-based coalitions on key economic and other issues.

Finally, congressional and administrative staff members, primarily women, have played a key role in advancing women's issues. They help build support for feminist-sponsored policy, alert lobbyists about proposed, potentially negative changes, and provide the type of information only "insiders" can have (Kolker 1983:216).

While both in the United States and Britain a variety of theoretical and practical approaches to feminism constitute movement politics, in America the pressure to build coalitions and seek reform through more or less traditional interest-group politics has been notable. As we have suggested, networking across ideological lines is still rare in the United Kingdom, although it is a concept gaining support from many feminist activists. Traditional women's groups do have a mass constituency base in the United Kingdom (at least in comparison with other groups), but they are usually reluctant to join forces with those perceived, with reinforcement by media coverage, as being lesbian and antimale.

The close relationship that has developed-in terms of resource sharing, political access, and even consensus on goals-between the so-called traditional women's groups and their reformist and radical feminist allies in the United States has no analogue in the political culture of Britain. The failure to seek advancement of women in existing political structures and the emphasis on sectarian politics have denied British feminists the mainstream voice their American sisters have been able to articulate (Weir and Wilson 1984; Coote and Campbell 1987:255). At the same time, the British movement has continued to be distinguished by its diversity and its capacity to celebrate difference and spontaneity.

THE ROLE OF WOMEN IN PARTIES AND UNIONS

As noted earlier, the resurgence of feminism in the latter half of this century has been characterized by the development of at least two wings of feminist organization. One wing, the autonomous feminists described in earlier discussion, has been more concerned with creating alternatives than with exerting political influence, particularly in Britain (Lovenduski 1986:63). The other wing has tended to emphasize rights and legal change and to operate within the decision-making process via traditional parties and unions or through a new set of lobbying-oriented interest groups. In this chapter, we explore two different approaches to legal and political change as manifested by British and American feminists, each constrained by the context of movement politics.

Parties: Britain

Despite the striking absence in British feminism of a counterpart to the dues-paying, mass-membership orientation of American feminism represented by such organizations as NOW, one way contend that in the British political system, such mass-based feminist groups are not necessary or even desirable. It may be argued that the functional equivalent of liberal feminism exists in Britain because, as suggested earlier, British feminists have historically been organized and influential as pressure groups within existing institutions, namely political parties and trade unions. Despite concern about co-optation and ideological dilution by male-dominated structures, feminists, especially on the left, have sought to develop alliances with these institutions to further their political goals. Nonetheless, this chapter suggests that increased activism by feminists has not ended a pattern of women's participation in these institutions that has been marked by "marginalization" and isolation from power. We thus share the view that existing political structures give little priority to feminists' interests; rather than seeking to solidify feminist strength and advancing women's interests, they have aided in their dissipation and fragmentation (Rasmussen 1983a, 1983b).

We will examine the role of women within party organizations in three ways: the role of women's groups within the parties, the role of women within the party hierarchy, and the party's approach to promoting women as candidates for political office. Underlying this chapter's perspective is the view that as Britain is becoming a more administrative state, the importance of feminist influence within groups whose major impact is on the legislative process may, in any case, be seriously debated.

Although women compose at least half the membership of the Labour and Conservative parties (Hills [1978] estimates a female membership of 40 percent in the former and over 50 percent in the latter), their role within party structures appears to be circumscribed. Women in parties and unions are organized into separate advisory groups having few powers and little ability to gain acceptance for resolutions they have passed. In addition, they are limited to reserved or set-aside seats on key decision-making bodies.

In the main, the more significant a policy-making body is, the fewer women it has on it. Somewhat surprisingly, the Labour Party (founded in 1906), though closer to feminists on some policy issues and in ideological terms, has had no better a record on representation and power sharing than its Conservative opposition. Women are poorly represented within the party's annual conference (11 percent in 1980) and are allotted five seats of 29 on the party's National Executive Committee (NEC), the dominant administrative and policy-making body (Hills 1981:17; Randall 1982:75). (Since 1960 only two women have been selected for the NEC by the constituency- or local-section of the party; none have been elected by the trade unions.) The principle of setting aside women's places on executive bodies is a well-established one in parties and unions, as we shall see. Because trade unions are dominant in the Labour Party and unions cast their vote in block fashion, in practice the set-aside women's seats are union controlled (Hills 1981). Hence, most women selected for the NEC are not independent feminists.

The Women's Section of the Labour Party is constituency based. Like other women's groups in similar institutions, it holds annual meetings and passes resolutions (interview, Gould, July 1982). Resolutions are forwarded to the NEC, which may or may not choose to consider them. (A National Labour Women's

Advisory Committee acts as a liaison with the NEC.) In essence; then, the women's organization is powerless to affect policy and has no direct representation at the party's annual conference.

Unlike the Conservative Party, the Labour Party is a confederal organization, with a vast array of women's groups (as well as countless other political factions). In recent years, women's Labour groups have grown and proliferated-from the Women's Action Committee (WAC), associated with the far-left Campaign for Labour Party Democracy (CLPD), to a Women's Rights Study group established with M.P. Jo Richardson as chair. A group called Fightback for Women's Rights is active at the party's fringes. It has been especially vigorous in pressing for more channels to the Labour Party hierarchy-advocating that five resolutions be sent to the party's annual conference by the Women's Section and that women members be elected to the NEC directly by the Women's Conference. Fightback and WAC both espouse an end to all-male parliamentary shortlists (lists of candidates for final consideration). A Woman's Charter has been developed and promoted by WAC.

A measure of the expanded interest in women's activities was the upsurge in the number of women's delegates-from 320 in 1980 to 650 in 1981-at the annual Women's Conference. This increase indicated an intensified resolve to use the conference as a forum from which to articulate concerns and press demands on the party hierarchy. In recent years, there has been growing evidence of serious debate on key feminist issues (Perrigo 1985:142). At the 1982 party conference, party feminists sought to establish a more significant policy-making role. Their resolutions (thus far unheeded by the party) called for the right both to elect the women members of the NEC directly and to send to the conference five resolutions that would be automatically considered. Surprisingly, the Women's Conference defeated an effort to make selection of women on candidate shortlists mandatory (Perrigo 1985:143; Vallance 1984:301).

The Labour Party hierarchy has responded to feminist pressure by appointing a national women's officer and, more recently, designating a shadow minister for women's affairs (with no counterpart in the present government), formerly M.P. Joan Lestor and now M.P. Jo Richardson. A women's subcommittee of the NEC has been created to formulate policy on women's issues. Its members are also members of a National Women's Committee elected by women at regional conferences around the country, thus providing a direct link between the NEC and grass-roots women. A National Women's Charter drawn up by the NEC in 1982 calls for greater women's representation at all party levels and for day-care services for women attending all party meetings (Perrigo 1985:143). Joyce Gould, the national women's officer, has sought to promote more female candidacies for office. As of the mid-1980s, the NEC recommended, though it did not mandate, at least one woman on each shortlist. Constituency parties were permitted to establish women's sections without prior approval from the party hierarchy (Coote and Campbell 1987:148).

The extent of feminist participation within the Labour Party is impressive and often channels socialist feminist energy into party activities, but because of the party's disarray at present, any victory may be a pyrrhic one. In addition, there is some suspicion that several groups seeking dominance within the party may be using the feminist issue to build their own power base-with little actual regard for feminist concerns.

And although the Labour Party committed itself (in its 1983 manifesto) to supporting abortion and contraception rights, measures against rape and wife battering, and equal pay for work of equal value, and to ending job segregation, promoting positive action, and strengthening the Sex Discrimination Act, it has yet to make these policies central campaign issues (Vallance 1984). Rather, as with women in general, such policies are isolated as women's issues and even treated as ethical matters on which M.P.'s need not be bound to party policy. Hence, it may be premature to contend that British women are emerging from a decade of isolation and an exclusive grass-roots focus to help unite the left and the Labour Party (Jenson 1982:343). In fact, though the party's feminist activity in recent years has expanded, it is not a new development. Nor is it clear that, at national-level party politics, major claims for feminist influence are supported by the evidence.

In the Conservative Party, women's participation in local politics is significant (perhaps 50 percent of constituency party chairs are women) but has not altered the pattern of "marginalization" we have suggested. While women are better represented at the party's annual conference (38 percent of the delegates were women in 1977-78), this body lacks the policy-making powers of its Labour Party counterpart (Randall 1982:74; Hills 1978:4, 8). Women constitute about 20 percent of the membership of the Executive Committee of the National Union, which is the highest point in the party hierarchy, although its policy-making and administrative powers are limited by the primacy of parliamentary leadership, consigning it to more of an advisory role. As of 1982, 50 of the 200 members were women, 19 of these being in statutory or mandated seats (European Union of Women 1982). At least one analyst (Hills 1978:6) has contended that although Conservative women are better represented than their Labour sisters, they have only limited impact at party conferences because they are not very vocal.

As in the Labour Party, there is a women's national advisory organization with its own annual conference, now called the Conservative Women's National Committee. This committee often discusses women's issues in the guise of such concerns as education (interview, Hooper, July 1982). Another group affiliated with the Conservative Party, the British section of the European Union of Women, is active on behalf of women's issues as well and was instrumental in stopping cuts in Social Security proposed by the Thatcher government (Rogers 1983:34). This group has pressed for a party rule to include at least one woman candidate on shortlists and for mandated interviews of women by candidate selection committees. It also recommended in 1982 that women's groups within the party undertake candidate education and training.

Prime Minister Margaret Thatcher's leading political role in the party has not altered the position of women in her party at all. She has consciously distanced herself from women's interests and has neither appointed other women to key positions (with the exception of Baroness Young, who spent a brief time as Lord Privy Seal) nor advanced policies of concern to women. (A vice chair, Emma Nicholson, charged with encouraging more women to join the party and Parliament, was appointed after the 1979 election [Vallance 1984:302]). Although Thatcher's campaign in 1979 stressed her image as a housewife and mother, she has made it clear that she does not view women's issues as a cause for concern (Rogers 1983:171). (In 1986, however, Thatcher announced that women must be shortlisted for all public appointments and that an explanation must be provided for failure to comply [Economist, Nov. 1, 1986:53]). Thatcher has openly suggested that women with children should leave the labour force, and her government has steadily reduced nursery and child-care provisions, maternity and child-care benefits, and women's work rights (Rogers 1983:161). It is difficult to disagree with Richard Rose (1986:159), who has written that of the four women in the British cabinet from 1964 to 1969 (Thatcher, Barbara Castle, Judith Hart, and Shirley Williams), in no instance was their political stature derived from their sex or from their expression of feminist views. Both Thatcher's critics and supporters see her sex as largely irrelevant and her political views as significant. As the only woman in her cabinet, Margaret Thatcher demonstrates that high positions for women are an exception (Rose 1986:160). Nonetheless, Thatcher is assessed favourably for leadership qualities, for standing up for Britain, for ability to communicate, and for crisis management, suggesting that as a role model her position may augur well for future women in British politics (Butler and Kavanaugh 1984:296). However, as an indication that many women find Thatcher's policies wanting and may tend to reject them, the 1983 election saw a move toward the Alliance-the Social Democrat-Liberal partnership-and away from the major parties among women voters (ibid., 296; Rogers 1983:159).

Finally, with regard to candidates standing for election, women have continually been underrepresented in both major parties. They have also been consistently underselected by constituencies; even when they are chosen, they are selected disproportionately for unwinnable or marginal seats (Vallance 1984:304; Hills 1978).

Although in 1983, for the first time over 10 percent of the party's candidates were female, a third higher than in 1979, it has been argued that with regard to selection women are worse off today than they were a century ago (Rasmussen 1983b:309). As of 1983, only 3.5 percent of M.P.'s were women, in contrast to 5.1 percent of representatives in the U.S. Congress

(Sainsbury 1985:4). By 1987, however, partially reflecting the effort by parties to reach out to women voters in a hard-fought campaign, over 6 percent of the M.P.'s selected were women.

In the Labour Party the "A" list is union-dominated. In 1972, two of 100 candidates nominated were women; in 1977, three of 103 (Hills 1978); and in 1983, seven of 153 (or 4.5 percent) (Hills 1978; Vallance 1984:306). The TUC's increasing sympathy for women's concerns (to be discussed later) may aid in the future expansion of women's role in the Labour Party, but there is little evidence that much change has occurred as yet. The limited support extended by unions to women denies them the crucial access to monetary and other resources enjoyed by men. In 1982, Labour with 11 women M.P.'s had just 25 women on a list of 250 candidates (Guardian, April 16, 1982). By 1983, Labour had increased its female representation on candidate lists to 15 percent, resulting in 12.5 percent female candidates, of whom just 10 (of the 78 who ran) were elected (Vallance 1984). As of 1987, of 85, or 16 percent, female candidates nominated, 21 were elected.

In 1982 the Conservative Party had just eight women M.P.'s (of whom one was the prime minister). In the past, according to Hills (1978:12-14), the Conservative Party may have attracted more women candidates than the Labour Party (perhaps more a function of class than party policy), but that did not seem to be the case in 1982. A centralized party office keeps a list of approved candidates. In 1982, of 600 names on the list, only 10 percent were women (down from 15 percent in 1977) (Guardian, July 18, 1982). The Conservatives shortlisted 10 percent female candidates, with 6.3 percent (or 40) selected, resulting in an increase to 13 female M.P.'s (Vallance 1984). In 1987 the party nominated 36 women, or 7 percent (a continued decrease), with 17 being elected.

The new Social Democratic Party (SDP) has recruited women discontented with the other parties' attitudes and practices, and its National Steering Committee has adopted two of three women-sponsored resolutions. These resolutions mandate that women be included on every shortlist (at least two of nine candidates) and that four of the eight members on the party's National Steering Committee be women. A mail ballot to party members resulted in the defeat (by 57 percent of the voters) of a resolution requiring equal representation by sex to the party's central decision-making body, the Council for Social Democracy (interview, Toynbee, July 1982). Despite this defeat, the SDP has gone a bit further than its better-established partisan colleagues in meeting some feminist demands for sharing power and issue concerns. Together with the Liberals, the SDP has disseminated endorsements of far-reaching policy changes related to women, including better child care provisions, strengthening of antidiscrimination legislation, parental leave, and rights for part-time workers (Coote and Campbell 1987:149). The SDP and its Alliance partner, the Liberals, also sought to increase female representation in 1982.

The SDP nominated 17 percent women to its shortlists, resulting in 14.4 percent female candidates, of whom, however, none won (Vallance 1984)! In 1986 the Alliance nominated 100 women (SDP, 20 percent; Liberals, 13 percent), although only two were elected. The Alliance and the Labour Party, apparently competing for the women's vote, thus nominated increasing numbers of women. The SDP threat (supported by pre-election surveys), though not yet translated into electoral power, may have galvanized Labour in particular to adopt a more "feminist" perspective in the most recent election.

Summary of British Women's Role in Parties

Each party seems to be firmly committed to the continuation of separate women's committees. These committees are endorsed by feminists as an important forum through which demands may be articulated and attention focused on women's issues. In each case, feminist party activists would like to see women's groups play a stronger consultative role. Dahlerup and Gulli (1985:19) have suggested that separate women's organizations within parties have five purposes: (1) to get women to support the party, (2) to recruit women members to the party, (3) to activate women and train them for top party posts, (4) to influence party policy, and (5) to create linkages to women in other groups.

Apparently few, if any, of these aims have been achieved by women's organizations in British parties. We will examine the degree to which separate Swedish women's organizations within four of the five major parties have affected nominations, party policy, and recruitment to leadership roles.

It seems that only limited benefits have accrued to British women as a result of separatist organization in parties. In 1973 the merits of retaining a separate women's conference were debated at the Labour Party Conference meeting, and its continued existence was endorsed as a mechanism to provide encouragement and training for female activists, as well as to promote solidarity (Holland 1984:62-63). However, women remain underrepresented in policy-making and leadership roles at all levels. In any event, parties appear to provide less of a link to policy-making in a system, such as the British one, increasingly controlled by bureaucratic functionaries. In addition, the hierarchical, mass-based structure of party groups in the United Kingdom is antithetical to the ideals of women's liberation, and so the relationship between many women and party activism is at best ambivalent.

While women in parties have called for mandated positive action with regard to candidate selection-as most obstacles to women's selection appear to exist at the local level-little change has occurred. In response to pressure, the parties have moved toward expressions of greater concern for the nomination of women, but they have not insisted on equality of representation in the final selection process or in any other aspect of party politics. The ability of the 300 Group to attract over 1,500 women to training sessions for political activism points to the continuing gap between rhetoric and reality in much of British party politics. As an all-party group that defies traditional British political dictates, its endurance and continuing appeal say a great deal.

Parties: United States

Political parties are less central to the political process in the United States than in Britain, and feminist interest groups such as the NWPC, NOW, and other groups have played an important role in recruiting women for political office, providing training and some campaign support, and actively campaigning for key political issues such as abortion rights and the ERA. In the United States, the tradition of separate women's groups and the principle of numerical reservation of seats for women in the party hierarchy within the parties have largely been viewed as anachronistic. However, in the Democratic Party, women moved to mandate equal representation of male and female convention delegates via the 1972 McGovern-Fraser guidelines.

The 1972 Democratic Convention had 40 percent female delegates, while the Republican Convention had 30 percent (up from 17 percent in 1968). Since then, women's task forces in both parties have pressed for women's concerns within the parties and the provision of some funding and training for women candidates (Mandel 1982:211-13). After the numbers of women delegates to conventions fell somewhat in 1976, the Democratic Party in 1978-80 moved to equalize convention representation by men and women and to provide support for such key feminist concerns as the ERA, election of more women to state and local offices, and even abortion rights. At the same time, the Reaganite Republican Party moved further to the right and away from commitment to feminist concerns. Nonetheless, in 1984, 48 percent of Republican delegates were women, as were about half of the Democratic delegates (Freeman 1987:236), an apparent response in both parties to Democratic-inspired rules reforms.

The increasing significance of feminist interest groups in the Democratic Party has been particularly striking during the past decade. Jo Freeman has pointed to the different political cultures that dominate the Republican and Democratic parties. In the Republican Party, power flows from the top down and delegates' relationship to party leaders and loyalty to the party itself tend to be significant. In contrast, in the Democratic Party, constituencies are seen as the party's building blocks, and power flows from the bottom up (ibid., 232).

These cultural distinctions help explain the important role feminist groups have been able to gain in the Democratic Party. In the Republican Party a Woman's Division was created in 1983, joining the (virtually defunct) National Federation of Republican Women, but its major functions were to mobilize, recruit, and publicize party accomplishments rather than to work as an advocacy group within the party. In fact, in the Republican Party, feminists are viewed as having competing loyalties and have been eliminated from leadership and administrative roles (ibid., 235-42). Instead, right-winger Phyllis Schlafly has become the major policy arbiter on women's issues.

In the Democratic Party, because of the different structure and mechanism for representation, feminist groups came to have a major role. Building initially on the turmoil surrounding the 1968 convention, which opened the Democratic Party to reform, feminists gained one vice chair for their ranks (one each also went to blacks and Hispanics) (ibid.). In 1976, disturbed by the falloff in female representation, feminist groups, especially the NWPC, together with the Women's Caucus of the Democratic National Committee and NOW, fought for a 50-50 rule guaranteeing equal representation to women and men. The Carter campaign, initially hostile to this idea, eventually acquiesced. Apparently Carter operatives felt that their refusal to support these feminist concerns would lead to a pro-Kennedy move. By 1980, over 20 percent of the Democratic delegates were members of NOW or of the NWPC (ibid., 230). They gained support for a proposal to deny Democratic Party funds to any candidate who did not support the ERA. NARAL, like the NWPC, had its own floor operation and lobbied successfully for the addition of another minority plank to the platform-one supporting government funding for abortions for poor women (ibid.).

Therefore, by 1984, feminists had demonstrated their political clout. NOW met with five of the Democratic presidential candidates and pressed them on their support for women's issues, female appointments, and willingness to select a female vice presidential candidate. NOW Vice President Mary Jane Collins was appointed to the platform-drafting committee and given the leading role on matters of concern to NOW (Freeman 1985). A coalition of women's groups presented a list of acceptable female vice presidential candidates to Walter Mondale (who had earlier received the endorsement of NOW and later got that of NWPC and NARAL as well). After the nomination of Geraldine Ferraro, a committed feminist, the feminist coalition had little to do at the convention itself.

At the time of this writing, it is not clear how Republican (and some Democratic) efforts to label feminism as an electoral liability-because of its identification as a "special interest" and because of the failure to deliver a "gender gap" vote on behalf of Ferraro-will affect feminist access to power at future Democratic Party conventions (Freeman1987:242).

Despite real gains in representation and support for women's issues (at least in the contemporary Democratic Party), the role of convention politics in the American policy-making process is limited and marginal at best. In addition, numerous (if not most) women seeking political office at all levels in the United States have by-passed traditional centers of candidate support and sought other routes to elective and appointive office. This contention is confirmed by a recent study of female candidates appointed to political office in state government: party-related factors were important for less than a third, with only 15 percent indicating that efforts by state and national party leaders had been very important (Carroll 1984:102). Younger women perceived party leaders as having played virtually no role in their appointments and, in contrast to some of their older female colleagues, had almost no history of party activism or campaign activity (ibid., 103). Crucial to women candidates is a network of women's political organizations, which provide financial aid, research and information, and financial campaign assistance, and generally encourage women's active participation in the political process. Especially prominent in this regard are the Women's Campaign Fund (WCF) and NWPC (Bomafede 1986:2178).

In the United States, once a candidate is elected to political office, partisanship is only one influence that defines his or her political behavior. In Britain, only the 300 Group, an all-party organization that trains and recruits women who wish to run for political office, is analogous to the American model (especially the NWPC).

In the United Kingdom it can no longer be claimed that the women's vote is more "conservative" than men's nor that women are more conservative in their political attitudes, but neither can it be claimed that they are more left-wing. To the degree that a "gender gap" is emerging in Britain it does not represent the result of a feminist organizing effort. What it does seem to represent is a slight movement away from the two major parties, neither of which has met feminist aspirations effectively (Norris [1988]:13; Edgell and Duke 1983:357-76; Rogers 1983:159).

In the United States, what had appeared to be a significant "gender gap" in 1980, involving female rejection of Reaganite social policy and, in particular, opposition to defense spending and support for domestic spending, was reduced in 1984 to 8 percent in the presidential race, although still providing evidence that fewer women supported Reagan (Light and Lake 1985:105). Nonetheless, despite the feminist movement's role in gaining a place for Ferraro on the ticket and efforts to mobilize against Reaganite conservatism, at the national level this strategy was not effective in attracting a majority of women voters. Feminist efforts in congressional elections and the women's vote at state and local levels in 1984 and 1986 resulted in greater evidence for the existence of a gender gap.

Unions: Britain

An early link between trade unions and the "new feminism" was evident in Britain in the 1970s. The NCCL held a conference in 1974 that brought together some 550 representatives of women's groups and labour, which was followed by the London Trade's Council's issuance of a ten-point Working Women's Charter drawn up by Communist Party feminists (Coote and Campbell 1987:56). Nonetheless, what appeared to be a promising relationship has not developed into a set of positive, concrete developments for feminist activists. In contrast to the United States, where about 15 percent of women are union members (fewer than 20 percent of all workers are unionized) and women compose about 30 percent of union membership, in Britain about 31 percent of women are union members and they account for about 40 percent of union membership (fewer than 50 percent of all workers are unionized) (Milkman 1985:300; Ellis 1981; Equal Opportunities Commission 1983a:11). Swedish women, reflecting the national trends, are among the most highly unionized in the world, despite their extensive part-time status.

In Britain, as well as the United States, the number of women unionizing has increased dramatically in the last decade. Of 12 million British TUC members in 1980, about 4 million were women (TUC 1982). Female union membership increased from 1961 to 1980 by 111 percent, while male membership increased by only 17.6 percent (Coote and Campbell 1987).

Table 3: Representation of Women in Unions and the Labour Party

Union*	Female Members (% of total)	NEC (Women and Total)	Full-Time Officers (Women and Total)	TUC (Women and Total)	Labour Party Delegates (Women and Total)
TGWU	15.5	0/39	7/500	4/82	1/40
GMWU	34	0/40	13/243	4/74	4/63
AEUW	13.5	7 nonvoting seats/66	1 district secretary	1/37	NA
USDAW	62	3/16	None	5/38	5/34
NUTGW	90	5/15	8/43	12/17	NA
NUPE	66	8/26	6/125	9/32	6/18
NALGO	50	14/69	11/165	11/72	NA**
NUT	72	4/44	17/110	4/34	NA
CPSA	73	12/28	4/NA	10/36	NA
ASTMS	17.5	2/24	6/63	4/31	5/28
TASS	15	NA	NA	4/18	2/17
APEX	56	1/15	1 national, 1 area/of 51	4/15	1/6

SOURCE: Women's Fightback, March 1982:6-7.

*TGWU Transport and General Workers Union

GMWU General and Municipal Workers Union

AEUW Amalgamated Union of Engineering Workers

USDAW Union of Shop, Distributive, and Allied Workers

NUTGW National Union of Tailors and Garment Workers

NUPE National Union of Public Employees

**Not available.NALGO National and Local Government Officers' Association

NUT National Union of Teachers

CPSA Civil and Public Services Association

ASTMS Association of Scientific, Technical, and Managerial Staff

TASS Technical and Supervisory Section [of engineers' union]

APEX Association of Professional, Executive, Clerical, and Computer Staff

While many socialist and nonaligned feminists have organized autonomously in their local communities and sought to develop specific feminist projects and activities-shelters for battered women, day-care facilities, self-help clinics, and the like-other socialist feminists have sought to forge links with trade unions in order to reach out to working-class women. Nonetheless, because of the largely middle-class composition of the movement, the separatist ideas that some union women find abhorrent, and the lack of time that plagues many working-class women, it has often been difficult for the women's movement to make headway with its working-class sisters (Hart 1982:161). It is unusual in Britain for campaigning organizations such as feminist groups to have links to trade union politics; particularly at the local level, there is suspicion of women's liberation (ibid.). But there has been an increase in exchange of ideas between union and other feminist women, facilitated by such groups as NAC and the NCCL, which have ties to both.

Efforts to politicize newly organized women workers (especially in white-collar unions, where their numbers have greatly expanded) have met with some success, and socialist feminists have gained support for some key issues from the trade unions. But, in the main, women have virtually no power in unions and have been unable to alter existing patterns of low pay and job segregation. Women lack representation in key union committees, among full-time officers, and at the local shop level as stewards and district committee members.

A 1980 survey by Coote and Kellner (1981) showed that while 38 percent of union members surveyed were women, only 11 percent of the executive members, fewer than 6 percent of the full-time officials, and under 15 percent of delegates to the TUC in these unions were women. Of 1,600 trade union officials, only 90 were women in 1983 (Holland 1984:66).

At the 1981 TUC annual meeting, 116 of 1,188 delegates were women, and at the 1983 meeting, 121 of 1,155 (Trades Union Conference 1982:1; New Statesman, March 23, 1984). Although a number of unions have a majority of women workers, men remain in control of top positions in individual unions and the TUC. For example, the National Union of Education, with

70 percent female membership, had only four women members on the Executive Committee of 44 in 1980. Several major unions, including the two largest, the Transport and General Workers Union (TGWU) and the General and Municipal Workers Union (GMWU) have not a single female executive member among them (Coote and Campbell 1987:52, 67, 145-67). (See Table 3.)

Feminists have sought greater influence in two ways.

One approach, as in parties, has been to advocate "positive action/positive discrimination," retaining or establishing set-aside or statutory seats on executive committees and seeking other types of special representation, through advisory committees, women's conferences, and the like. In some instances, such efforts do not represent a "new approach"; in the TUC, the Women's Advisory Committee and annual women's conference date back to the 1920s and 1930s, respectively (Randall 1982). In 1920 the Women's Trade Union League (WTUL), a women's labour union, merged with the TUC in return for two protected seats on the TUC Executive Committee. At the same time, another militant women's union, the National Federation of Women Workers, merged with what is now the TGWU. (In short order, the number of women officials fell from 16 to one. It has been an uphill struggle to regain strength ever since [Rogers 1983:31; Lorwin and Boston 1984:145].) In the late 1920s the TUC Women's Conference was created, essentially establishing a group without power. As is true for parties, advisory committees have a solely consultative role and depend on the (often lacking) sympathy of general councils and other policy-making bodies for acceptance. The TUC Women's Action Committee has ten members appointed by the General Council and eight appointed by the Women's Conference; hence, like similar party-related bodies, it is not truly representative of women activists (Breitenbach 1981). In 1981 the TUC, to which most British unions are affiliated, responded to a Women's Conference demand by increasing the number of statutory delegate places reserved for women on the TUC Executive Committee from two to five (out of 41).

However, among the white-collar unions, whose female membership is growing especially rapidly, there have been efforts to create special opportunities for women. Some unions have appointed a national women's officer (e.g., the Technical and Supervisory Section [TASS], of the engineers' union). Others have introduced the practice of setting aside executive council seats for women. Still others, including the GMWU and the Association of Scientific, Technical, and Managerial Staff (ASTMS), have established women's advisory committees or set up equal opportunities groups or women's rights groups at the district level. Even consciousness-raising and special-training sessions for women have been introduced into several unions-including the GMWU, TASS, and the TUC. But, in the main, what has distinguished these efforts has been their "from the top down" quality. In Britain, unlike the situation in Italy and, to a degree, in France, consciousness-raising and feminist groups did not emerge in the workplace (Elliott 1983:68-69). Except in a few instances (as in NALGO and the ASTMS, where several local women's groups were established, and in unions providing women-run courses "for women only"), most women's committees and efforts are institutionalized, segregating their concerns and removing them from grass-roots feminism (ibid.). The lack of a tradition of autonomous women's labour organizations, like those in other European countries and in the United States (to be discussed shortly), has lessened the impact of these efforts. The tensions created by efforts to develop autonomy yet gain influence have not seriously been addressed by trade union feminists in Britain.

The second approach feminists in unions have taken to increase their influence is their drive to gain union support for feminist-related issues. Even in the 1960s, prior to the activization of feminism, the TUC had lobbied for the Equal Pay Act. Later, prompted in part by the 1974 Working Women's Charter-the London-based effort to promote a minimum set of feminist demands in trade unions-the TUC set about revamping its own charter, "Aims for Women at Work." The feminist campaign for child care found expression in the TUC's Charter for Under Fives (1978), calling for comprehensive and universal child care and flextime. The TUC has recognized the "outdated" concept of the family wage and has called for positive action in employment and education. A 1979 TUC ten-point "Charter for Equality" for trade union women advocated special efforts to include women on decision-making bodies and supported child care and awareness-training programs to aid in increasing women's union participation. In addition, the TUC has held conferences on women's issues, established guidelines for positive action in employment, and taken an active role in supporting amendments to the Equal Pay and Sex Discrimination acts.

A dramatic instance of union support for feminist issues came in a massive demonstration-a joint TUC-feminist march in 1979-to protest the possibility of restrictive antiabortion legislation, then pending in the House of Commons in the Corrie Bill. This demonstration marked a unique expression of union support that moved beyond the rhetorical level to practical action.

In 1983, partially owing to pressure from the Labour Party Women's Action Committee, the biennial conference of the largest union in the country, the TGWU, supported a series of resolutions on positive action, including "a call for the extension and formal constitution of effective womens' organizations" in the union and in the Labour Party. It also instructed the union's Labour delegation to support proposals designed to improve

women's access to and participation in the party (Spare Rib, Sept. 1983:29). This action represented a victory because trade union feminists mobilized the delegates in opposition to the proposed platform, voted down a compromise proposal, and successfully pushed for a strong program of positive action (Rogers 1983:31).

Nonetheless, with regard to key feminist demands (also endorsed by the TUC and other unions)-equal job opportunity for women and an end to pay discrimination-only limited progress has been made. As suggested earlier, male dominance still exists in the unions at all levels, from regional councils to the shop floor to the industry-wide negotiating teams. In crucial negotiations with employers and with the federal government, bargaining priorities related to women have been neglected. The gap between stated policy in resolutions and its implementation in agreements and at the local and plant levels remains a key hurdle for union women (interview, Turner, July 1982). Hence, while unions have provided rhetorical support for "social issues" of concern to working women (e.g., abortion, welfare, housing benefits, day care), their impact has been minimal on economic and industrial matters such as pay and maternity leaves. It is those matters over which men still retain firm control and discretion, limiting possibilities for the implementation of the numerous resolutions passed in union conferences. To a large degree, women's interests are viewed as secondary to the larger concern for social and economic issues. The resulting subordination of feminist demands leaves male bastions of power and sexism untouched (Scott 1982; Bouchier 1984). The indifference with which unions treat women is reflected in a survey that found clear hostility to unions among women factory workers. They articulated the view that unions cared only for men (e.g., holding shop meetings early in the morning) and pointed to the exclusion from unions of part-time workers who are disproportionately female (Speakman 1984:44-45). Policies such as affirmative action ("positive discrimination") have been met with hostility and suspicion owing to high unemployment and concern for male jobs (Lewis 1983:221).

Several conclusions appear in order. The first is that, in the main, trade unions are unwilling to extend their purported support of feminist concerns to meaningful action in concrete areas. While they have endorsed and supported legislation related to women, they have usually not translated such support to other arenas of power. Although most unions are affiliated to the Labour Party, and effectively control its policies through their majority of votes, they have neither pressed for greater representation for women nor supported other efforts that increase women's power in the party. Nor have their representatives (female or male) on public bodies, such as the EOC (to be discussed later), been advocates on behalf of women's concerns. Hence, there is a need to move beyond the current stage of rhetorical support to a broadened perception of feminist issues in the unions themselves and in the larger society. As Labourite Audrey Wise has said, the aim of feminists is to feminize general issues of policy and generalize issues that are currently defined as women's issues (Perrigo 1985:143). (In our further discussion, we will see that the situation of Swedish women in trade unions has been similar to that of their British counterparts, with the dominant Swedish union being even more reluctant to deal with feminist demands in a climate that discourages "conflictual" grass-roots activity.) Given the analysis presented here, it is difficult to justify Hewlett's (1986:170) contention that the most effective women's groups in Britain are in parties and unions-not in separate feminist organizations. In addition, though women's committees, equal opportunity officers, and the like exist in most unions, their failure thus far to alter power relations and policy priorities leads to the conclusion, to be explored later, that autonomous women's groups, which organize outside the union structure, may have the best opportunity to produce meaningful change.

Unions: United States

Women compose 16 percent of the unionized labour force in the United States. If employee associations are included (in a work force that is less than 20 percent unionized), the number rises to 30 percent (Milkman 1985:304). As in Britain, the percentage of women currently unionizing is greater than that of men, although total membership in unions is declining precipitously. Like their British counterparts, few American women appear in leadership ranks, one exception being the National Education Association (NEA), a predominantly female union in which they constitute a majority of the board (ibid., 306).

In the International Ladies Garment Workers Union (ILGWU), where they also compose over three-fourths of the membership, they hold 25 percent of the board positions. In public sector unions, such as the American Federation of State, County, and Municipal Employees (AFSCME), which is 40 percent female, women's increasing membership and their participation in union activities have resulted in more of them running for office and becoming shop stewards (Bell 1985:288). In 1982, 33 percent of local presidents were women-up from 25 percent seven years before. In 1982, women also held 45 percent of local union offices (ibid.). Within the last few years, a woman was elected international vice president of the Service Employees International Union (SEIU), which has an estimated 45 percent women members, while two women were elected to the international board of the AFSCME. The SEIU held a conference in 1981 to discuss women's issues such as organizational roles, leadership, and collective bargaining; and several unions, particularly SEIU and AFSCME, have been active in fighting in the courts for women's concerns such as pregnancy disability insurance and comparable worth.

Table 4: Female Membership and Leadership in Labour Organizations with 250,000 or More Women Members, 1978

Organization	Women Members	Percent Female	Women Officers and Board Members	Percent Female
National Education Association	1,219,500	75	5	55
International Brotherhood of Teamsters	480,974	25	0	0
United Food and Commercial Workers	480,105	39	2	3
American Federation of State, County and Municipal Employee	408,000	40	1	3
Amalgamated Clothing and Textile Workers' Union	130,660	66	6	15
Service Employees International Union	312,500	50	7	15
International Brotherhood of Electrical Workers	303,518	30	0	0
American Federation of Teachers	300,000	60	8	25
International Ladies Garment Workers Union	278,704	80	2	7
Communication Workers of America	259,112	51	0	0

Source: Coalition of Labour Union Women 1980: Tables 3 and 5.

In general, women hold an increasing number of local-level union positions as stewards and officers-though there are still many more female secretaries than presidents. More women have been elected to high office and more resolutions passed on women's recruitment and promotion. Nonetheless, women do not hold top leadership positions in any unions and make up only a small minority of executive board members (Wertheimer 1984:298). In 1978, women held 31 of 655 elective or appointed offices in unions affiliated with the AFL-CIO and 109 of 662 positions in unaffiliated unions and employee associations. They constituted 7.2 percent of national executive board members in AFL-CIO affiliates and 35.3 percent of board members in employee associations where female membership is over twice that in traditional unions (ibid.).

Women's caucuses and committees have been created in a number of unions, and feminist activity has spurred a new interest in union activism among many women workers. Women in the ILGWU and the American Postal Workers Union (APWU) organized to gain support at union conventions for such issues as affirmative action (ibid., 309). Elsewhere, women's divisions have pressed for increased child-care and flextime provisions. As in Britain, the class separation between the larger feminist movement and the working-class women involved in union politics has resulted in considerable distance between these two groups. Nonetheless, despite a reluctance of union women to identify with "women's lib," they have adapted consciousness-raising and other innovative feminist techniques and have been especially interested in issues of gender equality in the labour force (Milkman 1985:307, 309). Efforts to organize around women's issues within unions have most often come from women themselves rather than from union leaders.

However, an aversion to the creation of special interests within unions, as well as the persistence of "male culture," has prevented women from gaining access to substantial internal power in unions, although as in Britain, the trade union movement has become an important ally of the women's movement in the political process. In the United States this support has gone beyond lobbying for legislation to active coalition participation in the Leadership Conference for Civil Rights and similar groups, in which the two movements have in many instances developed a joint agenda for policy. Such coalitional activity has been especially valuable with regard to the legal process and intervention in the administrative sector.

It has become evident that women compose a large segment of unorganized workers and, more importantly, are likelier than males to join unions. Evidence also indicates that unions win more representational elections when they stress women's issues (ibid., 310). Unions have therefore become more receptive to such issues, as they assess their options in a situation of crisis and decline.

However, the American tradition of feminist autonomy from established groups is evident in relationships with the trade union movement as well as with parties.

Feminists have organized within-but also outside-the labour movement. As in Britain, a tradition of women's worker groups, such as the WTUL, gave rise to networks of women at the perimeter of the organized trade union movement (Kessler-Harris 1985:131; Hyman 1985:24). But while some groups, such as the Coalition of Labour Union Women (CLUW), operate within the traditional labour structure, an alternate approach to organizing, untested in Britain, continues to exist outside the American unions.

CLUW

In 1974, after a set of legal challenges to force unions to comply with provisions of antidiscrimination measures (particularly the Civil Rights Act of 1964), the leading arm of the American labour movement, the AFL-CIO, helped establish a women's caucus within its ranks-CLUW. Like women's groups within British unions, CLUW has pressed for greater sensitivity to women's concerns, increased representation in leadership circles, and an end to job discrimination. (In addition, it lobbies for legislation and aids in organizing potential women union members.) CLUW has created a women's base and forum for networking within the labour movement, and the result has been more representation of women in union offices and the creation of women's departments and committees in some unions. CLUW has taken the union structure as a given, with the goal of advancing women's interests as workers and unionists within it (Milkman 1985:310). Membership in CLUW is limited to those who were already both union members and activists in the trade union movement along traditional lines (e.g., elected leadership and committees). Thus, CLUW functions as a means to network within union circles, creating pressure to act on women's demands. In the main, the group has served as a mechanism to promote women into leadership ranks; its chapters rarely include the union rank and file (ibid., 312). At present, CLUW's membership comprises only about 1 percent of union women members, themselves a minority of union workers. As currently constituted, the group serves best as an internal union "watchdog," effective at leadership levels and only nominally attentive to the unorganized and the rank and file (ibid., 315).

Like its British counterparts, the CLUW has largely met with an uneven response. Progress in increasing the representation of women in leadership ranks has been slow, but one visible result of CLUW's efforts was the selection of Joyce Miller in 1980 as the first woman on the AFL-CIO's executive council. Although union support has been generated for such issues as the ERA and the Pregnancy Discrimination Act and for coalitions formed to promote them, there has been limited progress in gaining support for matters like affirmative action. (In Britain the rhetorical level of support for some issues appears to be greater.) With 16,000 members and 72 local chapters, CLUW operates within the constraints of labour union politics and has avoided confrontation with the union hierarchy (Goodin 1983:146).

A SECOND ROUTE TO ORGANIZING WOMEN WORKERS

In the United States a second tradition of organizing labour women has developed, owing in part to the ambivalence of many professional Americans toward the organized labour movement and perhaps also to the absence of a vigorous socialist (feminist) presence. This alternate route involves independent organizations of working women, primarily white-collar workers-groups like Wider Opportunities for Women (WOW), Working Women, and Union WAGE. Unlike unions that concentrate on collective bargaining, these groups seek to enforce antidiscrimination and affirmative action legislation, demonstrate against employers, and engage in educational efforts to promote safety, organization, and job rights (Seifer and Wertheimer 1979:168; Gelb and Klein 1983:34). As unions have perceived the growing strength of autonomous groups of women workers, they have sought to establish links with them, such as the relationship recently forged between Working Women (office workers) and the SEIU, which created a new union, District 925, to organize women.

In the 1970s, a younger group of feminist activists, who had roots in the New Left and the seminal women's liberation movement but who were also critical of labour politics, organized among previously uninvolved office workers. The group Working Women, formerly called 9 to 5, was a particularly successful result. Rather than dealing directly with unionization, this group concentrated on consciousness-raising and public dramatization of issues involving union organizations as well as on developing participatory democracy (Milkman 1985:315). After 1975, Working Women moved closer to the organized union movement when Local 925 was organized in conjunction with the SEIU. The new "union" was charged with organizing office workers all over the country and, although a part of the SEIU structure, drew staff direction from Working Women and retained autonomy within the union structure (ibid.). Working Women has continued as a separate entity outside the union as well. In addition to concentrating on unionization, it has focused on other issues of concern to women, including age discrimination and bank and insurance company relations with women workers. The group's emphasis on participation by all members continues and visible public actions, involving media attention, are utilized (ibid., 316). In its emphasis on developing specifically female organizational forms and concerns, Working Women seems to be almost a direct descendant of the WTUL.

The dilemma for autonomous groups is how to maintain independence while at the same time influencing the larger union structure. If the Working Women experiment proves successful, it may point the way to the creation of a uniquely feminist worker's presence, with influence in the union and access to its resources and power.

Another approach to women's employment is WOW (Wider Opportunities for Women), which grew from a locally focused volunteer organization stressing part time work to a national nonprofit organization with several staff members. WOW has sought to combine service and advocacy, providing training programs and job placement in nontraditional occupations. Through monitoring, coalition building, and advocacy, as well as publicizing and documenting job inequity, WOW and other groups have sought to reach women who are not union members and are outside the traditional labour market (Fleming 1983). The independent tradition continues and autonomous groups of working women, together with groups such as WOW and Catalyst, have been active in finding jobs for women in all levels of the economic ladder and in fighting job discrimination.

Local Women's Committees: "Municipal Feminism"-A New Direction in British Politics?

Recent efforts at the local level of British politics suggest that in some instances it may be possible for feminist women to work closely with Labour councils and local authorities. New developments in numerous British urban areas have interacted effectively with the decentralized structure of British feminism. Since 1969, a variety of multifaced action groups have developed in many British urban centers, focusing on feminist collectives, rape crisis centers and shelters for battered women, health clinics, black women's groups, and groups of women in law, the media, and other professions (Bouchier 1984). Feminists have turned to local council governments for funding, access, and space to maintain their activities; and, fearing hierarchy and male co-optation, they have tended to prefer local-level dialogues to those at the national level. Since 1982, aided in part by the increased number of local councilors who are women (18.4 percent) (Equal Opportunities Commission 1983a:95), several local councils have created women's committees to promote representation of women and women's interests (Goss 1984). Such committees have been established by the Greater London Council (GLC), numerous London boroughs, including Camden, Islington, Southwark, and Hackney, and by 22 other British urban centers (including some in Scotland). Virtually all these constituencies are under Labour Party domination. In some communities, support for women's committees came from local councilors (e.g., London), while in others the initiative for commission establishment emanated from the women's movement itself. In Leeds, for example, a local conference that drew together Labour Party and SDP women, trade union members, and local women's groups (including Rape Crisis, Asian Women, and the 300 Group) resulted in the formation of a women's Subcommittee of the Policy and Resources Committee (Flannery and Roelofs 1984). This body strengthened the work already begun by the Women's Equal Employment Group, which had been established in 1982 by trade union and other local women. By 1984, the Leeds council had trebled childcare funding (Rowbotham 1984).

The greatest resources were those of the GLC, which in 1984 devoted nearly £8 million to funding local women's groups and projects (interview, Wise, July 1984). The GLC Women's Committee sought to involve a wide spectrum of women by holding open meetings and coopting women to represent such groups as lesbians, the disabled, and trade unionists (Goss 1984). Funding was given to Greenham Common women for day care and to a female transportation service, as well as to day care and health facilities-all to a generally hostile press reception (Flannery and Roelofs 1984). A major thrust of the GLC Women's Committee was to foster multiaction centers for women, thus bringing some order to the centrifugal politics we have described, perhaps building on the women's action centers that already existed in many British cities (interview, Wise, July 1984). At the GLC, efforts were made to emphasize participatory democracy and openness through public meetings, which received enthusiastic response and enjoyed large attendance (Flannery and Roelofs 1984:77). Meetings were open to all interested women and tasks were rotated, in accordance with feminist theory. Despite media emphasis on funding of "radical" projects, child-care subsidies, in fact, accounted for the bulk of GLC funding efforts.

The GLC budget for grants to women increased from £300,000 in 1982 to over £7 million in 1984 (Goss 1984:112). Between April and December 1983 alone, 227 projects were funded for a total of £4.5 million, an unusually large infusion of funds for previously impoverished feminist groups (Spare Rib, Feb. 1985:20). Nonetheless, the portion allocated to women still was only a fraction of the total GLC 1983-84 budget of £824 million-less than 1 percent, in fact (Livingston 1984:261). However, by 1986, the fourth and final year of the GLC Women's Committee's budget existence, its budget had grown to £90 million (Coote and Campbell 1987:105-8). In this committee, as in other women's committees, local councilors retained the right to outvote and override the interest of the feminist consultants (Spare Rib, Feb. 1985:19-20)-a situation that has led some observers to suggest that in this instance women's groups are relatively autonomous but lack effective power (Goss 1984:125). However, the GLC did provide a meeting place at County Hall for a wide variety of women's activities and purchased a building for the specific use of two feminist groups, A Women's Place and the Women's Research and Resources Center (Rogers 1983:173). In addition, the GLC Women's Committee played a campaigning or mobilizing role, aiding efforts related to working women, child care, and Greenham Common (Flannery and Roelofs 1984:80).

Women's committees established in the London boroughs of Camden and Islington have had varying degrees of success and funding. The Camden group, with strong support from local Labour councilors, has devoted considerable funding to women's efforts. A Woman's Bus has traveled the community to focus discussions and provide information and advice, circumventing the media by going directly to local women (Goss 1984; Flannery and Roelofs 1984). However, in Islington, as of 1984, the Women's Unit was all but defunded and defunct (interview, Potter, July 1984).

The women's committees have been unique in creating new structures that bring women into the political process. They have aimed at breaking down traditional hierarchical processes and, through innovative systems of publicity and participation, tried to seek out women who are not normally part of the political process. They have also attempted to broaden the framework of service provision from a feminist perspective. Some feminists, especially those wary of Labour Party practices in the past, fear that such efforts may co-opt the movement (Goss 1984:128). In fact, however, these committees may act as a bridge between the movement and both labour and governmental structures, if they are successful.

A major drawback to these promising efforts has been the attack of the Conservative government on both the GLC and local London council governments (12 of which have had women's committees) (Spare Rib, Feb. 1985:20). The GLC itself was dissolved in 1986 by the Thatcher government. Although the trend toward local-level support for women's efforts in Britain is still too new to measure, these efforts are notable in providing linkages between traditional, socialist, and radical feminist groups and in seeking to reach out to the vast number of British women who have heretofore been unaffected by the feminist movement. Can local-level priorities be reorganized and feminists given real power rather than just their customary advisory role? Can a modus vivendi be reached between feminist democracy and traditional hierarchical government structures? These questions are as yet unresolved.

This chapter has assessed two different approaches to feminist political organizing: the British one, in which movement activity has been contained within the existing parties and unions, and the American one, in which gender-based groups have sought to interact with a weaker party and union system. It seems evident that the British model of organizing women's groups within parties and unions has had only limited impact on representation and policy. Whether, as Coote and Campbell (1987:148) have recently argued, the new forces of radical activism in the Labour Party are sufficient to "break down some of the barriers that had stood between the women's movement and parliamentary politics in the 1970's" is not clear from the analysis presented here.

In the United States, independent groups such as NOW, the NWPC, and NARAL have gained a significant voice in the Democratic Party, pressing their views effectively on a still predominantly male leadership. The role of feminist movements as constituents in electoral politics appears to be clearer from the American case, although in Britain there have been some (more half-hearted?) efforts to mobilize them in order to create new alignments of political power.

Unions in both countries present an ambiguous picture, although in the United States the innovative model created by 9 to 5, emanating from an independent feminist base, has suggested new alternatives for workers and organizers. In Britain a new model of feminist activism, at the local level, has seemed to represent a fresh, more "political phase" of the movement where it has felt most at home. The effect of the abolition of the GLC, which had the most resources and influence of all local committees and working parties, is still undetermined.

FEMINISM IN GOVERNMENT: ADVOCACY AND POLICY-MAKING

We can test the impact feminists have made on national politics by analyzing public policy issues. We must explore: (1) agenda setting-the role of feminist groups in initiating and structuring public policy, (2) the influence of these groups on legislative and executive decision-making, and (3) the implementation of the policies enacted. Central to this analysis is an examination of the role played by feminist groups in any or all of these crucial steps in the policy-making process. Implicit in our discussion will be the question: Have the policies enacted made a difference?

In this chapter we analyze the role of two apparently similar bodies: the Equal Opportunities Commission (EOC) in Britain and the Equal Employment Opportunity Commission (EEOC) in the United States. In addition, we examine the structure of the policy-making process in both countries by focusing on abortion and sex discrimination politics. Finally, we assess the role of British and American feminist groups in affecting policy outcomes by looking closely at the politics of domestic violence, an issue first brought to public consciousness in Britain.

Not surprisingly, given the institutional setting, women are poorly represented in British political life. In 1982, only 23 women served in Parliament, although a record 210 stood for election (European Union of Women 1982). By 1987 a higher number-40 out of 221 candidates-had gained seats. In addition to the female (though hardly feminist) prime minister, Margaret Thatcher, there are three other women ministers in the present Conservative government, but they do not hold cabinet rank. Of 97 senior judges, only two are women. While women increasingly qualified as barristers and solicitors during the 1970s and 1980s, in England and Wales they composed only 3 percent of the Queens Counsels, from whom judges in the High Court and above are chosen (Lovenduski 1986:217). In 1983 only 4 percent of High Court judges were women. No women were represented among the higher-level appeals judges. In the senior civil service, in 1986, fewer than 4 percent of high administrative officers were women. In 1983, while women composed 47.1 percent of Home civil servants, there were no female permanent secretaries (ibid., 216). Few women are nominated to, or serve on, government committees, councils, or other public bodies. And, at the local level, in the mid-1970s there were only two chief women's officers out of 500 (Hills 1981:27). But more women are becoming local councilors-in 1982 they numbered 18.4 percent (Equal Opportunities Commission 1983a:95). However, as we noted earlier, the overwhelming structure of power in Britain is predominantly male.

GOVERNMENT-BASED ADVOCACY OF WOMEN'S ISSUES IN BRITAIN

The Economic Opportunities Commission

During the 1960s and early '70s, pressure arose in Parliament for the creation of a quasi-independent body to "act as an amalgam of recipient and investigator complaints relating to sex discrimination, conciliator where possible and prosecutor in the courts where this failed" (Byrne and Lovenduski 1978:157). The result was the creation of the Equal Opportunities Commission to enforce the Equal Pay Act and Sex Discrimination Act (to be discussed shortly). The EOC was given law enforcement powers, research and investigative capacity, and jurisdiction over a number of policy areas related to women (education, housing, and employment) (Meehan 1983b:70-71). Excluded from EOC jurisdiction were the social security, pensions, taxes, and nationality. It was hoped that the EOC would be a vigorous voice on behalf of women and would play a strong enforcement role. In practice, the EOC has not developed as robust a defender of equal rights as many hoped, although it does provide a forum and base for feminist-related issues, one of the few that exists in a system essentially closed to change-oriented groups.

The EOC is a quango, or quasi-judicial/legislative entity, and as such is not strictly accountable to the House of Commons or the executive branch. The agency therefore apparently has a degree of independence. In the United States, by contrast, appointments to commissions and agencies dealing specifically with women's issues-the Equal Employment Opportunities Commission (EEOC), Commission on Civil Rights, and Office of Civil Rights (formerly at the Department of Health, Education, and Welfare, later at the Department of Education)-are politicized, and feminist groups are consulted and vocal about their preferences.

As a quango, in fact the EOC relies on funding from the Home Office and is dependent on government departments. It also lacks the supportive constituency necessary for a successful confrontationist stance (Atkins and Hoggett 1984:196-97). It is therefore reliant on informal government contacts and, as a result, lacks a public image and awareness. Perhaps mindful of the restrictive role to which the Commission for Racial Equality was limited when it sought to build a stronger relationship with ethnic groups and develop a constituency, the EOC has been more cautious (ibid., 197).

In addition, a history of tripartism limits the role of women both at the EOC and within the judicial process. Secrecy pervades the appointments process and access is limited, except for established groups. Nominations to the agency are made by reference to lists of "The Great and the Good," on which few, if any, women are found; interests represented include those of party, region, and, especially, business and labour. Recommendations of women clearly identified with feminism were rejected until the late 1970s (Meehan 1983b:70-74). Until recently, when two women with a feminist orientation (Sandra Brown and Ann Robinson) were appointed, the commission reflected little input from women per se. In the main, female trade union representatives on the EOC have been more responsive to labour than to women's concerns (interview, Turner, July 1982). Meehan (1983a:182) points out that when in one instance a TUC representative on the EOC dissented from the union position on protective legislation, she was met with punitive action by the TUC, including denial of reappointment to the EOC and removal from her senior position in the TUC. Leadership roles on the commission have been given primarily to majority party representatives.

In addition to the lack of access to appointments and the policy-making process, the role of the EOC is limited by the neocorporatist structure of the legal system. British employment suits are first heard in industrial tribunals rather than in courts. Tribunals are comprised of representatives of industry and labour and are seen as part of the collective bargaining process (Meehan 1983a). In this process, there is limited representation for complainants by unions or groups similar to the American Civil Liberties Union (ACLU), which do not really exist in the United Kingdom. While the EOC and National Council for Civil Liberties (NCCL) provide some legal aid, there are no pro bono, public interest, law-related groups that play an advocacy role on behalf of the disadvantaged. Trade unions, which could aid complainants in bringing suits, usually do not. In addition, tribunal personnel are overworked and undertrained and lack an understanding of sex discrimination issues. The number of cases heard and upheld by tribunals is discouraging to feminist aspirations (a situation we will discuss later). Tribunals do not create case law; therefore their rulings result in a plethora of ad hoc decisions. The British judiciary is naturally conservative, and not surprisingly, has shown itself to be far from progressive on issues of sex discrimination (Jackson 1984:193) Of the cases that have been won, at least two important ones have been on appeal to the European Court.

Among them was a case of indirect discrimination brought by Belinda Price. She alleged that the Civil Service Commission's requirement of an upper-age limit of 28 for executive officers discriminated against women as childbearers and rearers during their twenties (Bruegel 1983:151).

Because of the limited legal advocacy structure and the tradition of bureaucratic neutrality, outside pressure and monitoring of compliance with the law are absent in the United Kingdom (Meehan 1983a, 1983b). In contrast to the United States, where the existence of policy networks is a key part of the process of influence, in Britain women have not developed similar networks for reasons of ideology and institutional structure. Hence, there has been little or no organization per se to bolster the enforcement of sex discrimination laws.

The style of the 15-person EOC itself has been to limit emphasis on enforcement and sanctions and to concentrate on research and publicity. It has sought to avoid confrontation in favour of consultation and persuasion and has been involved in few, if any, dramatic cases (Meehan 1983b). It has conducted several protracted informal investigations into equal pay and employment issues-with limited outcomes.

The House of Lords has prevented the EOC from mounting formal investigations into the general workings of organizations (Atkins and Hodgett 1984:39). As a result, the EOC has sought to influence government at higher levels, by submitting proposals and evidence to the House of Commons and relevant agencies, including royal commissions and agencies concerned with manpower services and education (Spare Rib, May 9, 1981). It has provided legal assistance and advice to individuals (its power is limited to backing cases brought by individuals) and brought several cases to the European Court. Perhaps most significantly, it has played a major role in educating public opinion on sex discrimination issues (Byrne and Lovenduski 1978a).

It has helped create consciousness of the need for change and has demonstrated the extent of discrimination. The EOC has issued films as well as pamphlets and other documents, held conferences, and played a key role in funding projects, even those of women's groups considered "radical." Among them have been grants to the Women's Action Group, the Women's Health Information Center, the NCCL, Asian women's groups, Women's Aid, the Women's Therapy Center, Sisterwrite (a feminist bookshop), the Women's Research and Resource Center, and unions (for analysis of sexual harassment) (EOC 1981). In a system where funding opportunities are limited, the EOC is a new and important source of financial support for emerging feminist groups.

The EOC may also play a role in building relationships among disparate groups concerned with women's issues. An example is the commission's large annual conference, to which 70 to 80 women's organizations are invited, thus providing a rare forum and meeting place for a wide variety of feminist activists (interview, Trembath, Aug. 1982).

Additional factors limiting the effectiveness of the EOC are its location in Manchester (though it does maintain a small London office) and the absence of regional offices as well as the high turnover rate among its chief executives-four different heads during its first five years of existence (interview, Lockwood, Aug. 1982).

The commission has had difficulty in maintaining traditional bureaucratic neutrality among a staff with feminist inclinations. The result has been tensions between commissioners and staff-unlike the situation in its American counterpart, the EEOC, whose staff and groups frequently consult and may be mutually supportive (Meehan 1983a:74).

The election of a more sympathetic government would undoubtedly help, considering that the Conservative government cuts forced the EOC to reduce its staff from 400 to 148 (Guardian, July 10, 1980). Some British feminists fear that having created a body with extensive purported power, although far less in actual terms, the commission may actually impede further action regarding sex equality (Byrne and Lovenduski 1978a:146). The creation of a feminist alliance that transcends ideological, party, and class bias and that could provide legitimacy for feminist-related concerns may be the only way to strengthen the EOC (Meehan 1983a:74). The EOC itself has concluded that little further progress can be made without "substantial amendment" (Glucklich 1984:108).

THE WOMEN'S NATIONAL COMMISSION

A second government-based potential advocacy group in Britain is even more limited by constraints than the EOC. The Women's National Commission (WNC) is a government-founded and sponsored organization that was established in 1969. It has two co-chairs, one government appointed and one elected by the commission itself.

The WNC's mission is "to ensure by all possible means that the informed opinion of women is given due weight in government" (WNC 1982). The commission has a requisite size of 50 organizations, which must be national bodies with a large and active membership. Current members include women's sections of unions and parties.

The WNC develops working groups to examine issues and has produced papers, often in response to government (consultative) Green and White papers. While superficially resembling such American federal agencies as the Women's Bureau in the Department of Labour and the commissions on the status of women, the WNC shares some of their weaknesses and then some! The WNC is constrained in its criticism of government because of its close ties to the incumbent administration. In addition, the scope of its membership is limited by the requirement that member groups must have been in existence a number of years and must have a national presence and membership.

These ground rules militate against inclusion of most-if not all-women's liberation groups that have no say; hence, the WNC lacks true representativeness of women's interests (interview, Tuomin, July 1982). Even such small London-based groups as the Fawcett Society are excluded by this policy, although nonmember groups are occasionally invited to participate in the WNC's deliberations on an ad hoc basis. In addition, the group's charter lacks a provision for changing its organizational membership. The WNC is run by the general secretary (a civil servant) and one staff member, limiting its role greatly. Moreover, the group's power, like many others discussed here, is strictly advisory. The group exists on a budget that makes up 3 percent of the EOC's (limited) resources (Stott 1978:277). Hence, while the WNC remains as a symbol of women's influence and a potential advocate for women's concerns, which no government will abolish for symbolic reasons, it represents a classic case of institutional powerlessness.

Government-based Advocacy of Women in the United States

In the United States by 1980 the number of women state legislators tripled in 12 years to over 14 percent, although they constituted only 5.1 percent (25 of the 532 members) of Congress (Bomafede 1986:2176). In the 1980s women mayors governed several of America's largest cities, including Houston, Chicago, and San Francisco, and the number of municipal officials who were women tripled (from 1971) to 13 percent (Flammang 1984:10). Especially under the Carter administration, women's fortunes in the administrative sector improved dramatically. The number of women in top policy-making jobs subject to presidential appointment (grades 13-18) increased from a pre-Carter 14 percent to 33 percent in 1979. In cabinet and subcabinet positions, women's representation improved from 4 to 8 percent. Carter also appointed an unprecedented number of women (15.8 percent) as federal judges, bringing female representation on the federal bench to 6.6 percent. Under Ronald Reagan's administration after 1980, however, these numbers dropped significantly to 4.4 percent of judicial nominations and 9 percent of senior federal appointments (Harrison 1984:149; New York Times, March 27, 1987:A12). By 1987, Reagan appointments of women to top positions had reached 15 percent, although, despite their gender, many could be classified as antifeminists.

In the United States, as in the United Kingdom, the activities of agencies addressing sex discrimination, especially the EEOC, have been limited by an insufficient budget and bureaucratic ineptitude (Greenburger 1980:11). Enforcement has been primarily left to individuals who face serious obstacles (lack of money, information, and support) in pursuing sex discrimination cases.

In the United States the Women's Bureau was for some 40 years the focal point for women in government. Its role was hampered to some degree by its advocacy of protective legislation for women and its accompanying antipathy to the ERA (Tinker 1983:11). Nonetheless, after it abandoned its endorsement of protection and came to support the ERA, it became both a resource (as it had been since its inception, providing statistics and data) and an advocacy agency on behalf of women's concerns. It has helped provide resources and a forum for a variety of women's (primarily economic) concerns.

However, though at one time it was the only federal agency charged with looking after women's welfare, it has been joined (at various times) by the federal commissions on the status of women, the Civil Rights Commission, and the EEOC. The significance of these bodies has varied with the particular administrative viewpoints and with the type of leadership provided at a given time.

The EEOC was created pursuant to the passage of Title VII of the Civil Rights Act of 1964. As Vicki Randall has pointed out, it initially had fewer formal enforcement powers than its British counterpart, the EOC. Nonetheless, it emerged as a relatively important tool through which major policy advances in equal employment might be made, although its effectiveness has varied with the commitment of different administrations to it. The initial EEOC had power only to seek voluntary compliance with the Civil Rights Act; it could not litigate, although it could file amicus curiae briefs. After 1972, largely owing to pressure from the organized feminist movement and from commissioners sympathetic to the movement (whose appointments had been pressed for by the organized women's community), its enforcement powers were strengthened (Randall 1982:189; Meehan 1983a:177).

For the EEOC, enforcement involves the resolution of individual charges and the elimination of "patterns and practices" of discrimination (ibid.). Executive Order 11375 amends the earlier Executive Order 11246 to include sex discriminatory employment practices among those prohibited to employers under contract to the federal government. Although the enforcing agency, the Office of Federal Contract Compliance Programs (OFCCP), has not been vigorous in enforcing policy, a 1969 order spelled out in detail what affirmative action would entail, in terms of goals, timetables, and monitoring progress. Under pressure from WEAL, the executive orders were applied to women in higher education as well.

Despite the unevenness of the enforcement process, nondiscrimination efforts have been aided in the United States by a variety of factors unavailable to the British feminist movement. Nonetheless, during most of the 1970s, major questions were raised by critics about the EEOC's administrative efficiency and the seriousness of its commitment to end discrimination. The backlog of unresolved cases seemed particularly indicative of inadequate efforts. But in 1977, Eleanor Holmes Norton, a new chair appointed by the Carter administration, instituted a complete overhaul of the commission in order to rationalize its structure and procedures. Even prior to that, though, the commission had demonstrated its ability to litigate effectively on behalf of individuals. Through issuance of guidelines and briefs, it was able in large measure to shape the nature of judicial response to the issues raised. Particularly noteworthy was the 1973 settlement with the American Telephone and Telegraph Company (AT&T), the largest such award ever made under civil rights legislation (ibid., 178). Hundreds of briefs were filed on behalf of individuals and also in class action suits. In 1977 alone, 35 class action suits were resolved.

A major factor in the EEOC's ability to change law was the establishment of a policy network that aided in the appointment of sympathetic staff and commissioners, consulted with the commission, and produced additional legislation to strengthen the functioning of the agency. A Washington women's policy network brought legislators, bureaucrats, staff, and feminist advocates together on a variety of issues. The emergence of the women's movement aided in expanding federal policies, and because the bureaucratic process in the United States is recognized as more explicitly "political" than that of Britain, the effectiveness and persistence of the Washington women's lobby helped to influence appointments, press for continuing antidiscrimination legislation (such as Title IX, banning sex discrimination in education), and monitor agency enforcement (Randall 1982). The appointment of an outspoken black woman leader (Eleanor Holmes Norton) to head the EEOC in 1977 was made in consultation with civil rights and women's groups. "With its amicus curiae briefs, strict guidelines and its power to litigate after 1974, the EEOC is thought to have become, in the 1970's, a strong and successful proponent of women's rights" (Meehan 1985:10).

Under the Reagan administration, funding for civil rights enforcement dropped, now constituting only 0.07 percent of the federal budget. The ability of federal agencies to conduct compliance reviews, investigate complaints, and attack discrimination in a systematic fashion has been severely curtailed (Braun 1984:99). Like the British EOC, the EEOC has experienced cutbacks in staff and budget, with clerical staff and legal (attorney) positions most affected. These reductions in turn have slowed the production of documentation needed to prosecute cases. Litigation activities have also been curtailed owing to reduced funding, with little money available for witnesses, special studies, and data processing (ibid.). Staff at the OFCCP has also been cut back, resulting in a backlog of individual complaints (ibid., 100). New regulations further curtail coverage (of small firms) and may discourage the bringing of systemic discrimination suits. For the first time, an administration has intervened as a "friend of the Court" against women and minorities in "reverse discrimination" suits, although the Supreme Court has generally upheld affirmative action in recent cases (Johnson v. Transit Agency, Santa Clara County, California). Women have not yet lost most of the equal employment gains of the last two decades, although they have been forced to expend enormous energy and scarce resources just to maintain the status quo. But the resignation under protest of government officials such as Joseph Cooper, responsible for compliance with affirmative action guidelines, have helped highlight the administration's failure to vigorously enforce the law (New York Times, Jan. 5, 1987:II4).

THE CONTRAST BETWEEN U.S. AND BRITISH ADVOCACY

To the degree that the EEOC has been a more effective force for change than its British counterpart-although its role depends in large measure on the sympathetic support of both the executive and judicial branches-several points of contrast appear significant. First, the federal courts in the United States have upheld and reinforced numerous claims pursued under Title VII. Second, American courts are more available to make and interpret policy and may provide another access route to policy change. Third, class action suits may result in more sweeping and effective remedies, and the growing litigation sector among women's groups has used its limited resources to aid in bringing such suits before the courts.

A final area of contrast is the policy toward affirmative action. Atkins and Hoggett (1984:199) suggest that four factors present in the United States regarding this policy are absent in the United Kingdom: 1) the public availability of requisite statistics, 2) the imposition of high damages in discrimination cases, 3) the powerful position of the EEOC in conciliating and monitoring out-of-court settlements, and 4) the willingness and power of the courts to uphold positive action (or affirmative action) orders. As we shall see, similar constraints limit the effectiveness of Sweden's machinery for equal opportunities. An additional factor limiting the impact of the British EOC may be that its power (and potential constituency) is separated from that of the Commission on Racial Equality (CRE) and its racial and ethnic base, so that joint efforts, such as those facilitated in the United States by the Civil Rights Commission and EEOC, are not feasible in Britain. A possible opening for more effective policy-making by the EOC may lie in its emerging relationship with the EEC, via the European Commission, European Parliament, and European Court of Justice (ibid.; Meehan 1985:189). (In 1984, for example, the EOC finally met its obligations as stated in an EEC directive of 1975, amending the Equal Pay Act to cover equal pay for equal value-or comparable worth, in American terminology.) But despite this potential support for a stronger EOC role, it is difficult to see the emergence of a greatly altered commission unless a more cohesive and politicized feminist movement can effectively intervene at the administrative level (Meehan 1985:189).

The absence of an organized British feminist movement, coupled with an institutional setting that makes monitoring of implementation far more difficult than it is in the United States, helps explain in part the considerably different outcomes in the two nations (Randall 1982:196). In the United Kingdom the ensuing separation between the so-called neutral bureaucracy and feminist activists has both reflected and reinforced the absence of a feminist lobby. In the United States, equal opportunity policies have had a greater impact than in Britain (and Sweden as well, as we shall see later) because they have been in effect longer and have been accompanied by more aggressive enforcement of antidiscrimination policies (Dex and Shaw 1986:14).

WOMEN IN POWER: MOBILIZING POWER IN THE LEGISLATIVE ARENA

Britain

Women as elected political officials may provide support for feminist issues. Consistent with our analysis of the EOC and the EEOC, British women M.P.'s have been reluctant allies of the women's movement, while their American counterparts have developed a bit more cohesion on certain issues of interest to the feminist community.

The women in Parliament who became concerned with abortion apparently did so only after a decision was visited on them by their male colleagues (Vallance 1979:88). Once limiting bills were introduced in 1974-75, the M.P.'s were galvanized into action and helped organize support in committees and through petitions, marches, and the like. (In contrast, the Sex Discrimination Act was given qualified support by women M.P.'s because many of them saw it largely as publicity concocted for International Women's Year [ibid., 93].)

But whatever the momentum created around the abortion issue, parliamentary women have no very clear and "certainly no very enduring sense of themselves as a group" (ibid., 96). The presence of Margaret Thatcher as the lone woman in her cabinet merely reinforces the view that there are "exceptional women" who occasionally achieve power and who rule in "splendid isolation" from their female colleagues.

In the House of Commons, women do not see themselves as having any "esprit de corps." Most Labour women may have a degree of camaraderie and unity of purpose about some, though not all, issues. The existence of separate Lady Member's Sitting Rooms by party has developed in recent years, accentuating partisan differences between women M.P.'s. In the House of Lords as well, party is a greater influence on behavior than is sex. Women peers are not united by a feminist ideology, nor have they provided any feminist input in Parliament (Drewry and Brock 1983:2).

In contrast, in the United States a congressional Caucus for Women's Issues founded in 1977 claimed a bipartisan membership of 127 (down to 96 in 1986-83 Democrats and 13 Republicans [Bomafede 1986:2176]), including a majority of men (Thompson 1984:2).

The group acts as a lobbying organization, with a bipartisan leadership and an all-female executive committee. The caucus aids in gaining electoral support for members and provides information to its constituents through a newsletter, Update. It prepares news releases and promotes legislation through meetings with administration officials and through media advocacy efforts. The caucus may be weakened by its somewhat partisan cast, and its failure to solicit support from all women members (of the 24 female members of Congress, two Democrats and seven Republicans are not members).

However, though women legislators in the United States do not necessarily or even usually behave as a bloc, studies have found that women are consistently more liberal, particularly on issues concerning women and consumer protection (Norris [1986]:6). Republican women and men in Congress exhibit contrasting behavior on such issues as abortion rights, child benefits, and the ERA (ibid., 9).

Women legislators also appear to favour decreased military expenditures and arms control, regardless of party affiliation. In this context it may prove especially significant that the caucus supports legislation such as that contained in the Economic Equity Act (EEA). The group has served as a source of information and consensus building (as it apparently did in the successful drive for Child Support Enforcement legislation in 1984 [Thompson 1984:221]).

THE POLICY PROCESS

Britain

Pym (1974:80-81) suggests that few promotional pressure groups have a meaningful impact on the policy-making process in the United Kingdom, although she views the case of abortion reform as having been almost unique. Most legislation relating to women has been submitted as a private member's bill, and depends on tacit to overt government support for passage.

The House of Lords and appointed select committees have often played a key role in mobilizing support for "women's" legislation. Many feminists in Britain are skeptical about the ability of equal rights campaigns and legislation to alter the balance of power between men and women (Perrigo 1985:137). Hence the passage of the Equal Pay Act (EPA) and subsequent Sex Discrimination Act (SDA) owed more to the parties, the TUC, and also the EEC (whose Article 119, promulgated in 1957, provided for equal pay for equal work) than it did to the women's movement. Women's groups have played an auxiliary-but not central role-in creating support for legislative enactments.

The EPA was enacted under the aegis of a Labour government committed after 1964 to the principle of equal pay for equal work (Randall 1982:183). After consultation with the CBI and TUC, it was agreed that the act passed in 1970 would take effect in 1975. Randall (ibid., 184) attributes the support of the TUC for equal pay legislation not to its concern for feminism but to its fear that lower women's wages would undercut those of men.

Lorwin and Boston (1984:146) point out that until the late 1960s, unions preferred to deal with matters of equal pay through wage negotiations rather than through the legislative process. (Swedish unions, in a similar manner, opposed equal opportunities legislation in the 1970s.)

The EPA provided that machinery for complaints would be the same as that for other industrial disputes: efforts to reach a settlement via the Advisory Conciliation and Arbitration Service (ACAS), recourse to industrial tribunals, and, as a last resort, employee appeals tribunals.

The passage of the act did not end the demand for sex discrimination legislation. Private member's bills were introduced after 1967 by Joyce Butler. A 1972 bill introduced by Willie Hamilton provided the basis for a bill placed by Baroness Nancy Seear before the House of Lords. It was then referred to a Select Committee; a similar Select Committee was established in the House of Commons.

The Conservative Party then in power announced support for an equal opportunities commission and some form of legislation (Randall 1982:164; Rendel 1978). The ensuing Labour government in 1974 pledged support for strong sex discrimination legislation. The SDA was passed in 1975, providing for expanded scope and enforcement and a more powerful EOC.

The legislative process involved in the sex discrimination bill suggests that there was little opposition to the idea of some kind of legislative action on the issue. "The most admirable feature of the debate was the generally sympathetic attitude of the opposition," at least as far as the principle of the bill was concerned; the bill survived the parliamentary legislative process virtually intact (Byrne and Lovenduski 1978b:137).

It may be argued that activity of women in the two major parties created both a pressure and political climate in which legislation was thought necessary. However, there was, in fact, little influence by feminists or female politicians in Parliament (Jenson 1982:365). The Labour government in power in 1974 did endorse the idea of an enforcement body with strong powers as opposed to an organization that, as envisioned by the Conservatives, would be largely devoted to campaigning. Among parliamentary groups, the NCCL, the TUC, the Fawcett Society, and Women in the Media, as well as a short-lived Women's Lobby, pressed avidly for legislation.

At the other extreme, the act's passage was greeted with total hostility by segments of the feminist community, who described it as "fraudulent," "hypocrisy," "a sellout," and "miserable tokenism" and conducted a National Day of Action against the bill, chaining themselves to the railings outside Parliament (Bouchier 1984:120). Their opposition was based on the loopholes in the act, its presumed middle-class bias, and the weakness of the EOC.

They viewed the SDA as a cheap concession, aimed at staving off more meaningful and expensive demands for economic and family equality (ibid., 121). In the end, however, it appears that "lobbying was relatively weak and what mattered was M.P.s' willingness to pay [the bill] attention" (Randall 1982:184). As was the case with equal credit legislation in the United States, M.P.'s may have perceived the bill's proposals as a bow to a growing "women's vote," somewhat in anticipation of organized demands (Gelb and Palley 1987). Other reasons for the easy passage were Britain's pending entry into the Common Market-and the EEC directives requiring equal pay and job equality-and, as in the United States, the relationship between action against race discrimination and action against sex discrimination (Randall 1982:185; Meehan 1985:82).

A third law, the Employment Protection Act of 1975, was supported vigorously by the TUC (Lorwin and Boston 1984:147). The act gave women, for the first time, statutory protection against the loss of jobs due to pregnancy and childbirth. Women now had a statutory right to paid maternity leave, protection from unfair dismissal during pregnancy, and the right to regain their jobs up to 29 weeks of giving birth (Coote and Campbell 1987:93-94).

However, in practice, the rights defined are so narrow that only a minority of women qualify; the majority cannot meet criteria regarding length of service and hours worked per week. No more than one woman in ten who leaves work to have a baby returns (Bruegel 1983:153). Only some 5 percent of women in manual work who took maternity leave and wished to return to their job have been able to do so (ibid.).

The record nonetheless demonstrates that the 1970s in Britain marked legislative acceptance of the principle of equality in several different areas. How well has the legislation worked in practice?

We have suggested that the role of women's groups in facilitating the passage of legislation was an auxiliary rather than central one. Their participation has been even more minimal in the implementation process. As suggested earlier in this chapter, the EOC, which was set up under the Sex Discrimination Act, has been limited in its role, and, reflecting the systemic constraints within which it operates, has acted cautiously. Neither unions nor feminist groups have pressured vigorously for increased action, either at the EOC or in places of employment (Glucklich 1984:113).

The EOC has used its power of formal investigation and its power to issue nondiscrimination notices "judiciously." In 1979 it issued its first (and only) nondiscrimination notice (ten have been issued by the Commission on Racial Equality) on equal pay to the Electrolux factory at Luton (Spare Rib, Sept. 1979:23). A lawsuit involving "indirect" discrimination (i.e., qualifying conditions were more often met by men than women) was successfully won in Price v. Civil Service.

The SDA leaves untouched existing protective labour legislation, except to require the EOC to report on it (Bruegel 1983:152). Hedged with "genuine occupation qualifications" based on sexual distinctions, it fails to provide any obligation to establish positive (affirmative) action programs (ibid.). It is difficult to escape the view that the EOC was not given adequate legal machinery to enforce nondiscrimination on any significant scale (Lorwin and Boston 1984:150). And, as suggested earlier, the EOC has been cautious about using those powers it does have, preferring to devote its major resources to research and publicity.

In the British system, the individual is responsible for bringing cases before the appropriate authorities, and there is the assumption of an equal balance of power between the employee and employer. The onus is on the woman to prove that discrimination has occurred. There is no right to obtain all documentation related to the case for the complaint. And individuals who can prove they have been discriminated against can obtain financial compensation but cannot regain their jobs (Ruggie 1984:118). The burden of proof is on the victim. Since 1976, between 50 and 70 percent of EPA and SDA cases have failed to reach a tribunal. This situation has been largely due to the intervention of the Advisory Conciliation and Arbitration Service, which, as the conciliation service for all industrial complaints, may intervene when there is a prospect of success or when either side requests its assistance. The majority of cases are "settled" at this level or withdrawn (Atkins and Hoggett 1984:28, 123).

The number of cases heard and upheld under both acts is discouraging to feminist aspirations. In recent years the number of cases brought to the EOC under the SDA has remained at a relatively low 250 annually, but EPA cases dropped from 1,742 in 1976 to 54 in 1981, which indicates that the EPA in particular has had limited impact (Guardian, June 16, 1982) (see Table 5) because women have become disillusioned with its ability to change their economic circumstances.

In most instances, under the SDA only a handful of cases heard by tribunals result in a positive finding for women. Of the cases that are conciliated, most are "settled," often for token sums, while a large and puzzling number are withdrawn with no settlement (Spare Rib, Sept. 1979:22; Ruggie 1984:123). The number of applications, never high, has almost steadily fallen, and from 1977 to 1978 almost one-third of the applicants were men (Spare Rib, Sept. 1979:22).

Table 5: Industrial Tribunal Statistics, 1976-81, on Equal Pay Act and Sex Discrimination Act

Applications to Tribunals Where Action Has Been Completed			
Year	**EPA**	**SDA**	**Total**
1976	1,742	243	1,985
1977	751	229	980
1978	343	171	514
1979	263	178	441
1980	91	180	271
1981	54	256	310
Outcome of Cases Heard			
1981			
Total heard		50.0	34.8
Dismissed		38.9	28.5
Upheld		11.1	6.3
1980			
Total heard		28.6	38.3
Dismissed		24.2	30.6
Upheld		4.4	7.8

Source: Equal Opportunities Commission 1982: Appendix 3, p. 32.

Amendments to the EPA and SDA might strengthen their significance by clarifying the meaning of "work of equal value," allowing for greater use of "positive action," and permitting the institution of class action suits. Such amendments are supported both by the EOC and the TUC Women's Advisory Committee (Ruggie 1984:130). Efforts to reformulate the legislation have also been endorsed by the EEC. In 1982, the European Court of Justice struck down the EPA, saying that Britain has failed to broaden its definition of equal work to conform with the EOC's requirement of equal pay for work of equal value. When the Conservative government declined to comply with the ruling, Jo Richardson in 1983 introduced a private member's Sex Equality Bill, which would extend the definition of equal pay and bring under its aegis the growing number of female part-time workers (Perrigo 1985:138). The bill was defeated, but it could serve as a model for future legislation if a Labourled government in conjunction with feminist campaigners pressed for its passage at a later time. As noted earlier, in 1984, after nine years, the government finally complied with the 1975 EEC directive that mandated equal pay for equal value. The ensuing amendment to the EPA resulted in several hundred new complaints over the next two years.

By 1980 a new Employment Act had eroded the maternity rights awarded to women in 1975. The act qualifies the right to maternity leave by limiting it to women who work 16 or more hours and have had two years of continuous service with their firm. Part-time workers rights are qualified even more. The size of the firm is now also taken into account in the act; exemptions are given to firms with fewer than six employees. Notification requirements of intent to return to work are made more stringent. Finally, employers are no longer required to provide identical work to returning employees; rather they may offer "suitable alternative work" (Spare Rib, June 1981:9). The act also makes it more difficult for women to claim unfair dismissal.

Under these circumstances, the implementation of equality acts and subsequent legislative process have undoubtedly been a distinct disappointment to women's aspirations. In the absence of a sympathetic judiciary, committed at least in principle to equal rights, and of a government agency with strong powers devoted to antidiscrimination concerns, much of the legislation enacted remains inadequate. Feminist campaigning groups such as the ROW, the NCCL, and the Women's Liberation Campaign for Financial and Legal Independence have pressed for legislative change and the extension of principles of equality in terms of focus (e.g., positive, or affirmative, action) and scope (e.g., extension to social security and tax law). Nonetheless, it is difficult to disagree with the view that "only the organization of women for women" can help reverse existing labour market inequalities (Meehan 1983a:103). This course would involve the creation of policy networks, at this time lacking in the fragmented feminist political culture of Britain.

What of legislation dealing with social and moral issues? Cases in point are abortion reform and policies toward battered women. Abortion reform was brought before Parliament as a private member's bill, although lobbying by the Abortion Law Reform Association (ALRA) was important in gaining the bill's passage. Pym and others (Pym 1974:91; Rivers 1974:206) have argued that this is one of the few instances in which a promotional group has successfully "penetrated" the legislative process. Marsh and Chambers (1981:1) also contend that "interest group activity on abortion is unparalleled. There are more interest groups concerned with this topic and they are more politicized than on any other social issue." Randell (1982:183-85) concludes that, as in the case of sex discrimination legislation, developments within Parliament were crucial in facilitating the measure's passage. Again, the House of Lords played a key role when Lord Silkins' bill provided an important precedent. In the House of Commons, the sympathetic Labour government gave the bill extra time, while the pro-abortion vote on a Third Reading came primarily from a Labour majority that was reform oriented, young, and middle-class (other moral reform issues that gained support during this period were eased divorce and censorship rules, abolition of the death penalty, and legislation decriminalizing homosexuality) (Marsh and Chambers 1981:3).

Because the issue was "unwhipped," it reflected something other than a straight "party" vote. At the same time there was a strong relationship between Labour Party membership and a pro-abortion vote. (In the United States, similar trends regarding abortion are evident in the stance of liberals and conservatives and in congressional voting [Gelb and Palley 1987:138]). David Steel, who introduced the bill, proved an able parliamentarian who consulted widely and made concessions to the medical profession to gain support (Marsh and Chambers 1981:19). Opposition forces were not well organized, while the "benevolent neutrality" of the Labour Government supported the reform effort (ibid., 20).

The act that was finally passed authorized abortion up to 28 weeks of pregnancy in cases where two registered doctors agreed that the life of the mother or other children would be at risk, or that the baby was likely to be born handicapped. At the time of passage, numerous feminists opposed the act as inadequate because it failed to establish the principle of "abortion on demand," and they decried the definition of abortion as a medical rather than a woman's right. However, since the act's passage, the women's movement has been actively involved in efforts to defend it against restrictive provisions and limitations of its scope (Jenson 1982:356; Perrigo 1985:134).

In the aftermath of the act's passage in 1967, as in the United States after the 1973 Supreme Court decision legalizing abortion, groups formed either to oppose or preserve the legislation. These efforts have been described as "a near classic case of parliamentary lobbying-possibly unrivalled in the post-war era" (Marsh and Chambers 1981:40). By the mid-1970s, ALRA had been more or less eclipsed by the National Abortion Campaign (NAC), the women's liberation group described in earlier in our discussion.

NAC was less committed to parliamentary lobbying than to politicizing public opinion on abortion-related issues. Its strategy was largely extraparliamentary, emphasizing proselytizing through demonstrations and picketing (ibid., 47). As radical socialist feminists, NAC members also maintained close ties with the Labour Party and trade unions. This relationship produced TUC support for defeat of the anti-abortion Corrie Bill in 1979.

In March 1981, NAC and other groups were surprised when, in the absence of parliamentary debates, the DHSS issued new forms concerning abortion that contained no nonmedical grounds for termination of pregnancy (Kingdom 1985:148). NAC and other groups have thus far been able to prevent any prosecutions for noncompliance with this administrative edict. In 1981 as well, a bill to make NHS facilities mandatory for abortion was introduced in Parliament, failing by 215 to 139 votes, but nonetheless indicating considerable support for this initiative (Randall 1982:174). An important factor in stopping antichoice restrictions was the Coordinating Committee in Defense of the 1967 Abortion Act (Co-Ord), founded in 1976. By 1980, with 50 member organizations, this unique organization had developed a strong defensive posture, unifying such diverse groups as ALRA, medical groups, unions, and the Labour Abortion Rights Campaign (LARC) (Marsh and Chambers 1981:48, 53). Labour Party women, including M.P.'s Jo Richardson and Oonagh

McDonald as well as Chief Women's Officer Joyce Gould, helped greatly in defending abortion reform in Parliament. Vallance (1979:75) argues that abortion reform produced a rare example of collective action by Labour women in the House (although some Labour women-for example, Shirley Williams, a Catholic-opposed the measure). In addition, opposition forces were not well organized. The anti-abortion movement in the United Kingdom has lacked unity and mass support, in contrast to the strong pro-abortion organization in Parliament coordinated with extraparliamentary forces.

As in the United States, the feminist viewpoint has been incorporated in the liberal perspective (Marsh and Chambers 1981:94). Nonetheless, party affiliation is a better predictor of abortion policy-making in Britain, and because of the importance of Parliament in decisionmaking on this issue, attention has focused on that body. In the United States many more levels of government have been involved in abortion policy-making, including the courts, whose role has been central, as well as state and even urban legislative bodies.

A final case of women-related social legislation to be considered is policy toward battered women. The concept of state aid and public concern for battered women originated in the United Kingdom in 1972. By 1975, the National Women's Aid Federation (NWAF) had been formed to act as a communications and support network. In 1976, the Domestic Violence and Matrimonial Proceedings Act was passed in Parliament. As in the case of abortion, it was introduced as a private member's bill by Laborite Jo Richardson and enjoyed (some) support from the Labour government (Coote and Gill 1979). The NWAF and the NCCL aided in building support for the act's passage. The issue was first raised during deliberations by a Select Committee in the House of Commons (as in the case of other women-related legislation), at which testimony was presented by women's aid organizers and women victims of domestic violence. The committee found existing criminal and civil laws weak and recommended change. (As in the United States, police had frequently refused to intervene in what the state viewed as "domestic disputes," and appropriate legal remedies were often not available.) The act that was passed in 1976 (and put into effect in 1977) was a modest effort that sought to strengthen procedures by which a woman could obtain a court injunction to restrain a violent husband or cohabitee.

The 1976 act offers valuable protection in the county courts, permitting exclusion and nonmolestation injunctions without recourse to other judicial proceedings (McCann 1985:74-75). The 1978 Domestic Proceedings and Magistrates Court Act extended similar protection to that which existed in county courts, but for married women only. The 1977 Housing (Homeless Persons) Act obliged local authorities to provide abused women with alternative accommodations.

However, according to McCann and others (ibid.; Hanmer 1977:101), since the enactment of the new laws, the judiciary has favoured a limited interpretation of them, largely returning the position of abused wives to their pre-1976 role. The police response has indicated a similar reluctance to utilize the powers inherent in the new legislation. Funding, criminal justice reform, and therapy for victims of violence play a lesser role in the United Kingdom than the United States (Dobash and Dobash 1984:177).

There is absolute discretion with regard to a "power of arrest" attached to injunctions; the Home Office has limited powers of arrest to only three months (Rogers 1983:142). No national government funds have been committed thus far to provide financial aid for shelters or victim's related costs; local refuges are funded by local authorities.

Although Women's Aid has never seen legislation as particularly important in altering power relations between men and women (ibid., 146), the group did campaign not only for the 1976 act but also for the Housing Act of 1977, which gave priority to women and children for access to housing if they left home because of violence.

This brief survey of legislative enactments pertaining to feminist concerns leads to the conclusion that feminists have been able to influence public policy primarily as an auxiliary resource for parliamentary actors who are responsible for initiating and passing the legislation. As our analysis has demonstrated, most legislation in the United Kingdom came about through pressure, not from feminists, but rather from parties and unions, frequently through the vehicle of private members' bills in, Parliament and often with considerable support in the House of Lords.

As we have indicated, legislative support for measures involving women's equality and welfare has left parties and unions free to pursue issues of equality in the workplace and in their own decision-making bodies at their own (snail's) pace and on their own terms, leaving basic structures of power and male dominance largely untouched (Scott 1982:180). Further, it appears that in Britain implementation of policies enacted regarding equal rights has often been more difficult to secure than the legislation itself. Given the nature of the administrative process outlined earlier, there is virtually no mechanism for interested groups to ensure compliance with enacted policy. This analysis suggests that the impact of policy aimed at women's concerns in Britain has been less than impressive, while at the same time legislation may serve as a convenient symbol muting further demands for political change.

The United States

In the United States an Equal Pay Act was enacted in 1963, with little conflict. As suggested earlier, after the Civil Rights Act of 1964, other women's rights legislation was passed with greater input from feminist groups. In addition, in the implementation process, feminist groups have been vigorous, often acting to strengthen legislation through administrative intervention or judicial proceedings.

Easy passage of legislation on equal rights in regard to education and credit in the 1970s may be attributed to the presence of a policy network in Washington after the ERA. Coalitions of women's groups specialized for specific policy areas lobbied both behind the scenes and overtly to promote legislative efforts and prevent the erosion of legislative gains once secured (Gelb and Palley 1987:53-56). The absence of strong party input on equal rights issues and the vulnerability of representatives to pressure from organized constituents created an atmosphere different from that in the United Kingdom. In addition, as we pointed out earlier, the politicization of the bureaucracy led to continued activity by organized feminist groups and their allies at the administrative level to ensure continued commitment to statutory aims.

To a greater degree than in Britain, feminists have continued to present legislative initiatives even during the 1980s, in a less hospitable political atmosphere, achieving some degree of success with portions of the Economic Equity Act. In Britain, efforts to interact with the political process have been more defensive and reactive.

As in Britain, the activity of grass-roots groups engendered a changed public consciousness regarding domestic violence, the result being the creation of over 700 local shelters. But unlike the case in Britain, grass-roots women "forged alliances with Congress, the administration and national women's organizations" (Zeitlin 1983:266). Although federal legislation was initially defeated and finally resulted in only modest funding, the effort to pass a federal law generated the coalescence of a new policy network. And although federal legislation fell short of feminist goals, in several important ways the movement to gain public support for the policy area succeeded. First, although it was short-lived, a federal agency, the Office on Domestic Violence (ODV), was created in the Department of Health, Education and Welfare during the Carter administration, and it helped focus attention on wife abuse as a serious political concern. Second, federally based lobbying efforts galvanized the movement against domestic violence. Third, legislation was passed at the state and local levels that provided, as in Britain, for increased responsiveness by the legal process, but, in addition, other policy initiatives were undertaken that increased support for victims of domestic violence.

In 1977, in the wake of the 1975 establishment of NOW, hundreds of interested representatives from all over the country attended a meeting of the Task Force on Domestic Violence in Milwaukee. This gathering led to the creation of a new group, the National Coalition Against Domestic Violence (NCADV), which began to mobilize on a national basis and press for legislation. The issue was further highlighted by the International Women's Year convention in 1977 and by hearings conducted by the U.S. Commission on Civil Rights. In response to pressure from feminist groups, the Carter administration created the ODV, with the mission of disseminating information and funding technical assistance and demonstration projects.

Another federal agency, the Law Enforcement Assistance Program (LEAA), had been supporting and funding direct service and mediation programs for domestic violence victims since the mid-1970s.

In 1977, legislation to combat domestic violence was introduced in Congress. Female members of Congress, as well as such congressmen as Democrat George Miller of California, endorsed federal funding of community-based shelters (Gelb 1983:255). The bill failed to pass in 1978 largely because of concern over procedural issues in the legislative process. Further objections were raised, as they would be with increasing frequency, to the concept of federal intervention in domestic life and the creation of yet another federal social program.

The bill was reintroduced the following year, in the 96th Congress, with support from an extremely broad coalition of supporters, including feminist and traditional women's groups, the police, prosecutors, religious groups, the National Football League, and the Junior League (Zeitlin 1983:271). By this time, the NCADV had established headquarters in the capital and comprised some 350 groups and 25 state coalitions.

Although the group had developed a national lobbying presence, it continued to support the concept of community control of shelters by affected women in accordance with feminist principles of participatory democracy. Support for the bill was also forthcoming from female members of the congressional staff and feminists in the bureaucracy, particularly from the ODV and a large number of co-sponsors in Congress itself.

The bill passed the House by a vote of 292 to 106, with all congresswomen voting in favour of it-a key reason for the victory being "the work both by the sponsors with their colleagues and by shelter providers and other groups in their home districts" (Gelb, J., 1983:258). As passed, the bill would have provided for $65 million over a three-year period to supply "seed money" for local shelters. A similar bill was approved in the Senate, but by this time it had become the object of a concerted attack by right-wing forces.

The bill passed the Senate narrowly, and a House-Senate Conference Committee was convened to resolve the differences in the two bills. The conference report passed the House easily, but a massive lobbying campaign by the "New Right" continued to oppose the bill's passage in the Senate. The Senate did not take up the bill until after the election of 1980, when a major shift in power took place. Under threat of a filibuster, and lacking sufficient votes to invoke cloture, the bill was never brought to the floor again and died. The failure of the legislation to pass meant the death of the ODV as well, although some of its functions were merged into the National Center on Child Abuse and Neglect.

This significant defeat at the national level was accompanied by numerous cutbacks in federal aid to victim-related programs. In 1984, Congress appropriated $6 million for shelter funding, in a more modest version of earlier legislation (and a far cry from the defeated bill's proposal of $65 million over a three-year period). In subsequent years such funding has continued, and several additional federal programs now also provide support for victims of wife battering.

Given the nature of the federal system, however, prospects for change at the state level have appeared much brighter. In recent years three-quarters of the states have altered their policies regarding battered women, usually providing some funding for shelters and improved access to a more responsive legal system (ibid., 251). By 1981, 49 states and the District of Columbia had passed some form of reform legislation to combat domestic violence (New York Times, Jan. 27, 1986:A13). Most states have created new civil and criminal remedies for abused victims. States and numerous cities have specified in detail the duties of police who respond to domestic violence calls mandated better recordkeeping, and often created special training programs for police and judicial personnel. Police departments in more and more cities yearly report an increasing number of arrests for domestic violence (Gelb, J., 1983:250-51).

In addition, and most importantly in the short run, states have provided funds for shelters and other victim-related services, including job training, child care, and legal and psychological counseling for abused women (Temkin 1986: 26-29). Some states have raised additional revenue for their programs through surcharges on marriage licenses and divorce filing papers. Significantly, the policies leading to such improvements have been promoted largely under the aegis of state coalitions against domestic violence, which have lobbied for change in conjunction with a wide group of coalition supporters and carefully cultivated legislative support. These groups have continued to monitor the implementation of policies after their passage. It seems accurate to conclude that in the United States the scope and significance of legislation on domestic violence has been greater than in Britain, largely owing to the existence of a feminist lobby and a newly created policy network focusing on wife abuse.

While in both countries the grass-roots orientation of the battered-women issue has been maintained, resources have been more readily available in the United States, thanks to lobbying and legislative pressure. Even grass-roots American activists have moved in the direction of coalitions (often via state coalitions against domestic violence), greater organizational strength, and more avowed politicization than their British counterparts.

A similar point is made by Jennifer Temkin (ibid., 38-39) in her analysis of law reform for rape in Britain and the United States. American women's groups lobbied tirelessly for reform and developed liaisons with media representatives and politicians of all political persuasions. They engendered public interest and support through newsletters and other efforts, creating laws that resulted in a larger number of arrests and convictions in cases of sexual assault and improving the treatment of victims within the legal process. In contrast, similarly radical law reform in Britain "in the mid-1980's ... is as remote a prospect as ever" (ibid.).

In the absence of a cohesive and powerful women's lobby, as well as the general absence of women from corridors of power, recommendations by the House of Lords were modified to permit judges to consider the victim's sexual history and to extend efforts to gain anonymity for the victim and for the defendant as well. A 1984 Criminal Law Revision Committee similarly permitted rape to be viewed within a narrow perspective (Edgell and Duke 1983), providing for little change, particularly in comparison with U.S. legislation.

Political Opposition to Feminism in the United States and Britain

In both the United States and Britain the past decade has seen the ascendancy of conservative political administrations that have sought to reprivatize political issues, particularly those affecting the family and dependent women. There can be little doubt that the policies articulated by both British and American conservatives have a disproportionately negative policy impact, both on public sector employment and on availability of necessary public services especially important for dependent women (Lewis 1983:11). To what degree does the emergence of a New Right suggest negative future outcomes for feminist aspirations?

Recent politics in both countries have been marked by attacks on the role of the state in the economy and by the reassertion of traditional values regarding the family and the role of women (Conover and Gray 1984:91). In the United States some of the same forces that led to the emergence of feminism as a social movement have led to its antithesis, the New Right and the anti-abortion "pro-family" movement. Galvanized in part by the Supreme Court decision in Roe v. Wade, which helped create one sector of the feminist movement, antifeminists mobilized to oppose the ruling. They have viewed the expansion of government activism as threatening to traditional values and have organized effectively to combat what they regard as pernicious social tendencies. Aided by reforms in campaign financing (leading to an extraordinary growth in Political Action Committees [PACs]) and the relative decline in political parties, they have organized effectively to lobby at the congressional and administrative level and to seek to achieve change via the electoral process.

The New Right has been extremely adept at using direct mail to raise large sums of money, at grass-roots lobbying and indirect lobbying, and at influencing politics primarily through efforts to affect the outcomes of elections (Lewis 1983:14). In the United States, one arm of the New Right has linked antifeminism to a religious base (the Catholic Church and fundamentalist religious groups), which has provided powerful support for religious conservatives. The other arm includes such groups as Phyllis Schlafly's Eagle Forum, dedicated to restoring women to their traditional role in the family and in society, and the anti-abortion "Right to Life" movement. These forces were able to converge effectively with the Reaganite Republican Party in the 1970s and 1980s, gaining a significant role both in the party and in the Reagan administration.

It is probable that one source of the greater opposition to U.S. than to British feminism is the American women's movement's greater visibility and impact. Hence, antifeminism may constitute a larger segment of New Right politics in this country, although at the same time it remains only one interest group within the current Republican orbit. Other groups include some elements of the eastern establishment, cold warriors, and economic conservatives. The somewhat uneasy coalition erected during Reagan's reign may prove to be too fragile to endure. It appears, however, that in the United States both the women's movement and the New Right are strong (Light and Lake 1985), and it is by no means clear that feminism has been routed. Support for Reagan's personal leadership has apparently not meant a significant shift to the right among the American public; rather, judgments about Reagan's leadership qualities and personality and about the state of the economy appear to have been most significant in aiding his electoral victories (Conover and Gray 1984:16). Nor have candidates backed by the right wing continued to sustain the electoral momentum they seemingly had in the late seventies and early eighties.

There is little evidence that the election of either 1980 or 1984 constituted a conservative mandate or that the two major symbolic issues of the New Right-abortion and the ERA-had any impact on the outcome of the vote (ibid., 15). Nor does it appear that the outcomes of most House and Senate races are attributable to New Right efforts. The power of this new coalition in shaping mass attitudes and political behavior does not seem particularly great. Nor has public opinion regarding abortion and the ERA shifted to the right (ibid., 158). Single-issue voting by members of the New Right does not seem to have a major impact on outcomes either (Ferguson and Rogers 1986:45-46).

Regarding abortion, for example, an NBC News exit poll in 1984 found that two-thirds of the electorate endorsed the legalization of abortion, with the decision "left to the woman and her physician," while only a quarter did not. Soon after the election, an ABC News poll found the share of Americans supporting the relatively radical position that women should have a right to abortion on demand, "no matter what the reason," actually increased over Reagan's first term, rising from 40 percent in 1981 to 52 percent in 1985, while the percentage opposing abortion on demand declined from 59 to 46 percent. According to a Los Angeles Times poll, only 23 percent of the electorate supported a constitutional amendment prohibiting abortion, and only 32 percent of those who voted for Reagan endorsed his policy on abortion. Louis Harris reports that Americans support passage of the ERA by 60 to 34 percent. And few Americans are enthusiastic about Jerry Falwell, the most prominent leader of the religious right. A 1984 Los Angeles Times exit poll found that only 16 percent of the voters approved of the minister (ibid.).

Recent trends in public attitudes toward affirmative action merit special notice because of the Reagan administration's sustained attack on affirmative action and repeated insistence on the public's impatience with such "special interests" as women and minorities. In 1978, Louis Harris reported that only 45 percent of the public agreed that "if there are no affirmative action programs helping women and minorities in employment and education, then these groups will continue to fail to get their share of jobs and higher education, thereby continuing past discrimination in the future"; 36 percent disagreed. By September of 1985, 71 percent agreed and 27 percent disagreed. Those favouring a "federal law requiring affirmative action programs for women and minorities in employment and education, provided there are no rigid quotas," numbered 67 percent by 1984, and those opposed, 18 percent; by 1985, support had risen to 75 percent (opposition was 21 percent). Here, too, the trends in public opinion have been directly opposite to the trends in public policy.

Partially as a consequence of Reagan's failure to extend his coattails to other offices, primarily in Congress, his strategy has been to seek only marginal policy changes, regardless of his rhetoric. This approach has tended to moderate the impact of New Right forces on the actual policy process, as compromise and incrementalism dominate the need to operate in the practical world. The prospects for continued Republican ascendancy rely far more on economics than on the conservative social agenda, which lacks broad public support and even endorsement from many coalition members (Jacobson 1985:232-33). Although right-wing activism has had a major impact on administrative appointments and consequently on policymakers as well, the long-term effects on policy remain unclear. What is clear is that while feminists have been forced into a more defensive political role, and subject to considerable harassment in the legislative and administrative process, they have not been totally defeated. The fragmentation of American politics, both at the federal level and in state and local initiatives, as well as the degree to which feminism has been institutionalized as a legitimate interest group continuing to intervene effectively in policy-making, would suggest that all is not lost. Examining the organization and mobilization of the pro-family movement versus the feminist movement, Conover and Gray (1984:176) found that the feminist network is far better organized at the state level, having almost twice as many organized groups as the.right in the 40 states they surveyed. In general, their analysis suggests that the significance of right wing organizational power is far less than the media and New Right itself would lead one to believe, although in terms of financial resources they are formidable adversaries (ibid., 203-5).

In the United Kingdom, while similar shifts in the postwar consensus regarding the scope and direction of the welfare state exist and have been epitomized in the Thatcher government, several differences appear significant. First, given the importance of the party structure in Britain, the Thatcher government may represent a more coherent and tough-minded partisan bloc than Reagan's somewhat uneasy coalition (David 1983:198). Some observers perceive in Mrs. Thatcher's approach a significant break with traditional conservatism as well as with social democracy-an approach that has transformed the nature of British policies (Gelb, N., 1983). There is considerable evidence that the British public, particularly the skilled working class, has swung somewhat to the right, but nonetheless what has been called "authoritarian populism" may not reflect a complete or even significant rejection of the welfare state in

Britain (Butler and Kavanaugh 1984:293). Nevertheless, there is support for some privatization and greater individualism as well as resentment of taxation and waste (ibid.).

In British politics it is clear that support for the Conservative party manifesto means decreased spending, including reductions in funding for housing and education; cuts in some state benefits (e.g., maternity and unemployment) and abolition of others as well, including supplementary benefits; reduced levels of public service and reduced subsidies to those services; and the privatization of public assets, including council housing and some industry (Edgell and Duke 1983:358-59). Most of these policy areas directly affect women as employees and clients of the state. Both the electorate and popular ideology have shifted to the right regarding abortion, women's rights, and welfare (Robertson 1984:293). However, results of a recent poll indicate that the overwhelming majority of British women view abortion as legitimate if the woman's health is endangered, if the child is likely to be born deformed, or if the woman is a rape victim. Abortion is opposed if the child is not wanted or if the woman wishes to abort because she is unmarried (Langford 1980:11).

Anti-abortion views, in the absence of a religious base, have never gained the same political resonance in Britain as in the United States. While Prime Minister Thatcher holds views hostile to women's liberation, including her insistence that women with children remain out of the work force and her policy of defunding such areas as child care and state aid to dependent women, her rhetoric is not specifically antifeminist. However, the concern of her government for family policy- particularly via the all-male family policy group that has taken over important cabinet functions (Rogers 1983:44), most notably in the absence of consultation with women's groups (even such traditional ones as the Women's Institutes and Townswomen's Guilds)- implies a tacit antagonism to feminist issues (ibid., 108).

In contrast to the situation in the United States, and perhaps because of difficulties encountered by all promotional groups in the political arena, neither the Society for the Unborn Child (SPUC) nor LIFE, another anti-abortion group, has ever been able to gain a foothold in the political arena. Pro-choice groups such as NAC have been more effective in establishing relationships with M.P.'s and mounting campaigns for popular support. SPUC lacks a connection comparable to that of anti-abortion groups in the United States with the Catholic Church, which in any event denounced a SPUC effort in 1983, saying that the "ends don't justify the means" (New Statesman, June 24, 1983:4).

The church itself lacks the numbers and fervor of its American counterpart and seems less avowedly political, particularly with regard to the abortion issue. Rogers (1983:157) reports that wide differences exist between the M.P.'s of different parties on social policy, 83 percent of Labour M.P.'s favouring free child care and 86 percent of Conservatives favouring the view that women be obliged to care for their children. The partisan cast of views on feminism is obvious and points up the possibilities inherent in the election of a more sympathetic government.

Only a future general election will reveal whether the vacuum left by the disarray of left-wing politics, created by the internal disorder of the Labour Party, will be filled either by the SDP or by a reconstituted Labour Party, permitting a different political attitude toward women to prevail.

ASSESSMENT

We have examined the policy process in the United States and Britain to determine the relative impact of the feminist movement in each nation. In the United States, while administrative agencies such as the EEOC have not always been effective and their enforcement strength has varied with political commitment, they have played a significant role with regard to nondiscrimination policies. The EEOC has benefited from the existence of a feminist policy network that has not only influenced both policy orientation and political appointments, but has also been instrumental in gaining substantial judicial and public endorsement of principles of affirmative action. Such a supportive network has been lacking in the United Kingdom, where the superficially comparable EOC has been isolated politically in the absence of political and material resources.

In Britain, policy has generally been initiated by private members, and, in the case of sex discrimination, prodded by the EEC. Feminists have played the role of secondary activists, given their ambivalence about political participation in national-level politics and their frequent lack of information regarding the policy process. The absence of policy networks, combined with the highly centralized and closed system described earlier, prevents any significant feminist presence in the implementation process. Nonetheless, we have seen that feminists have intervened successfully in collective action on the abortion issue, where they have continued to maintain a political presence and sustained a sometimes uneasy alliance with such groups as labour unions. Abortion-related efforts point the way to coalition building on other issues, although it is not clear whether similar congruence may be achieved on economic policies. American feminists have engaged in extensive lobbying, networking, and coalition building on a variety of policy issues at the state, local, and national levels of politics, even making some policy inroads during the conservative Reagan era.

New Right opposition to the type of social change represented by feminism has developed in both Britain and the United States, necessitating a reactive and defensive role for feminist groups, as well as lessening their ability to set political priorities. However, Mrs. Thatcher's third electoral victory and British public opinion data indicate an even more substantial right-wing shift in the United Kingdom than in the United States. Given the considerable political and ideological obstacles to feminist political mobilization addressed earlier, the persistence and reinforcement of Conservative Party strength do not augur well for feminist influence in British national politics.

CONCLUSION

This study has examined the different directions taken by feminism in three nations, emphasizing the importance of external factors, including political institutions, cultural traits, and values on the resulting movement structures and goals.

Swedish politics, we have found, presents a model of consensus and corporatism, as well as an all-encompassing state that directs most citizen-related activity and tends to incorporate those activities existing outside the boundaries of state policy. The British system is distinguished by a centralized bureaucratic state and a "dichotomous" ideological context in which conflictual politics tend to predominate. In the United States a less organized, somewhat adversarial pluralism reigns in a system distrustful of centralized power and welfare policies. In turn, the character of feminism has been shaped by the character of the state as well as economic factors and the strength (or weakness) of traditional values and attitudes. Thus, we have argued that in Sweden a form of state equality concerning women exists in the absence of an organized movement (albeit with a feminist "presence," primarily in the sphere of elective partisan politics). In Britain, ideological/left-wing feminism is in part a product of the closed and conflictual political system. In the United States, a less ideological and more pragmatic political setting has led to a mass-based liberal/ equal rights feminism. The prevalent mode of activism has been interest group lobbying for power rather than integration in parties and unions in the manner of the European movements.

In this concluding topic, we assess the societal impact and success of each approach to equality and self-determination for women.

Definitions of what constitutes social movement "success" may vary. Success may refer to legitimization of a group's goals, change in individual or group consciousness, and/or change in public policy outcomes involving redistribution of social goals and changes in power relations (Jenkins 1983:544). For some, political access for hitherto excluded groups constitutes success. Success may also refer to the mere fact of survival, and/or the creation of alternative sources of power through the development of new organizational forms (Rowbotham 1983:136). It is evident that the movement in each nation has succeeded in different terms, partially because of different goals and the systemic factors that constrain political activism.

We have shown that the most active part of the British feminist movement emphasizes expressiveness, personal transformation, consciousness, and changed belief systems. It eschews formal structure and hierarchy and is centered in small groups that stress life experience and self-help politics. In Gerlach and Hine's (1970:55) terms, it is segmented-localized, autonomous, and ever changing-and decentralized. Nonetheless, it lacks the reticulate, or networking structure that they see as inherent to movement groupings. Largely as a result of ideological conflicts and the consequent failure to coordinate action and permit the sharing of resources, networking efforts, particularly important at the national level, are absent. Social movement organizations in the United States have been far more likely to form coalitions in order to realize their goals (McCarthy and Zald 1977).

As several researchers (Zald and Ash 1966; Curtis and Zurcher 1974) point out, movements adopt different forms depending on their goals, with personal change movements adapting decentralized structures and exclusive membership, while institutional change movements are typically centralized and inclusive. Although the goals of grass-roots participation, service, and transformation of aims are more likely to be realized in decentralized structures, the costs may lie in the failure to influence the larger political system, as in the British case. Bureaucratic structures provide skill and coordination but may sacrifice participatory goals, as is sometimes true of the American movement (Zald and Ash 1966). One trend in the United Kingdom that may effectively interact with the structure and values that predominate among women's groups is the growing interest of local council governments in aiding feminist efforts.

Clearly, the British movement has succeeded in creating local activities emphasizing consciousness and life-style transformation in numerous (primarily urban) centers throughout the country. British feminism has also defied traditional sociological rules regarding the origins and maintenance of social movements. Rather than becoming bureaucratized and less radical, the British movement has retained its ideological fervor and commitment and has continued to seek new alternative structures (Bouchier 1984:179). The degree of activism and commitment is impressive, even to the casual observer. Movement groupings and activist outposts created in the 1970s survive. These include Women in the Media, NAC, the NWAF, Rights of Women (the voluntary legal arm of British feminism), and the Women's Rights unit of the NCCL, as well as Women Against Violence Against Women (WAVAW) (Van der Gaag 1985:137). As Jenson (1982:373) has observed, the movement's main contribution may be simply its survival, in contrast to the largely esoteric state of the formerly active French and Italian (as well as other continental) movements. The British movement remains the most vital and important one in Europe, although the numbers involved in some grass-roots groups may have declined since the 1970s (Coultas 1981:36).

Although the British movement's origins were in many ways similar to those in the United States (even prompted initially by infusions of Americans who served as catalysts), the movement was never characterized by either mass demonstrations (other than the Corrie effort discussed earlier) or a strong national presence. Its internecine struggles, largely between sectors of radical and socialist feminism, remain unresolved. One effort in conjunction with the TUC-the march to fight restrictions in the abortion act, demonstrated both the mass potential of the movement and its internal conflicts. This march was probably the largest demonstration over a social issue that Britain had ever seen (Bassnett 1986:157).

Nonetheless, it revealed the chasm between women and the trade union movement and between socialist and radical feminists. The radical feminists resented what they perceived as male usurpation of the movement (as women were placed fifth in a seven-place march) and ran to the front with their banners. Three women were arrested in a later scuffle with police for hoisting the women's liberation banner; a feeling of hostility was thus one result of the day's effort, though not the only one. The effort at the Greenham Common missile installation three years later resolved some of these conflicts through a separatist, women-only protest. Thirty thousand strong, it helped to bring women from all groups together and to generate widespread awareness of the dangers of nuclear proliferation. A major question for British feminism remains the centrality of "cultural" versus "political" feminism, a question we will return to because of its significance in the movement's failure to create a meaningful national presence.

In the United Kingdom, parties and unions occupy a major-if declining-political role, and a tradition of left/socialist thought has been strong. Although activity in party and trade union politics may be viewed as equivalent to the American liberal/equal rights movement, little evidence for this perspective exists. This analysis is thus in considerable disagreement with the view expressed by Hewlett (1986:170), who argues that in both England and Sweden the most effective women's groups have been embedded in parties and unions, not in separate feminist organizations.

Rather, it appears that women's participation in established British institutions has been marked by marginalization, with women organized into separate advisory groups and limited to a handful of mandated seats on executive committees. The major union force, the TUC, has endorsed, lobbied for, and even demonstrated for numerous progressive policies on behalf of women (especially in the case of abortion, referred to earlier). Nonetheless, where issues of economic and political power are involved, there is greater hesitancy.

In addition, tensions exist between socialism and feminism and between the hierarchical unions/parties and feminist ideology, as the march against the Corrie Bill demonstrated. However, at their most effective, women's groups within parties may serve as forums through which women's demands and concerns can be highlighted. Nonetheless, Jenson's (1982:370) contention that British feminism has emerged from a decade of political isolation and an exclusive grass-roots focus to help unite the Left and the Labour Party seems premature, based on the analysis presented here. The energetic activity of women within Labour and the organized Left notwithstanding, thus far their policy-and decision-making impact has been limited.

Despite the existence of numerous progressive policies pertaining to women in the United Kingdom, the absence of a feminist movement that can set a policy agenda, speak for itself, and engage in dialogue regarding specific policy initiatives has resulted in serious gaps between policy and implementation. The upshot: a strangely limited vision of feminist goals and ideals, which has, in fact, led to less societal change than might be expected.

In the United States a tradition of reform, the absence of a strong socialist Left, and the impact of interest groups in decision-making have combined to produce a different type of movement. In part reflecting the increased weakness of parties and unions politically, feminists have organized as separatist or gender-based groups outside established structures (Adams and Winston 1980:104). This approach has given them significant autonomy in strategy, as a recent trend in the direction of electoral efforts demonstrates. American feminism is characterized by far greater inclusivity of different views than its British counterpart; coalition building and networking are movement watchwords. The American movement has also forged an accommodation between the more "radical" women's liberation movement and the middle-class reformist one (it has also developed strong linkages with traditional women's groups, such as the League of Women Voters and the YWCA).

The most visible manifestation of American feminism is the traditional interest group, organized as a hierarchical structure with staff dominance. Groups such as NOW have moved in the direction of mass membership, while such feminist groups as WEAL, the Center for Women Policy Studies, and the NWPC fit the McCarthy/Zald model of funded social movement organizations relying on "conscience constituencies" or contributors for resources and staff for day-to-day decision-making and long-term strategizing (Handler 1978:8; McCarthy and Zald 1975:11).

As the history of the movement against domestic violence demonstrates, even nontraditional groups with grass-roots origins are pulled toward political engagement and greater professionalization. American feminists have been eclectic and pragmatic in their use of strategies-from protest to litigation and campaigning. Nonetheless, although American feminist groups have moved much further than British ones in the direction of traditional organizational structure (which most reformist lobbying groups have always utilized in the United States), they have not abandoned feminist policy goals in the interests of organizational maintenance. Thus, although different from their British counterparts in structure and ideology, the movements have each remained firmly committed to their own feminist vision of the "good society."

In Sweden, feminist movement politics per se has played a minor role, although "equality" and "family" issues have been given primacy by the SDP and other parties. Women's federations in four of Sweden's five parties have provided a context for some policies pertaining to women and for recruitment of women to party and political office. Although various data in this chapter suggest that women are dissatisfied with Swedish efforts to achieve "equality," at present apparently no mechanism exists to capitalize on this discontent and move beyond the egalitarian rhetoric (so dominant a feature in Swedish society) to a new stage of political endeavor on behalf of women.

So far in this chapter, we have examined the role of women's politics in changing individual consciousness, creating alternative political structures, and simply surviving as organizational structures. Hence, we have been concerned with movements (or their absence) primarily at the individual and structural/organizational level.

Now, recalling our initial definitions of movement success, we will examine other facets of the success, or impact, of women's politics: 1) the impact on changed policy outcomes and 2) the impact on group and societal consciousness as well as the legitimization of group goals (see Table 9).

Table 9: Impact of Changes in Individual and Group Consciousness

	Sweden	U.K.	U.S.
Legitimation of group goals	-	-	+
Access to power structure	+	-	+
Changes in power relations	+	-	+
Public policy outcomes	++	+	++
Group survival	-	+	++
Creation of alternative sources of power	-	+	++

Note:— little or none; + = somewhat; ++ = significant.

To assess the latter, in particular, we rely on attitudinal and economic data on the three nations under consideration. We will try to distinguish between those gains that have been made in the welfare state and those that have involved a changed role for women in society because of increased economic opportunities. We will divide our discussion into 1) attitudes that demonstrate consciousness of the women's movement and support for feminist issues, 2) attitudes toward child care and domestic work-or the persistence of traditional attitudes toward sex roles, and 3) evidence of changed economic roles for women as a result of more employment opportunities.

EXTENT OF SUPPORT FOR FEMINIST MOVEMENTS

We have already noted that the British movement has succeeded in changing the consciousness of its individual members and in creating new, localized alternative power and service structures. With regard to other measures of success-for instance, those involving the larger society and policy outcomes-the movement's achievements have been less impressive. Efforts to increase collective awareness of movement goals and to gain broadened support within the political system may involve potential members, allies, and the general public. Measured by this standard, the total membership of British feminist activists has been estimated as one-tenth of 1 percent (or 20,000) of the female population, indicating a huge distance to go to reach even a fraction of the women in the United Kingdom (Bouchier 1984:178). In contrast, membership in traditional British women's groups is close to a million (ibid.). Only a small segment of British women have been reached by the women's liberation movement in its various manifestations, and the movement remains isolated, both by deliberate design and because of the obstacles created by British economic and political institutions. Despite the mobilization potential evident in the case of abortion rights and Greenham Common, the movement remains on the fringes of British life, its marginal position reinforced by media emphasis on the movement's domination by antimale radical feminists. The failure to reach more traditional women may be seen in a 1981 Spare Rib poll that compared the responses of Spare Rib readers (associated with the women's liberation movement) with women in the more traditional Townswomen's Guilds (see Table 10).

Similarly, despite the media attention given the women's protest at Greenham Common in December 1982, there is little evidence that most women have changed their opinion about the cruise missile as a result of that effort. The balance of women had the same opinion after the demonstrations as they had had three years earlier (Spare Rib, May 1984:18). A Guardian poll in January 1983 showed about 23 percent of women to be in favour of the Greenham Common activists' goal-that Britain abandon nuclear weapons-which was actually 10 percent fewer than four months earlier (before the protest). Spare Rib rightfully concludes that Greenham has not especially raised women's awareness of the

Table 10: Attitudes of Spare Rib Readers and Members of Townswomen's Guilds Toward Work by Women

	SR	TG
Bad for children	7%	75%
Undermines the family	16%	71%

Source: Spare Rib, November 1981:24.

nuclear threat, at least as measured by national polls. In conducting their own, more limited poll, most women interviewed by Spare Rib objected to the all-female nature of the protest, and the magazine's survey found that working-class women were less supportive of the Greenham Common protest and of feminism than their middle-class sisters (ibid., 19-20).

The American movement has grown in size and heterogeneity, particularly in the Reagan era, where apparent disaster has been turned to advantage in terms of group mobilization. NOW, for example, grew from 125,000 (in 1978) to 250,000 in several years. This number has fluctuated considerably as the attention of the public has wandered from one issue to another (similar phenomena have been observed with regard to other reform groups) (McFarland 1984:203; Bomafede 1986:2175). As of 1985, the dues-paying membership of the feminist movement numbered about 300,000 (Gelb and Palley 1987:26). Despite the relatively small membership (augmented considerably if the million-odd members of the more traditional women's groups allied with feminists are added), support for feminists among the American populace appears to be far broader and more significant than is the case in Britain.

American women's support for feminism also appears to be substantial: 56 percent of them said in 1986 they considered themselves feminist, 28 percent said they were not, and a mere 4 percent indicated they were antifeminists (Newsweek, March 31, 1986:51). A majority of women also indicated that the women's movement had affected their lives positively (18 percent very much, 53 percent fairly much).

A 1981 poll indicated that 4 percent of women and 2 percent of men contributed to the women's rights movement (about 4.5 million people), and that one of every 300 women is active in some type of feminist activity (Bouchier 1984:180). A survey by Janet Boles (1984:84) as far back as 1974 found that the total membership of women's rights groups (including the NWPC, NOW, the League of Women Voters, and the National Federation of Business and Professional Women's Clubs) was 56.77 per 10,000, indicating a fairly significant pattern of participation, which is likely to be much higher a decade later, given the trends we have outlined.

As Ruth Mandel (quoted in Bomafede 1986:2175) has noted, "The women's rights movement is in a process of diffusion. It is spread, assimilated and incorporated throughout society at various levels and [has] become part of the social fabric." Underscoring acceptance of many feminist views were the results of a recent New York Times poll. Twenty-eight percent of those surveyed indicated that the women's movement had made their lives better, and these respondents were most likely to be young and educated.

Among those who responded favourably, improved job opportunities were cited most often as being a result of the women's movement (New York Times, Dec. 19, 1983:316). Similarly, while strong differences separate college-educated women from their more traditional (and more numerous) sisters, over the past decade the more egalitarian views of the former have begun to make inroads among the latter (Poole and Zeigler 1985:vii), and we contend that American sex role attitudes have become increasingly egalitarian.

Growing numbers of less-educated women were found in a recent study to be more receptive to egalitarian views, although not necessarily to what is perceived as the more "radical" women's liberation movement (ibid., 10-24). In the United States a 1980 survey found that, on a five-point scale, attitudes changed from 3.2 to 2.9 toward liberation, while in Britain rightward shifts on women's rights, abortion, and welfare were more evident (Robertson 1984:236).

In Sweden, as we noted earlier, women's liberation is viewed as anathema by many men, hostility to the movement apparently existing out of all proportion to the limited strength of feminist organizations and views, at least among elite males. In any event, Swedish surveys do not reveal women's attitudes regarding feminism, because the movement in Sweden has been oriented differently.

In the United Kingdom there appears to be considerable ambivalence regarding the movement, its accomplishments, and the potential role of women (despite the political success of a female prime minister), although British women are only a bit less opposed to traditional role constraints than are their American counterparts (Dex and Shaw 1986:25).

While four-fifths of Americans say they would vote for a qualified woman for president (up from one-third in 1937) (Bianchi and Spahn 1986:238), in Britain, after Thatcher's election as prime minister, 64 percent agreed that it made no difference whether a woman held the office, while 25 percent said a woman was "not as good."

Support for the notion of "greater confidence" in a woman as a member of Parliament has dropped (from 5 percent of men and 12 percent of women supportive in 1975 to 2 percent and 4 percent, respectively, in 1983), perhaps reflecting some defection of women from Thatcher's social policies (International Gallup Poll 1981:177, 273).

Table 11: Favourable Feeling Toward Women's Liberation Movement

Country	Parents	Offspring
United Kingdom	43%	38.1%
United States	45.7%	51.8%

Source: Allerbuck, Jennings, and Rosenmayr 1979:497.

Studies comparing attitudes toward feminism and women's social role in the United States and Britain also offer some striking differences. One study found British youth much less supportive of women's liberation than their European or American counterparts, suggesting that generational change has been far more limited in the United Kingdom (see Table 11).

Of particular note is the limited nature of value change that has taken place in the United Kingdom. Inglehart (1977:34) found that Britain exhibited the smallest amount of generational change of any nation in his cross-country survey.

Another report of intra-European opinion on feminism reveals British women (and men) to hold a higher proportion of negative views than citizens of any other European nation except Italy. The degree of polarization cutting male/female lines is notable (Hernes 1983: Table 6). Although strictly comparable data are difficult to obtain, a 1979 poll showed 63 percent of Americans and only 40 percent of the British agreeing that the part played by women in their nation had changed a lot (International Gallup Poll 1981:272). Britons are reported to have the poorest opinion of women's liberation of any Europeans (Euro-Barometer 1983:179).

Attitudes Toward Sex Roles

A 1983 survey found more Britons "disagreeing with women who claim there should be fewer differences between men's and women's role in society" than in any other European nation surveyed, as well as profounder disagreements regarding female family roles (e.g., housework and child care) than elsewhere in Europe (ibid., 134, 137). More British men preferred that their wives not be in paid employment (ibid., 164). These findings are confirmed by a recent survey that found that British husbands were not supportive of working wives: only 41 percent of women said their husbands were enthusiastic about their working. While in many instances working wives were tolerated by their husbands, this was true only if their employment did not interfere with their domestic life or the husband's work (Employment Gazette, May 1984:206).

Female attitudes toward work have undergone considerable transformation, with only 25 percent of women indicating that women's place should remain in the home; a majority believe that work is beneficial for women (ibid., 203). Among younger women, a vast majority say they wish to return to work after having children.

However, 53 percent of British women (in contrast to 21 percent of American and 35 percent of Swedish women) say that women should quit their jobs when they have children and return to work only after their children are grown up (Hastings and Hastings 1985:714).

At the same time, British women accept the view that work is beneficial, but only if it can balance with and accommodate their primary domestic role (Employment Gazette, May 1984:203). Opposition to feminism may combine with the poor economic conditions in Britain to reinforce the concept of the "family wage" discussed earlier and keep women in a secondary role in the labour force.

British women consider their career less important than their home. Eighty-nine percent of surveyed women of working age felt that a woman's first duty was to home responsibilities, 61 percent said that a woman's first duty was to her marriage, and only 31 percent thought they could be loyal both to marriage and to a job.

For 69 percent, their husband's career had priority-and 55 percent of the respondents were under 25 (Rose 1986:159)! While a poll of Townswomen's Guild respondents did reveal that a majority (69 percent) supported the view that it was good for women to work, 75 percent indicated that such work was "bad for children" and 71 percent thought that it was undermining the family (Spare Rib, Nov. 1981:24).

Forty-eight percent of men and 38 percent of women interviewed in 1979 agreed that women should remain at home with children under 10 (International Gallup Poll 1981:272).

In contrast, in the United States, 63 percent of women interviewed in one poll indicated that they would want to work outside the home in the future, even if they had enough money to live comfortably without working.

Another poll found a majority of American women indicating they wished to combine home and career, while slightly under half of men and women interviewed said they favoured a new concept of marriage in which husband and wife share work and domestic responsibilities (Ms., July 1984:60; Roper Organization 1980:30-33).

By 1982, 75 percent of Americans said they approved of women working outside the home, and over 80 percent favoured joint responsibility for raising children (Bianchi and Spahn 1986:239).

In 1985, only 22 percent (down from 57 percent in 1967) of American college freshmen interviewed said they believe the activities of married women are best confined to the home (Chronicle of Higher Education, Nov. 5, 1986:32).

Even women's Political Action Committees are increasingly approved by the American public-with favourable responses rising from 11 percent in November 1982 to 64 percent in May 1984 (Hastings and Hastings 1985:374). (In 1985, support for union PACs was recorded as 34 percent.)

In Britain, compulsory military service for women is favoured by 35 percent of the public; in the United States, by 53 percent (Hastings and Hastings 1982:262-63). In all three of the societies under study, women continue to perform more household tasks than men, but in the United States, particularly, there is some evidence of more equal sharing of tasks, especially child care and economic roles (e.g., bill paying) (Bianchi and Spahn 1986:231).

Data collected by the University of Wisconsin's Comparative Project on Class Structure and Class Consciousness indicate similar attitudes by U.S. and Swedish respondents toward sex roles, with one exception.

As the data in Table 12 show, the exception is that whereas 66 percent of American women believe that traditional learned sex roles benefit the family, almost 60% of Swedish women disagree. Egalitarian attitudes toward housework are similar in both countries.

Perhaps reflecting the economic stratification in Sweden that we will discuss later, even more Swedish than American women would like to see a larger role for their sex in business.

Table 12: Attitudes Toward Sex Roles (Percentage of Respondents Agreeing)

	U.S.	Sweden
Traditional roles benefit family	66%	41%
Housework should be shared equally	95%	97%
Not enough women are employed in business	77%	85%

Other Swedish data reveal some division between parties on ideological lines-and, increasingly, divisions between men and women-on women's issues. The data over time suggest a trend toward conservatism regarding some issues, a trend that may affect women adversely in the welfare state. Growing imbalances in the economy appear to make cuts in public expenditures inevitable (Erickson and Aberg 1987:13).

Conflicts in discussions of distributive policy have become sharper as well, so that the very real gains women have enjoyed as beneficiaries of the policies of the progressive Swedish welfare state may be in question.

The absence of an organized feminist movement to press for continued commitment of social policies may be critical, although the trend toward advocacy by joint groupings of women's organizations from the different parties may lead to collective action on this front. To date, collective action has been limited to "sexual" or "woman-specific" matters (e.g., rape and pornography), which do not directly affect the parties' socioeconomic policy commitments.

Since 1976, of the two leftist parties, the VPK has been especially supportive of such issues as day care and the six-hour work day.[*] In 1985 over 80 percent of the VPK and about 70 percent of the SDP favoured the building of more day-care centers and the six-hour workday.

Swedish surveys reveal that the concept of equal representation in Parliament for men and women has received little backing from any quarter. Principles loosely related to "affirmative action" are viewed with considerable apprehension by the Swedish public. Interestingly, given the state commitment to economic equality and independence for women, 46 percent of men and 48 percent of women in 1979 indicated that men should get jobs first. Another response that may signal difficulty ahead for the welfare state was the considerable support for reducing the public sector and social welfare commitment in 1982 and 1985.

Prohibition of pornography, an issue initially supported by the more conservative parties, has come to reflect a dichotomy between male and female views. From 1979 to 1985 women consistently supported a ban in far greater numbers than men (in 1982, 51 percent of women, 28 percent of men; in 1985, 68 percent of women, 43 percent of men).

There appears to be a growing awareness of this issue, which was highlighted by an all-women party demonstration in Stockholm. Eduards (1986) has noted that a majority of women (but not men) also favour the use of quotas to gain election to the Riksdag for women and oppose jobs for men first. (Some data also suggest a gender gap on the issue of abortion, with more women against [Eduards 1986; Sainsbury 1983]!)

Whether these trends augur a new feminist consciousness that may be translated into group activism is questionable, given the continued prevalence of norms related to Swedish political consensus within the corporate state. What is worth noting, however, is the apparent emergence of a separate female consciousness about some key women's concerns.

Opinion polls in the early 1980s found some contradictory responses to survey questions among the three nations (Hastings and Hastings 1985:707). Whereas 63 percent of Swedish respondents and 59 percent of American ones felt that men and women were treated equally, only 47 percent of British respondents thought so (and 40 percent replied that men were treated more favourably). Nonetheless, it is difficult to measure whether these data reflect a more truly egalitarian role for women in Swedish society or simply acceptance of the well-known institutionalized rhetoric. Table 13 presents a comparison of responses regarding 1) sexual equality in politics and 2) general customs and practices.

The data in the table indicate, perhaps somewhat surprisingly, that a far higher proportion of Swedish than

American women perceive that equality has not been attained in politics or social life.

Table 13: Attitudes Toward: (1) Politics; (2) General Customs and Practices

Country	Men Treated More Favourably		Both Sexes Treated Equaly	
United States	(1) 58%	(2) 20%	(1) 38%	(2) 70%
Sweden	(1) 78%	(2) 60%	(1) 15%	(2) 28%
United Kingdom	(1) 94%	(2) 71%	(1) 5%	(2) 22%

Source: Adapted from Hastings and Hastings 1985:707-17.

Table 14: Distribution of Household Responsiblities (in Percentage)

	U.K.	U.S.
Household repairs:		
Done by men	76	39
Shared partially or equally	11	47
Cleaning house:		
Done by wife	66	46
Shared partially or equally	31	45
Cooking:		
Done by wife	73	55
Shared partially or equally	22	35

Source: Hastings and Hastings 1982:239; 1983:285.

A crucial measure of egalitarian views is the distribution of household responsibilities (see Table 14).

In Sweden, despite the legal encouragement given to sexual equality, few husbands participate in child care, and other traditional sex roles appear to have remained entrenched.

Thus, it appears that labour force participation per se has little impact on sharing of customary sex roles, particularly given the high incidence of part-time work among women, which is likely to reinforce existing patterns of domestic responsibility.

According to a 1976 study on Swedes at work by the Swedish Central Bureau of Statistics (cited in Scott 1982:78), in families where husband and wife were both employed full time:

---

67 percent of women did all or practically all the cooking;

50 percent did all or practically all the washing up;

80 percent did all the laundry;

53 percent did all or practically all the shopping; and

55 percent did all the cleaning.

As for the time spent by Swedish men who did "some" of the cleaning, shopping, cooking, and so on, a sample survey of 7,000 women made by the Committee on Equality in 1978 revealed that, overall (including families with women who were not employed full-time), men spent less than half as much time as women in daily routine household tasks. Sex segregation and "ubiquitous part-time work" have reinforced women's almost full responsibility for the household (Erickson and Aberg 1987:9).

Although the role of women in the domestic sphere still completely overshadows that of men, recent data demonstrate some movement toward leveling. From 1974 to 1981, men doubled their share of the family domestic responsibilities from a minute 7 percent to 14 percent. Differences between age groups are remarkably small and gender roles still very strong, although a larger percentage of men share household tasks with fulltime working wives (Tahlin 1987:238). Recent Swedish survey data demonstrate that sex role differentiation in the home remains marked. Women are almost exclusively responsible for care of clothing (e.g., laundry, mending, and ironing). They are disproportionately involved in cooking, cleaning, and washing up and in child care as well (Equality Ministry 1985:57-58), while men engage in repair work, gardening, and car and boat maintenance.

Nonetheless, the distribution of household responsibilities reveals a more egalitarian division of labour between husbands and wives in Sweden and in the United States than in Britain, where, for instance, a larger majority of wives clean house. Similar patterns appear with regard to washing dishes, although in the United States, children are the most likely to help out (Hastings and Hastings 1985:712). American women are also the most likely to undertake such male-oriented tasks as gardening and lawn mowing (ibid.). (Nonetheless, in a recent survey of women only a fraction of U.S. respondents thought that real householding decision-making power was shared equally by both partners; and the Swedes were the fewest of all respondents to agree that males should be the major breadwinners and women should stay at home, which at least demonstrates the prevalence of the full-employment philosophy in Swedish culture [Hernes 1983:49].)

The data suggest that strong patterns of gender polarization and traditional sex role socialization persist even among the sons and daughters of the welfare state. Earlier we noted similar patterns discernible with regard to the taking of parental and sick leave. Data on political participation by women also demonstrate a continued separation between the public and private spheres among all socioeconomic classes in Sweden (Szulkin 1987:207-9), although the differences have narrowed somewhat in the last decade. However, union-meeting activity among women in Class I (primarily SACO/SR) and the proportion of women holding office in the LO declined from 1974 to 1981-perhaps a reflection of the increased growth of the part-time sector and lessened attachments to the workplace. Women's participation in corporate channels lagged behind men's by at least 10 percent. But data from the 1970s reveal decreasing gender differences in union and party activity and other efforts to influence the political process, especially in the 16-24 age group. Whether these patterns may continue to survive the demands of domestic responsibilities and counter prevalent trends in which males "out-participate" women is open to speculation (ibid., 201; Sainsbury 1983).

Clearly, support for some of feminism's basic goals, including sex role modification, has met with great resistance not only in the more traditional United Kingdom but even in the "egalitarian" society that Sweden has forged. In turn, as we have seen, the persistence of traditional values has constrained political opportunities for feminists and, together with the rigid nature of the political system, has limited their options. The British movement in particular has a long way to go in gaining support of women who do not enter into competition with men, and therefore do not feel unequal, and in convincing the vast majority who are married, have been married, or expect to be married that the feminist movement they perceive as antimale is relevant to their lives (Hills 1981:104).

Impact on Public Policy

Public policy reflecting feminist concerns has resulted in Sweden, the United States, and Britain; in each of the three nations, legislation on equal pay, sex discrimination, abortion, and domestic violence is in effect. However, the policy process both leading to and involving implementation of legislation has been significantly different in each nation, thus influencing policy impact. In the United States, policy has largely been the result of lobbying by gender-based groups. As noted earlier, gender-based policy networks are made possible by the emphasis on coalition formation and the relative openness of the political system to group participation.

Even though public policy in the United Kingdom on such movement goals as equal pay, sex discrimination, abortion, and domestic violence has reflected feminist concerns (if not direct influence) via trade union and Labour Party politics, the impact of policy change has been minimal. Some of the efforts made toward these goals were prompted at least in part by EEC directives requiring equal pay and job equality. A major exception is in the area of abortion policy, where a coalition of trade unionists, feminists, and Labour Party activists has effectively intervened to prevent weakening of the existing law. (In addition to demonstrating against the Corrie Bill, in 1979, they mobilized after 1981 to lessen the impact of a restrictive interpretation of the Abortion Act by the DHSS that would limit circumstances in which doctors could perform abortions.) The EOC, TUC, and women's groups have also succeeded in expanding public consciousness about such issues as positive action and "equal value" (pay equity) (Atkins and Hoggett 1984:198). In Britain the continued efforts by such activists as the women's rights officer of the NCCL (since 1975), increased strength in white-collar unions like the NUPE (where training courses and baby-sitting services have been established for working women, with a resultant increase in the number of shop stewards and TUC delegates) (Vallance 1985:30), as well as efforts at the local council level provide evidence of ongoing attempts to achieve policy change. However, whereas in both the United Kingdom and the United States it has been more difficult to secure policy implementation than the legislation itself, in the United States opportunities for intervention in bureaucratic politics are far greater.

In Britain, owing to ideological purism and localized structures, women have not developed political networks comparable to those in the United States. Institutional factors such as the growth of administrative power and executive dominance and secrecy, combined with the strength of parties and Parliament, have limited opportunities for direct intervention in policy-making and made monitoring of implementation well-nigh impossible.

The women's liberation movement's emphasis on "women-specific" issues, such as abortion, rape, and domestic violence, while of utmost importance, has sometimes obscured the significance of issues involving work and the family ("organization of daily life" issue) so crucial to change for women.

When the Conservative government came to power in 1979, the tone was one of de-legitimization of women's right to work, as exemplified by the opinions of Lord Spens who, opening a debate on unemployment, said that married women should leave paid employment to make way for men (Huws 1985:57). Shortly thereafter, this view was reinforced by Thatcher's secretary of state for social services, who contended that women should look after their children full time and that state aid be restricted to very needy cases. As noted earlier, state provision of nursery and child care has never been adequate in Britain, and when other benefits were also cut, stipends to dependent mothers and children became even more meager. These events were not greeted with any mass response by the feminist movement in Britain.

In contrast, the positive changes in laws relating to violence against women were in part a response to women's campaigns, although these were often marked by the feminist ambivalence and the inaccesibility to the political system, as discussed earlier. As van der Gaag (1985:137) has correctly pointed out, Women's Aid never perceived legislation as particularly important in altering women's position in society and in the family.

Nonetheless, feminists did intervene when they pushed for the Housing (Homeless) Persons Act of 1977, which gave priority in local housing to women who fled their homes because of violence. They also campaigned for changing the law on injunctions, discussed earlier. But there have been massive difficulties with enforcement in the face of a hostile judiciary and police force and the feminists' inability to monitor implementation (Williscroft 1985:103). Sums made available to the shelter movement by local and central government grants have been minimal, for the same reasons.

Similar difficulties have ensued with regard to the Sexual Offences (Amendment) Act dealing with rape. Funding problems and failures of enforcement and interpretation remain. British feminists have concluded that the act has appreciably affected neither the way in which trials are conducted nor their reporting. Williscroft (ibid.) concludes that legislation at the local and national level has been of marginal importance. The failure of legislation to produce significant gains may result in either political quiescence or heightened cynicism regarding the political process, reinforcing the isolation of British feminists in any case.

We have argued that though the Sex Discrimination Act and the Equal Pay Act were potentially important pieces of legislation, they have not been implemented effectively enough to challenge inequality. The absence of coalitions and the failure to create a feminist infrastructure that might transcend ideological differences have been crucial. These deficiencies have to some degree been averted in the United States, where affirmative action practices are much more widely practiced than in Britain, reflecting a major difference between the American EEOC and the British EOC created by the Sex Discrimination Act (Dex and Shaw 1986:4). Affirmative action is viewed with suspicion and hostility in a Britain dominated by high unemployment and economic strain, while in the United States, women have benefitted from more vigorous implementation of equal opportunity and affirmative action directives.

Three factors account for more effective enforcement of sex discrimination laws in the United States than in Britain or

Sweden: 1) legislative and judicial commitment to the principle of affirmative action or positive discrimination, including the use of sanctions against offenders; 2) greater public acceptance of and mobilization for affirmative action principles; and 3) monitoring and intervention by a feminist network. In addition, the range of legislation that the EEOC can call on is impressive, as are the resources at its disposal, particularly in comparison with the United Kingdom and Sweden. The EEOC employs 3,100 people in a Washington office and 48 district or local offices (Grant 1984:52). It is thus far more accessible to the public than the minute British office (170 employees, primarily in Manchester, in 1984) and the even tinier Swedish version (7 employees). Federal guidelines appear to have produced significant gains in hiring and promotion in companies that do business with government, particularly if supported by vigorous organization and litigation (Law 1988:31, 33).

The American tradition of litigation for equal rights has provided a securer foundation for equality than has the British approach, even in a period of conservative rule. There has been less erosion in the U.S. public policy arena because it has been buttressed by strong public support for affirmative action (64 percent in 1984) (Hastings and Hastings 1985:541), the concept of "indirect discrimination," the ability to bring class action suits (minimizing individual costs and providing relief to large numbers), a professional feminist litigation sector, and continual feminist lobbying and networking. As Grant has found, there is extraordinary support among American business for the practice of affirmative action, in part because this provides far more utilization of human resources and opens the workplace to new talent and ideas (Grant 1984:60). Unlike the unions in Britain and Sweden that opposed national legislation against sex discrimination and remain lukewarm toward it today, in the United States the initially hostile business community strongly supports the continuation of aggressive federal affirmative action and equal opportunity guidelines.

In particular, the employment of black women, especially in firms with federal contracts, increased significantly as a result of EEOC policies. The major impact of equal opportunity policy has been at the professional and managerial level. It is at this level, as we shall see, that American women have achieved gains that exceed those made by women in Sweden and Britain (Dex and Shaw 1986:224).

It is undeniable that because of the largesse of the Swedish welfare state, benefits to single-female heads of families, to female members of the labour force, and to their children are far superior to those offered in the United States and Britain. Over 50 percent of Swedish children were in child-care facilities funded and regulated by the government in 1980, but only 15 percent of American children were similarly advantaged in 1984 (although a large number of American women relied on private-sector group and individual day care, bringing overall coverage to about the same level) (Bianchi and Spahn 1986:230). While 40 percent of American women have maternity coverage through their employment, 76 percent of Swedish women have that benefit (through the state) (Jonung 1984:50). Generous family rent and maintenance allowances, paid parental and sick leaves, in addition to special subsidies for single parents, have created a system that provides a far higher standard of living, without stigmatization and without long-term dependency and work disincentives, than in the United States (Kamerman 1984).

Swedish parties have proven receptive to women's sections' views on such issues as day care and leaves. but in fact the inception of many of these issues predates an active role for women's groups. Because the unions and parties sought to discourage further economic inclusion of immigrant groups, the participation of women in the labour force was encouraged in the 1960s. Policies related to women were therefore not informed by a feminist perspective, although they clearly sought to create equal opportunity for all, primarily through full employment. Both the SDP and the powerful unions, especially the LO, have opposed state intervention in order to strengthen institutional guarantees against sexual discrimination and have continued to view voluntary agreements between labour and employers as more significant than legislation. As we have noted, "equality" policies on sex discrimination and on lack of employment opportunities for women met with a tepid response from the unions and Social Democrats, so that these policies have been narrowly defined and limited to employment-related issues. Given their lukewarm attitude, there has been scant impetus to gain compliance with anti-sex discrimination efforts through the effective application of government policy since the resumption of political power by the Social Democrats and their labour allies in 1982. At present, in an atmosphere in which the dominant political view is that "equality" already exists, women's sections within the four parties that have them appear to be playing a quiescent role. Though in the past they provided women with an opportunity to voice their special concerns, today women's sections may "ghettoize" participation and prevent fuller inclusion in decision-making.

In the main, women lack independent resources with which to seek further implementation and discussion of their concerns, including intransigent issues such as part-time work, occupational segregation, and limited mobility. We have seen that Sweden represents a society in which women have been politically incorporated without being fully mobilized; so their demands as claimants in the political system have been dealt with by the male-dominated corporatist power structure on its terms. Women, unlike men, have been unable to create a basis for organization in the labour market owing to their lesser numbers and representation and to the active discouragement of women's groups in the labour force. Nor have they effectively created independent groups related to other aspects of their lives.

Despite Sweden's official policies mandating change in men's roles as well as women's, absence from work because of child-care needs is almost exclusively restricted to women. Nearly eight out of ten men transfer their parental leave to women (mothers), and family life is organized so that women work part-time in order to care for children and home. Work, society, and politics are still organized on patriarchal lines despite the existence, of "equal opportunity" (Equality Ministry 1985:11, 79-83).

Policies concerning what we may call the "organization of daily life" (e.g., child care and parental leave) have proven costly and difficult to implement in the absence of a significant movement continuously advocating for them. The result: Sweden remains highly sex-segregated in politics, work, and the home. In the absence of a feminist frame of reference, women's issues have been subsumed under "equality" and "family policy" and no longer regarded as a problem. Women-only issues involving "sexual" or "body" concerns have been belatedly recognized and incorporated into state policy mechanisms; they are treated as minor problems despite their relatively high incidence in a society viewed as violence-free. The fact that a grass-roots voluntary movement has arisen with regard to wife abuse indicates that the pervasiveness of male violence against women is a key social issue even in consensus-oriented Sweden. Similarly, the emerging differences on such issues as affirmative action for women may demonstrate increased consciousness of feminist concerns among Swedish women.

Swedish women have in fact not really left their homes; their major domestic responsibilities and very partial attachment to the labour force (to be discussed further) has resulted in the continuing primacy of traditional sex roles and society. The socialization of traditional women's roles in public-sector paid employment and the existence of benefits that help support women's part-time status may reinforce rather than change sex roles over the long run.

In examining the Swedish policy process, it seems clear that Swedish unions and parties have "literally preempted feminist demands and have put their political clout behind numerous proposals to advance equality between women and men" (Scott 1982:53). Enactment of public policy has in large measure left the unions and parties free to pursue issues of equality in the workplace and in their own decision-making bodies at their own pace and on their own terms, and issues of power sharing and male dominance have largely been left untouched. As Verba and Orren (1985:130-31) point out, the SDP has worked "deliberately and successfully to make gender equality a subset of the general issue of equality and not a separate, isolated set of demands.... In Sweden, the Social Democrats ... shaped feminist demands; in the United States feminist demands transformed the Democrats."

We have indicated that the issue of wife beating and abuse, identified in the American context as the more neutral policy arena known as "domestic violence," illustrates a good deal about the nature of the American political process and the receptivity of the system to feminist issues. Although the shelter movement began in England and exists belatedly in Sweden as well, it has been most successful in a number of ways in the American setting. The creation of shelters under the aegis of feminist groups legitimized the issue as a policy agenda matter, and by 1982 there were at least 300 shelters (plus hundreds of "safe houses") in operation (Pleck 1987:199).

Coalitions were created to combat treatment of battered women in 48 states. State funds became available, largely owing to pressure from shelter staff and residents, as well as other coalition members. Federal aid was forthcoming from a variety of sources, although it was not until 1984 that federal funding ($6 million) was finally appropriated for shelter support specifically, after several years of strident attacks from the New Right, which feared what was perceived as the weakening of the nuclear family. Since 1985, Congress has appropriated additional funding for shelters, and several additional federal programs have come to the aid of victims of domestic violence. In almost every state as well, laws

have been enacted to improve reporting procedures, mandate police intervention, and establish more effective criminal court procedures (ibid., 192-98). As Pleck (ibid., 199) points out, the process of gaining legitimization for intervention in domestic violence meant some dilution of the original radical feminist ideas that gave rise to the shelter movement. The inclusive coalitions involved in pushing for reform were often pressed to compromise because of the broad-based nature of the movement as it developed strength. Thus, a price was paid for success in gaining funding, legislation, and new legal enforcement: feminist rhetoric and control of shelters and even the movement's direction were affected. Nonetheless, the conclusion reached in this analysis is that the new coalition spurred by autonomous feminist movements allied with legislators, the judicial enforcement process, and other activists, including the social work profession, produced gains that made domestic violence a priority issue and helped achieve significant change. Women as claimants in this policy arena have had considerable success, and the diffusion of feminist ideas into the political culture seems evident.

The reluctance of British feminists to engage the national political system on the issue of battered women provides a clear contrast. The ready co-optation by the Swedish political system of the issue, at the same time as it was placed on the policy agenda, may have muted the important process of conflict and controversy, leaving in question both the fate of the grass-roots voluntary efforts that helped raise the issue initially and the vigor of the implementation process in the absence of an autonomous feminist movement (Lundqvist 1980:196).

In the United States the existence of numerous channels to influence policy-the executive, the courts, the states, and the legislature-may facilitate the diffusion of issues at different levels and permit pressure to initiate and enforce policy. We therefore contend that the relatively permeable American political system permits more choices than that of Britain or Sweden for change-oriented groups such as feminists and helps provide numerous reinforcements for the activity of independently organized and funded groups. Even though the policy process is characterized by incrementalism, with regard to a once "radical" issue such as wife abuse or domestic violence, it seems quite responsive to demands for change.

CHANGING ECONOMIC ROLES FOR WOMEN

A final area for examination is the significance of women's increased presence in the labour force as a vehicle for personal and societal change. Two different types of public policies must be considered to understand the increased mobility of American, as opposed to Swedish, women. Policies of the first type facilitate labour force participation-these are the policies provided much more generously by the Swedish state than by the American one. Policies of the second type foster greater economic opportunity by expanding the possibilities and choices available to women. In this second arena, characterized by commitment to affirmative action and widespread feminist consciousness, the United States (and even Britain, with a longer and somewhat more meaningful commitment to equal opportunity enactments) appears to have surpassed Sweden.

In an earlierdiscussion it was shown that women's labour force participation in each of the three nations discussed has increased phenomenally during the post-World War II period and continues to grow annually in each nation.

Table 15: Part-Time Employment of Women and Men

Country	Women	Men
Sweden	46.2%	7.3%
United Kingdom	42.4%	3.3%
United States	23.3%	7.6%

Source: Equality Ministry 1985:12.

In 1983, 58 percent of British women, 61 percent of American women, and 77 percent of Swedish women were employed (Equality Ministry 1985:12). Nonetheless, although the employment of Swedish women was the highest of all three, so was the percentage of women employed part-time (see Table 15). As Erikson and Aberg (1987:9) have pointed out, "It is to part-time work in the public sector that newly employed [Swedish] women have moved. Women are overrepresented in unqualified work, have little independence at the job, and are underrepresented in supervisory positions. Both sex segregation and the ubiquitous part-time work are the reasons for their low income."

In the United Kingdom and Sweden, women are disproportionately employed by the public service sector, and there they are increasingly employed in part-time positions (Dex and Shaw 1986:122). In Sweden, 90 percent of the women who work do so in the service sector, a vast majority being employed by the government, in contrast to about 75 percent in the United States and Britain (Mailler and Ross 1987:34-35; Hernes 1984:32). Forty-five percent of all women were employed in the social welfare sector in Sweden, 28 percent in the United States, and 26 percent in England. As Rein (1985:46) and others have shown, the social welfare sector is also the most highly segregated, with Sweden and Britain having the highest patterns of sex segregation (82 percent and 76 percent, respectively) and the United States the lowest (66 percent).

Occupational segregation is a problem in all three countries, but probably the greatest amount of change can be discerned in the United States, where there has been a decrease in occupational segregation and downward mobility after childbirth (Dex and Shaw 1986:80-107; Bianchi and Spahn 1986:182). In Sweden, especially, occupational choice has been very much an extension of the traditional role of women (i.e., child care and service roles), and sex segregation remains a persistent problem.

Another obstinate problem affecting women's role and power is that of wage differentials between men and women, in large measure a function of part-time work and occupational segregation. In Britain, women's hourly earnings were 74 percent of men's, while gross earnings were 61 percent whereas in the United States they were 83 percent and 65 percent, respectively. Among American women ages 26 to 34 this gap has narrowed to 75 percent of men's income, and for ages 20 to 24 it has narrowed even further to about 86 percent (New York Times, Feb. 6, 1987: D2; Coote and Campbell 1987:18; EOC 1983a: 89; Money, Dec. 1986:62). In Sweden, full-time female workers earned about 80 percent of male income, but because of the large part-time component of work force, total female earnings are in fact about half of men's (Eduards 1981:210).

A significant measure of the economic role of Swedish, British, and American women is the disparity between women in each country who hold managerial and supervisory positions. Even accounting for differences in data-gathering methodology, the differences are striking. In contrast to the United States, in which over 35 percent of managers and administrators are female, the comparable numbers in the United Kingdom and Scandinavia are 18.8 and 11-15 percent (Davidson 1985:91). In Sweden, women occupy only 0.2 percent of the managerial positions (men occupy 7 percent), 3 percent of executive positions, and less than 1 percent of the top positions in companies and public authorities (Equality Ministry 1985:20). Four percent of the senior government executives and officials are women. In the United States the female share of executive, administrative, and managerial jobs rose from 20 percent in 1972 to 35 percent in 1985, almost doubling (Bergmann 1986:68).

The United Kingdom occupies a middle position: women slightly decreased their role as managers in 1983 and now hold 17 percent of the administrative and professional positions

(EOC 1983a:97). However, in the private sector in 1986, women held only 0.3 percent of the top positions in companies and only six percent of senior managerial posts (EOC 1987:2; New York Times, May 6, 1987: C1). British women hold 18.5 percent of appointments to public bodies, but are only 2 percent of the directorates of private sector firms. Only 25 women are found among the top three grades of the senior civil service (of 658) and only nine women among the boards of the hundred largest companies, while in the United States, 36 percent of corporate boardrooms had female members in 1982 (New York Times, May 6, 1987: C1; Economist, Nov. 1, 1986:58; Cooper 1985:16). Hernes (1983:17) shows that British women held from 8 to 12 percent of the country's top administrative positions, whereas in Scandinavia in general and Sweden in particular no more than 2 percent of the top managers were women.

Table 16: Occupational Stratification

Occupational category	U.K.		Sweden		U.S.	
	M	F	M	F	M	F
High-prestige professional and technical	4.8	2.3	8.5	6.2	11.1	6.7
Administrative and managerial	6.1	0.9	5.2	0.4	10.4	3.0

Source: Roos 1985: Table 3.3.

A comparative analysis of occupational stratification of women in Britain, Sweden, and the United States suggests trends similar to those described here (see Table 16).

Although strict comparability is not possible because of the absence of incisive cross-national data, the available data reveal that "professional employment [has] widened more rapidly and significantly in the United States, as females have during the last generation made serious inroads into a wide range of professional occupations" (Mailler and Ross 1987:46). Although this quotation refers specifically only to Britain and the United States, our analysis indicates that the Swedish case may demonstrate greater resistance to women, particularly in senior administrative and managerial roles. The virtual absence of women in such positions in Sweden may be attributable to women's marginal attachment to the labour force-owing both to occupational segregation and to part-time work, which continually reinforces the role of women as responsible for the domestic sphere-and Swedish cultural norms that appear to decry assertive, individualistic women as beyond the pale of consensus politics.

The pattern of higher education in each country buttresses the economic role of women. In Sweden, although 66 percent of university graduates in 1982-83 were women, postgraduate work was dominated by men (Equality Ministry 1985:34). (In 1986, only 23 percent of postgraduate students were women, down from 27 percent in 1982.) The proportion of female university students is largest in the United States, and they now reap more than half of the bachelor's and master's degrees and one-third of the doctoral degrees awarded (New York Times, Feb. 6, 1987: D2). In the more elitist British educational system, 5 percent of women held bachelor's or advanced degrees, whereas in the United States the number was 20 percent (Dex and Shaw 1986:34).

Women in all three countries have greatly improved their representation in medicine. (Is it perceived as an extension of the "caring" role?) The high number of Swedish female dentists (34 percent) is particularly notable (Statistical Abstract 1987). However, in the United States, 11 percent of engineers are women, in the United Kingdom only 3 percent, while in Sweden women hold about 5 percent of construction-related positions (a category including architects and engineers) (ibid.; Tomes 1985:77). Only 10 percent of American women planned to major in education in 1985; business was now the most popular undergraduate major for both men and women. The proportion of M.B.A.'s awarded to women rose from 3 percent in 1965 to 30 percent in 1986 (Bianchi and Spahn 1986:119). American women have made particular strides in the field of law, where they earned 38 percent of degrees awarded, up from 15 percent in 1975 (New York Times, Feb. 6, 1987: D2). In Britain, 11 percent of the barristers in 1983 were women (a number that rose to 17 percent toward the end of the decade) and 14 percent of the solicitors (Williscroft 1985:100). In Sweden, about 11 percent of lawyers and jurists are women (Statistical Abstract 1987); in the United States, almost 20 percent.

American women compose 27 percent of university faculties and about 12 percent of all professors; in Britain, female professors number less than 4 percent (Economist, Aug. 23, 1986:14; "Equality Between Men and Women" 1987). In 1982, 5 percent of Swedish women were professors (Chronicle of Higher Education, Sept. 10, 1986:26; Tomes 1985:74). The contrast between the growing economic and professional gains of American women and to a lesser degree, their British sisters, seems to highlight continued inequities in Sweden. While as many Swedish women as men interviewed by a survey said they would like to be promoted, only 5 percent thought they would be (Equality Ministry 1985:20). Through the division of labour, then, Swedish "men are able to preserve a dominant, superior position. Men still occupy practically all positions conferring power and influence in society.... Women do not compete with men because they live on different terms" (ibid., 79).

ASSESSMENT

In this analysis we have argued that structural factors, including political, cultural, and economic constraints, narrow the possibilities for women to become policy claimants. We have marshaled evidence to demonstrate the importance of women articulating on behalf of their own interests and own concerns, contending that the "strident" tones of women's liberation decried by some are a necessary, if not sufficient, condition for societal change (Hewlett 1986:166).

A causal relationship between movement politics, policy enactments, and the growth of a professionally active group of women with economic and political potential is not fully demonstrable, but it is evident that the American feminist movement has had a profound impact on changing expectations and possibilities. In 1984, 49 percent of the women surveyed by Ms magazine (July 1984:54) indicated that they would continue to work even if they did not have to do so for economic reasons, while 57 percent indicated that they felt the "women's movement has just begun." The evidence of the continued vigor of the American feminist movement seems fairly conclusive, suggesting that reports of its demise are premature and unfounded.

This analysis has stressed the significance of several major factors that appear to limit the role of British feminists: the closed and inflexible nature of British government, particularly the administrative process; the reluctance of key institutions such as parties and unions to go beyond rhetoric in meaningfully sharing power; and the localized, purist nature of the women's liberation movement, which has failed to create coalitions and an enduring national presence. In Sweden, the anomaly of progressive policies pertaining to women, despite the lack of an independent, feminist movement, has resulted in a set of political contradictions. Not withstanding the greater hospitableness of the Swedish party system in particular to pressure, in practice the system permits little ideological or political space for nonproducer groups.

Issues drawn from the feminist agenda have found their way into the public policy arena and have profoundly influenced expectations, particularly regarding women's role as labour force participants. But in the absence of an autonomous independent movement that could structure dialogue on its own terms, much of the policy enacted appears to have had little impact on gender-based roles. The continued existence of a huge part-time female work force, the extraordinarily high degree of labour force segregation based on sex, and the apparent persistence of traditional sex roles imply that the general labour force policy that benefits women is not enough.

This analysis has sought to demonstrate the interaction between the "political opportunity structures" and mobilization by feminist social movements. In turn, the product of this interaction has affected the success of feminist claims and the degree of social change possible in each nation. Although the concept of success utilized here has emphasized policy outcomes, it has not neglected other manifestations, such as movement survival, changes in individual consciousness, and diffusion of group values. The results of these developments include acceptance of the group as a legitimate political organization, with ensuing gains for its members.

We have argued that policy impact may often rely on implementation efforts by a coalition of feminists and their political allies, and that the efforts may best succeed if these feminists are members of autonomous groupings that enjoy access to the political process, as is the case in the United States. American feminists also seem to have achieved the most public support for movement goals and ideals, now broadly diffused throughout the culture. With regard to individual consciousness, we contend that feminist ideology has had a profound impact on women in all three nations, although it has sprung from different sources. In the context of its self-defined goals British nondirected "liberationist" movement politics is remarkable for its continued vigor and survival.

In his analysis of social movements and policy change, Tarrow (1983:8) has observed that "the range and flexibility of its tactical repertory is often a good predictor of movement success." We have contended that the American movement has enjoyed the greatest autonomy in choice of tactics because it has been unconstrained by the necessity to work through the intermediation of existing groups, such as parties and unions. This freedom has permitted the use of a variety of tactics from protest to participation in existing power groupings. British feminist participation has been constrained by the rigidity of the political system and the ambivalence of movement activists about engaging in national politics in a coordinated fashion. Swedish women have, in the main, been limited to behaving as participants in existing institutions.

In all three nations, the relatively unstable nature of traditional electoral coalitions and the declining relationship between unions and the working class have produced new opportunities for women as potential recruits and bases of strength. In Sweden and the United States, these new opportunities appear to have produced the most responsiveness to new policies for women, although they have created different results.

The crucial factor appears to be the greater availability of allies or coalition partners in these two countries. In the United States in the last two decades, relationships have been cemented between feminists, other like-minded groups, and the Democratic Party, while in Sweden electoral instability created new opportunities for political access for women, particularly in the 1970s.

As Tarrow (ibid., 45) puts it, political "reforms may be more reversible when they are substantive only, creating no new vested rights of participation or veto in the population groups newly enjoying them." This hypothesis argues, then, for the idea that reforms producing institutionalized participation may be the most significant of all, largely because they help create resources for future mobilization and ensure continued attention to substantive policy concerns. Seen from this perspective, the American movement, now recognized as a legitimate group in the pluralist system, may be in the strongest position to endure as a significant political force.

From the examination of substantive policy gains, this analysis has found that Americans have achieved the most in expanding economic opportunities, while the Swedes have been most successful in creating a support structure that facilitates female labour force participation. Substantive rights, such as access to equal employment, are, as we have seen, limited by support from government and willingness to use sanctions, the sympathetic response of the public and political allies, and continued intervention by an activist feminist policy network. Legislation, it appears, is not enough, as it is necessary to have continued access to the implementation process in order to consolidate policy gains and achieve further political success. In the final analysis, all three nations demonstrate the limitations of their "political opportunity structure" as it affects the role of women. In the case of Sweden, gender-neutral policies have not yet been able to encompass the special needs and experiences of women and liberate them from their traditional roles. And, in the United States and in Britain despite the strength of the independent feminist tradition that has acted from a collective position in the name of collective goals, individual women have been forced to struggle with family responsibilities still squarely rooted in the private sphere.

BIBLIOGRAPHY

Beaver, R. Pierce: *American Protestant Women in World Mission: History of the First Feminist Movement in North America*, Grand Rapids, W.B. Eerdmans, 1980.

Bowie, Fiona: *Women and Missions: Past and Present: Anthropological and Historical Perceptions*, Providence, Rhode Island: Berg, 1993.

Brouwer, Ruth Compton: *New Women for God: Canadian Presbyterian Women and India Missions, 1876-1914*, Toronto, University of Toronto Press, 1990.

Burton, Antoinette: *Burdens of History: British Feminists, Indian Women, and Imperial Culture, 1865-1915*, Chapel Hill, University of North Carolina, 1994.

Chaudhuri, Nupur: *Western Women and Imperialism: Complicity and Resistance*, Bloomington, Indiana University Press, 1992.

Clancy-Smith, Julia Ann: *Domesticating the Empire: Race, Gender and Family Life in French and Dutch Colonialism*, Charlottesville, University Press of Virginia, 1998.

Dutta, N.C.: *Politics of Identity and Nation Building in North-East India*, New Delhi, South Asian Press, 1997.

Gagan, Rosemary Ruth: *A Sensitive Independence: Canadian Methodist Women Missionaries in Canada and the Orient, 1881-1925*, Montreal, McxGill-Queen's University Press, 1992.

Georgi-Findlay, Brigitte: *The Frontiers of Women's Writing: Women's Narratives and the Rhetoric of Westward Expansion*, Tucson, University of Arizona Press, 1996.

Gopalkrishnan, R.: *Insurgent North-Eastern Region of India*. New Delhi, Vikas Publishing House, 1995.

Grewal, Inderpal: *Home and Harem: Nation, Gender, Empire, and the Cultures of Travel*, Durham, Duke University Press, 1996.

Hogan, Anne: *Womcn of Faith in Victorian Culture: Reassessing the Angel in the House*, New York, St. Martin's Press, 1998.

Ishii, Noriko Kawamura: *American Women Missionaries at Kobe College, 1873-1909: New Dimensions of Gender*, New York, Routledge, 2004.

Kwok, Pui-lan: *Chinese Women and Christianity, 1860-1927*, Atlanta, Scholars Press, 1992.

Lawes, Carolyn J.: *Women and Reform in a New England Community, 1815-1860*, Lexington, University Press of Kentucky, 2000.

Lodwick, Kathleen L.: *Educating the Women of Hainan: The Career of margaret Moninger in China, 1915-1942*, Lexington, Kentucky: University Press of Kentucky, 1995.

Oliver, Caroline: *Western Women in Colonial Africa*, Westport, Conn., Greenwood Press, 1982.

Pascoe, Peggy: *Relations of Rescue: The Search for Female Moral Authority in the American West, 1874-1939*, New York, Oxford University Press, 1990.

Robert, Dana Lee: *American Women in Mission: A Social History of Their Thought and Practice*, Macon, Georgia, Mercer University Press, 1996.

Scales, T. Laine: *All that Fits a Woman: Training Southern Baptist Women for Charity and Mission, 1907-1926*, Macon, Georgia, Mercer University Press, 2000.

Stern, R.: *Changing India*, Cambridge University Press, Cambridge, 1993.

Thomas, Mary Martha: *Stepping Out of the Shadows: Alabama Women, 1819-1990*, Tuscaloosa, University of Alabama Press, 1995.

Wexler, Laura: *Tender Violence: Domestic Visions in an Age of U.S. Imperialism*, Chapel Hill, University of North Carolina Press, 2000.

Yohn, Susan M: *A Contest of Faiths: Missionary Women and Pluralism in the American Southwest*, Ithaca, Cornell University Press, 1995.

INDEX

L

M

N

O

P

R

S

T

U

V

W

❑❑❑